THE HIPPIE
TRAIL

THE HIPPIE TRAIL

AFTER EUROPE, TURN LEFT

ROBERT LOUIS KREAMER

FONTHILL

For Elizabeth

Fonthill Media Language Policy

Fonthill Media publishes in the international English language market. One language edition is published worldwide. As there are minor differences in spelling and presentation, especially with regard to American English and British English, a policy is necessary to define which form of English to use. The Fonthill Policy is to use the form of English native to the author. Robert Louis Kreamer was born and educated in the United States; therefore American English has been adopted in this publication.

Fonthill Media Limited
Fonthill Media LLC
www.fonthillmedia.com
office@fonthillmedia.com

First published in the United Kingdom and the United States of America 2019

British Library Cataloguing in Publication Data:
A catalogue record for this book is available from the British Library

Copyright © Robert Louis Kreamer 2019

ISBN 978-1-78155-736-5

Typeset in Sabon 10pt on 13pt
Printed and bound in England

Contents

Introduction

The overland route between Europe and Asia has been in use by people for trade, migration, and war for thousands of years, and its ancient cities are strung out along the way like mileposts—Istanbul, Damascus, Jerusalem, Bagdad, Tehran, Kabul, Varanasi, and Kathmandu. The youth of Western Europe had a freedom of movement denied to their Eastern counterparts for many years. It was adventure on the very cheap and your very own front-row seat to just a very small yet interesting part of this planet—that is if one's money, luck, and wits held out.

When I first heard about the hippie trail, I was drinking and hanging out in the bars of the Untere Strasse as a nineteen-year-old student. Listening to drunken late-night stories of other people's adventures awakened a childhood dream of visiting Kathmandu. Then, one day, some friends went down the hippie trail, came back, and told my friend, Dave, and I all about it. After considering going, I discovered almost every major city in Europe had a bus service of some sort to New Delhi, the Magic Bus and the BlueBus, though I am not sure which one started in London and which in Amsterdam. The advertised twenty-one-day, straight-through ride to India seemed like cheating.

Airfare in 1977 was ridiculously expensive; however, Dave said he heard something about driving vehicles to the Middle East for money.

By 1977, the word "hippie" and the character it represented had long become *passé* and a cliché, and it was even used as an insult. The '70s were almost over, and the hippie was as old-fashioned as big band music and shunning greed. It took only ten years for the mass media to shift the prevailing view of a hippie towards something more negative, unpleasant, and unseemly than it had once been.

By the early 1960s, the route became well-trodden and traversed by the youth of the western world. By the early '70s, it was legendary, and dubbed "the hippie trail" long before I got there. By 1977, the closed road to Baghdad was just one of many diversions one had to navigate around like a pothole, but this harbinger of the future had yet to resonate. The hippie trail had closed by the end of the 1970s, and it seems it will remain so until further notice. The rising level of violence and war in the region—and the world over—could keep the overland route closed to the casual traveler for the next century or longer.

1

And So It Begins

August 17. Elvis is dead. We heard the news on a car radio while hitchhiking to Munich. The news said he had overdosed sometime yesterday. He had been on the radio a lot lately with a new song called "Way Down Low." I guess when you are dead, you do indeed end up somewhere way down low. That song seems weirdly poetic now. The news of Elvis passing made me think of my childhood.

This news started quite the lively conversation between the driver, his passenger, and us. It gave us all something to talk about for a time. The couple that picked us up along the Autobahn on ramp seem cool and nice enough. It was a welcomed exit from the rain as we climbed into their VW Bus. Dave and I talked about our plans as we approached the outskirts of Munich and, like in a film, the sun burst through the German rain on cue. Everything looked fresh, new, and shiny, washed in the summer sun.

We hope to travel with any westerners if we find a convoy, at least until we find our footing. Dave sort of knows the going rate for importing and driving various sized vehicles to the Middle East—or he says he does. That knowledge has made him the self-appointed and anointed leader of our gang of two. We plan on sticking to our plan and act like we have done this many times before.

We talked before about importing these supposed and imagined vehicles to the supposed auto dealership, where rumor placed it in Amman or Istanbul. We imagined driving a new Mercedes-Benz with the radio blasting all the way to nirvana. But really, our plan boiled down to a basic arrangement: we stick together and do not do anything stupid. While heading south, the VW Bus we ride in is being passed by every machine

with four wheels on the *Autobahn*. Dave is asking me what I am writing in my notebook. My reply that I plan to keep a journal and write everything I can remember down is met with howls of laughter and derision.

We thought it would take us all day to get here. Found a cheap hotel and dumped off the backpacks and went to a few of the cafes, killed time, hanging out, talking to people, and drinking coffee until my teeth rattled. I drank enough coffee to wake up Elvis. We were directed to another cafe, and there we met a man who called himself Sammy. He was sitting in a sort of kebab house-type cafe booth with a couple of other people, and we remained standing. We were really getting the once over from many pairs of eyeballs. He said he was looking for drivers to Damascus. It turned out we had eventually found our man, and after looking over our passports and international driver licenses and then handing them back, he gave us his business card.

I took the card and looked it over. His eyes followed it into my pocket. I think he wanted his card back. In truth, we took the first gig we stumbled in to. Sammy informed us we were leaving right away—that meant first thing tomorrow morning. Something about this guy tells me he can be trusted, despite how slippery he seemed at times while he was trying to be a tough guy with his hole-in-the-wall gang. Neither one of us wants to wind up in a shallow grave somewhere along a lonesome highway in some lonesome country. Holy shit, we are driving to Syria.

August 18. Cheap hotel, paper thin walls, lots of late-night shouting from the street below, drunks and the drunken fights of the neighbors, and the unanswered questions before the very early dawn all added up

Business card for Sammy. (*R. L. Kreamer © 1977, 1978, 2019*)

to no sleep, and life is a twenty-four-hour clock. I stayed up writing in my journal, followed by a lot of watching the ceiling and smoking cigarettes. My traveling comrade slept and snored. The coming light seems to have quieted the night but not the thoughts running through my head. The traffic now picks up as the morning moves on. I can hardly believe it. If I am going to chicken out, now is the time.

We went to the address we were given, and it turns out to be something akin to a wrecking yard. We met the rest of the drivers in our convoy and Dave and I are the only Americans. Two German guys who have done the trip before, many times as it turns out, are the only other westerners. One of them hands me a business card. This must be the year of the business card. I am surprised the junkies are not handing them out.

His card reads "Ursin Heino Von B_____" and under that is what I assume to be his name printed in Arabic script. Now that is very cool. His card has his address in Bremen. He says to call him Heino. Dave and I introduce ourselves.

Heino commented on my name and that Bob sounds like the Arabic word for door. "Ah, Bob," he says, "Knock, knock"; it was quite funny now that I think

back on it, but at the time I was not amused. I replied: "Heino sounds like one of the Marx Brothers." He looked puzzled and Dave shot me a dirty look. The other dozen or so guys are all from somewhere in the Middle East and seem like nice guys.

I get my first lesson in culture and geography. I am an idiot that knows less than what I think I know. I just assumed they were all Arabs, but, no, that was just my muddled misconception. I should have taken some Middle East studies. Persians are not Arabs. A few of these guys were from Syria, Egypt, Jordan, Lebanon, Iran, and one guy from Iraq.

The guy from Iraq Dave dubbed "Joe" because he was wearing a tee shirt that had a print of the U.S. flag on it. Joe seemed pleased with his new nickname. What a collection of trucks we are driving. Most seem like museum pieces. So much for the new car with the radio blasting all the way to nirvana. The convoy is made up of all trucks except for the boss man's station wagon. I am making less money than Dave on this trip. Sammy said to put our luggage in that truck and pointed. We threw our backpacks in the back of another truck, the one driven by Heino's German friend, Bernard. The truck we piled into is a white

Mercedes Benz dump truck, with a car sitting in the bed. Dave is driving and I am shotgun. Leader says so. For now, my job is to have one of these trucks on my passport when we travel through Turkey and to be an occasional relief driver. Sammy was busy supervising some work going on under the hood of our truck and filling the radiator with water. He starts shouting "Let's go, before the water runs out!" All these trucks are at least ten years old or more, and all seem to be Mercedes Benz trucks. Heino is driving an old water tanker, or milk tanker, that is bright red. One truck has a bright blue tarp on it. Other trucks are green, blue, white, and grey. I imagine from a distance these trucks look like children's toys, scattered on the floor waiting to be picked up and put back in the box. The racket of a dozen of these relics being fired up at once is both deafening and choking. The mad rush to get out of the wrecking yard almost results in a huge pile up, though at least we were in the right place for a smash up truck wreck. We could just leave them in place. Sammy got out of his car shouting and spitting. It is like lining up in the schoolyard. Sammy is first, driving the new station wagon with the tape player blasting out a Middle Eastern lament all the way to nirvana. Heino and Bernard are next, followed by most of the hole-in-the-wall gang I saw with Sammy at the cafe. Dave and I were last in line in our dump truck. After much swearing and horn blowing, our unlikely convoy was snaking its way through the suburbs of Munich in search of the Autobahn. We laughed with the contemplation of dropping back and stealing the truck. I mention our luggage is in another truck, and that was Sammy's doing and Sammy is not stupid. It is a mini capitalist assault on wheels thanks to Sammy. Everyone is in it for the payday money, but Dave and I are in it mostly for the adventure of the road, and to get us closer to our ultimate objective. Our convoy comrades have families and need to do this for the bread. For me, this is going to put us at least a quarter of the way to India and on the road to Kathmandu. Oh, and the money is nice.

August 19. We have been driving like bats out of hell all day, only stopping for gas, bratwurst, and beer as Austria and Western Europe fade in our side mirrors like a John Ford sunset. We are blasting through Graz. I think I drank too much. We are on the fucking road for fucking real. In the sky, the lonesome sound of a jet at 20,000 feet is muffled by the clouds, and then a glider comes into view, peaking at the apex of a loop, hesitates, and then slides over. I am now writing in a bumpy truck in bumpy script again. Our Mercedes Benz dump truck

has a car sitting on the bed, and from the rear-view mirror, it appears to be a flying car that is following very close. It is not tied down at all, and the only thing holding it in place is the tailgate. The tailgate is banging on the underside of the car's gas tank with every bump. It is banging a small hint of a leak along the seam of the tank. It is sure to go from seeping to weeping soon—not good. I imagine a flaming dump truck streaking down the Autobahn. I must stop throwing my cigs out the window. Joe has been now dubbed "Crazy Joe" by Dave after a bizarre incident on the Austrian autobahn. Every member of the convoy now calls him that, even the ones who do not speak English.

We watched him miss the autobahn exit for Graz; we could see the convoy out in front of him, and they were peeling off the exit like synchronized swimmers, and Joe just kept going straight, like he was asleep. Sammy had to chase him for miles and miles before he would pull over and turn around. It took them six or five hours to catch up, hence all the time Dave and I had for beer and bratwurst in between what seemed like manic bursts of driving from roadside bar to roadside bar. Joe was caught somewhere in the mountains two hours after taking his wrong turn. Then they had a long way to double back. He always has a look of childlike wonder on his face and he must have, in truth, wondered and marveled at the convoy disappearing and the question of where everyone had gone off to.

We all met up at a gas station, and after a good telling off, he was then instructed to follow a certain truck and no one else under any circumstance. He seems to have taken that quite literally. For the next couple of hours, as anyone in our convoy tried to pass him, he would swerve into the fast lane of the Autobahn to cut them off, almost setting off a chain reaction of crashes behind him.

We imagined him shouting, "Hey, I'm told follow this guy, not you!" This alarming lack of sane judgment at high speed went on and on, and at first seemed quite funny—Dave and I could not stop laughing. After the fourth or fifth time, we backed way off, expecting to pass the smoking ruins and twisted metal of his misconception at any time.

At the next gas stop, he was knighted "Crazy Joe" by Dave and was subjected to howls of abuse in many different languages by everyone. Boss man Sammy howled the loudest. Poor Joe looked truly hurt by it all.

During our madcap dash from roadside bar to roadside bar, Dave seems to have put his asshat on. I really hope this was not my glimpse into the future. I mean, I have known this guy for a couple of years now

Above: Somewhere in Germany, heading for the Austrian border. (*R. L. Kreamer, Kodachrome 35-mm print film,* © *1977, 2019*)

Below: Somewhere in Austria the blue truck tries to pass. (*R. L. Kreamer, Kodachrome 35-mm print film,* © *1977, 2019*)

and he seems cool—we even did a trial run hitchhiking to Berlin and London, although I have a feeling this trip will make the trial run seem like a bus ride. I should be on my guard. Good lesson. Do not let your guard down.

Speaking of guard. It is an overcast night and I am left alone to guard this truck, so I write. I am not sure what "guard" means. If some well-armed pirate wants the truck, fuck it, they can have it. The word guard implies a little too much responsibility for my liking. One of the Germans we are traveling with, Bernard, just finished filling us with stories of travels to the east gone wrong—very wrong. He was telling his tales like campfire ghost stories, albeit with a heavy German accent. Dave has crashed out in the back of another truck. I think he is trying to pick up Heino's girlfriend, or possibly Heino, or maybe both.

I am poised on the edge of the world as I know it and it is nothing but the inexplicable ahead. We are 10 km from the border of Yugoslavia on the outskirts of a town called Leibnitz. I am glad I brought along a road map. The night closes around me. I feel like Dylan's Mr. Jones.

August 20. Into Eastern Europe, chasing rain and rain chasing us. It has been damn cold since Austria and it still is. This is weirdly cold weather for late August. Stopped at a few of what seemed like small-village or small-town grocery stores along the highway. They were noticeably empty but for few jars of jams, pickled things, and some bread—I am currently living on bread, cheese, cigs, and beer. Crossed the border into Yugoslavia and the change was instant. Yes, we have no bananas. The wealth and consumerism of Western Europe is a thing of the past. Yet only a few miles away and behind the border it remains with all the fruit and vegetables. This is like time traveling. Past, present, and future tense all in one go. Anyway, there is none of the preening and prissy dressed-up and self-conscious fashion. Everyone is dressed like peasants or cheap suited thugs. Granted, my scrutiny so far has been restricted to gas stations and small cafes and small towns, but even the towns and cities that pass in a blur seem depressed.

Not just economically, there is something else as well. Everyone is so serious and suspicious towards outsiders. People seem to be even more guarded and rude towards those in our convoy with dark skin.

Maybe our gang is scary to look at. If so, that is good, as no one is going to fuck with us. It really seems like the 1950s around here and it is more than just fashion. The racist bastard stink is the same everywhere. I am getting a bit of that same look from people until I open my mouth to speak, then they know I am an American. They ask, so I tell them. Suppose I could lie just to see how I am treated. I realize my mother's Mediterranean genes have given me a look more akin to my fellow drivers from the Middle East than from anywhere else. My bushy oversized mustache, my big nose, and great tan completes the disguise.

Dave and I stopped along the road in a field to play Frisbee under the blue summer sky. Soon, a small crowd from the nearby village gathered to watch. Like hicks from the sticks, they told us they had never seen a Frisbee before and marveled like it was magic. An old man approached with tears in his eyes and begged us for the Frisbee. I told him no fucking way. It was so unkind. Shit, sometimes I am what I rail against. Should have given the old man the toy, but some deeds cannot be undone. I will probably lose this worthless toy somewhere in the future and think nothing of it.

We are now somewhere in Turkey. Transit visas obtained at border crossings. It is all drive, piss, eat, drive, shit, drive, sleep, drive, piss, and then drive some more. The huddled masses of people on foot or in cars, buses, and trucks all want to move through as quickly as possible. It is heavy on the borders man, as armed guards stare, searching for anything and everything and everyone, and they are ready for you if you fuck up and get caught at something. Everyone in our convoy has each other's back. Our strength is in our purpose.

The objective of this convoy is a simple one. After money changes hands and that in turn is changed into transit visas, we get back in the trucks and drive border to border as quick as we can. We do not linger at gas stations—get in, get out. The road goes ever on. Capital to capital. Munich to Graz to Belgrade to Sofia to Istanbul was driven as fast as possible and filled with lots of asphalt and bad drivers in between. The older trucks top speed is around 60. With the extra car on the bed of our truck, our top speed is 50. To get anywhere we gotta push the gas to the floor and hold it there for a long time. To go any faster, we need to be rolling downhill. God, the politics at the gas station alone would make you cry. The border crossings had more uptight searches than I had ever seen. What are they looking for? Guns, drugs, stowaways, spies? Stopped in some towns and some villages, but for the most part, the convoy moved fast. Munich to Istanbul clocked in at around 1,200 miles. I have completely changed my mind about these trucks. They drive and run like a top and will run for years after the thousand miles plus we put on the clock. They are reliable, easy to

Southern Bulgaria and the turn off for Asia. After Europe, turn left. (*R. L. Kreamer, Kodachrome 35-mm print film,* © *1977, 2019*)

Opposite: Visas for Netherlands, England, East Germany, Yugoslavia, Bulgaria, Turkey. (*R. L. Kreamer* © *1977, 2019*)

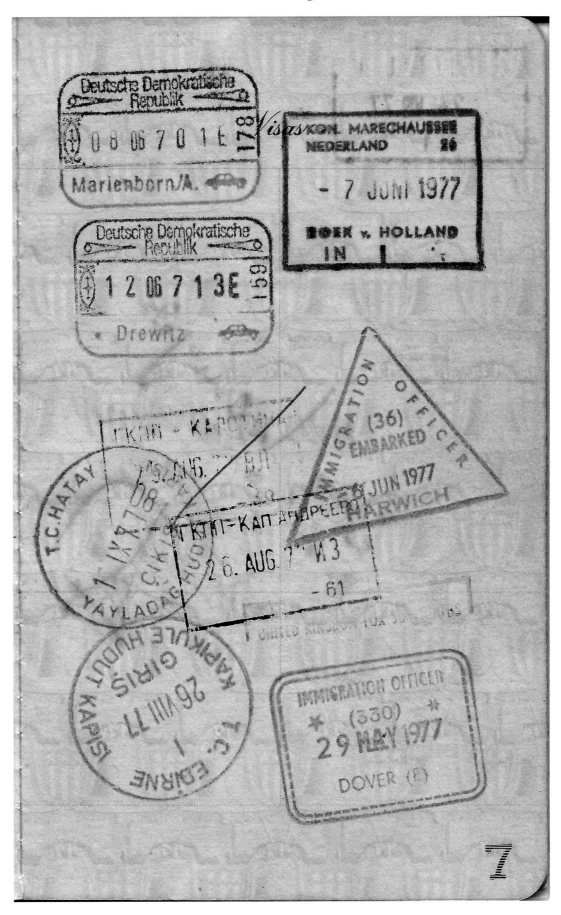

Approaching the bridge across the Bosporus, Istanbul. Where the west meets the east. (*R. L. Kreamer, Kodachrome 35-mm print film,* © *1977, 2019*)

work on, and when people see you coming, they get out of your way.

Driving across the bridge over the Bosporus, I felt a sense of exaltation and real adventure. Very weird and surreal scenes were seen on the bridge as well. Some sort of police checkpoint pulled the convoy over. I watched Crazy Joe get out of his truck and walk over to the police. After a brief exchange between Joe and the cops, I saw the cops were taking turns kicking Joe hard and chasing him back to his truck. Dave and I yelled some shit at them from our truck and they left Joe alone and turned their attention towards us.

A couple of cops pulled our doors open and started to rummage through our stuff. They were looking for drugs—anything. They found my stash of Marlboro cigarettes. They wanted them. They wanted pens. They

wanted money. I said no. They got angry. I offered them a couple of packs of cigs each. They took it and then they went away laughing. What a bunch of corrupt fuckers.

Then a man holding a goat waved down a taxi, and after a brief exchange of words and money with the driver, he put the goat in the back seat, closed the door, and watched the taxi speed away. The goat was sitting up in the back seat, window rolled up, and staring out. It looked so at ease one would think the goat hailed the cab on its way to work.

Dave got into a shouting match with some old dude driving a station wagon. Somebody cut somebody off in traffic and Dave gave him the Italian version of the middle finger. The dude went crazy, got out of his car, leaving wife and kids and car door open and blocking traffic, and ran over to our driver's side and pulled the door open and was screaming with purple rage. Dave laughed at him, knowing it was all show, though I got freaked out; I was sure Dave was going to get an ass kicking.

The real crazy bit was the border crossing into Turkey. Everyone was trying to leave Bulgaria at the same time. Anyone trying to cross the border whilst behind the wheel pulls up to this insane version of an orderly line to get the ol' passport stamped. It was hours and hours, sixteen in total, spent in a huge jam of trucks and cars all trying to squeeze at once from twenty lanes of traffic down to one lane. No police or handy markings on the road to help us merge. It was dog eat dog with no time for fear, so gun the engine, get through this line, and hope no one gets hurt. In the dead of night, tranquil sleep was broken by a truck starting up, somewhere in the queue, somewhere in the distance, and was soon followed on by more and more engines roaring to life. Surrounding us were hundreds of vehicles starting in a deafening bellow followed by thick dust and smoke as everyone claws for a spot another 5 to 10 feet closer to the border. Soon, the need for petrol to be conserved while in line allows for things to quiet down for an hour or so before the game of chicken with the other drivers begins again. It seems to start up once again only after the dust has settled. The road goes ever on, but so does the waiting and the political bureaucracy and money backhanded *du jour* of the typical border crossing.

After Istanbul, it was wide-open road to Ankara and was hellish busy with crazy traffic in that town. Once through Ankara, it was empty desert. We skirted a large inland salt sea called Tuz Gölü in blazing heat.

A hundred miles further southeast, a lone mountain in the distance was basking in the setting sun. My map says the lone mountain is called Hasan Daji. It looks like something out of the book *The Hobbit*. This is real open road—the kind that can swallow a person and never spit them out. Heading due south and it is getting warm again. It reminds me of the American Southwest, and my hometown—all that beautiful desolation. I am with the truck that is on my passport and I cannot let that truck out of my sight. What I did not know when I signed on to this circus was after entering Turkey, any vehicle noted on your passport better be with you when you try to leave, or you have to pony up the value as some sort of tax.

Cash for gas is doled out by Sammy. Sammy got connections on this route, and he is always ready to pay the petrol bill to the nickel. Sammy does not trust nobody with his spare change. Sammy will convert your money, though, nice but at a price. Sammy picks and chooses the highways and byways and we roll along as quickly as we can to keep up with the speeders in the convoy. Sammy's tape player is busted and has been since entering Bulgaria. Sammy is hitting the bottle, and he is looking a bit rough.

Another truck has a busted engine. Rumor also has it that one of the Germans hit a pedestrian somewhere up the road after entering Turkey. The word seems to be that much money will have to be paid to get out of this, now that the law is involved. Our windshield is covered in dead bugs, and we have not cleaned it in days—we can barely see out of it.

August 26. The days are hot and dry. We are camping on the outskirts of Adana and a hot wind is blowing towards the nearly full moon. The moonlight is bright enough to write by. The wind rocks the truck like a cradle. At night, when I try to recall the events of the day, my mind first wanders to visions of the road, lined with cities, villages, cultures, brown fields, and children begging for money. Mountains in the distance beckoned like some vaguely remembered lover. Languages, suspicions, love and hate, governments and ordinary people, gas stations, police, soldiers, and travelers, all have come to watch or join or impose order over the spectacle. It is all spinning by fast. The convoy is taking a repair break and Dave and I heard of some nice beaches to the south, so we are waiting out the delay in İskenderun and have been joined by one of the German dudes.

Sammy has finally trusted us enough with his trucks, so we have been let off the leash. It is like a small village on the outskirts, beautiful beaches, no tourists, and all with a slow, sleepy feel to it. Lots of time for reading, writing, eating, and sleeping. Everyone else is complaining about the delay and waiting is costing pocket money. A couple of funny incidents occurred that have kept me entertained.

We have been camping out along the deserted beaches in the truck and we found a small outdoor cafe nearby, which is really someone's house who wants to serve us some food for money and that really is the setting—it is just an outdoor area to sit in the shade. Toast and coffee. "Got any fresh fruit?" The owner did not understand a word and registered a look of surprise complete with rolling eyes. No English. We clucked like chickens. "Ah," said the man. We cannot speak the local dialect, but we seem to speak chicken. He came back ten minutes later with an axe in one hand and a flapping chicken in the other and a big

Above: Tuz Gölü Lake. With a surface area of over 600 square miles and an average depth of only 2 feet, Tuz lake is one of the world's largest hypersaline lakes. (*R. L. Kreamer, Kodachrome 35-mm print film,* © *1977, 2019*)

Below: Hasan Daji. A 10,000-foot-high inactive stratovolcano straight out of *The Hobbit.* (*R. L. Kreamer, Kodachrome 35-mm print film,* © *1977, 2019*)

grin on his face. He was ready to do the deed right on our table in front of us and chop the chicken's head off. Dave shouted no. He started saying "Eggs man, eggs." Dave squatted and started to make sounds like he was constipated. The owner was really rolling his eyes now. I drew a picture of an egg. Then I drew a picture of a fried egg and showed it to the guy with the axe. "Ah," said the man once again and started to laugh and jabber loudly to his wife. Fifteen minutes later, he came back with two plates of scrambled eggs, fresh tomatoes, toast, and a pot of coffee strong enough to strip wallpaper. Nice.

A couple of days later, I sold this cafe owner a new pair of Levi 501's I had been carrying around in my backpack. The buyer was pleased with his new fashion status in the village and promptly put them on and commenced to parade around in them despite the heat. My backpack was lighter, and I covered the expense of hanging around southern Turkey and got what I paid for it in change.

Some local guy who has been hanging around us the past couple of days went with us to the beach. God knows how the conversation started, but when I started to pay attention to Dave and this other guy, they were talking penis, specifically circumcised *versus* uncut. The local guy said he had never seen one cut, or maybe it was the other way around, so Dave was happy to further his education.

August 31. The days are hot. It is now two weeks on the road. I feel as though I am approaching closer to the edge. The waning moon is peeking over mountains, silhouetting and casting its light on blue-painted hotels like a thin pane. Cats howl in the alley. The night has settled the thick dust and cooled the thicker heat. Tomorrow we leave for the border and Syria. We flew by a lot of what I would like to have seen at a stroll. I am spending money on a hotel room for a good night's sleep and outside my window the howling cats are drowned out by fireworks and loud music blaring from the cafes. The music is beautiful and strange. The singer is amplified with a lot of echo, and flutes and drums provide the backing.

We are staying in Antakya; Antiochian is this town's ancient name. Today, to escape the heat, Dave and I ventured into the nearby mountains on a detour. We found a swift cold mountain stream to bathe in. No one was around. I stood naked in the waterfalls and dried myself lying on huge stream boulders in the hot sun. It was like a spa. In the city of Antakya, people enjoy staring because they are not used to seeing tourists, so I am told, or westerners, or whatever we are. They stare

a lot. Dave and I did a lot of jabbering while stuck in these trucks like cellmates. We talked about life, music, books, philosophy, women, living in West Germany, drugs, and the war in Vietnam now over, politics, bars, the road out ahead; you name it, we blabbed about it. Not much said about the pool game weirdness. Dave insists I am still being a bad sport. A sore loser. Yeah, we talked a lot about a lot of stuff, but we are not talking much now.

I went to a Turkish barbershop and got a shave. It was weirdly old-fashioned, or what I think old-fashioned is—something I imagined the '50s to be like. The hot towel wrapped around the face and the straight razor was expected. The head massage and fingers in the ears to wash them out was not.

Later, Dave and I went to what we thought was a bar, then we thought it was a brothel, and it then turned out to be neither. It was some sort of a dime a dance joint, but it was more than a dime they wanted. For an exorbitant fee, a rather large and funky woman who reminded me of someone's mother would sit at your table and let you talk to them. All the women seemed like the type that, by the time they reached their fifties, would need a shave. We were laughing about how stupid it all was, and the women, management, and other patrons were not amused at us being amused and us not being impressed with their club really started to piss them off. I guess I was laughing at how stupid I was. I was laughing at how stupid Dave was. Dave felt somehow cheated over the price of his beer and cheated at not getting laid. I thought it would make a good story.

I remembered some of the stories Bernard told us earlier at the beginning of our trip. He said the road we were about to travel is called "Death's Highway." The past couple of weeks revealed that not to be an exaggeration. After Austria, the road to the Middle East is primarily a two-lane black top. The route is dotted here and there with the twisted and smashed wrecks of head-on collisions and burned out cars and trucks, left alongside the road like some monuments or tombstones of many personal, yet anonymous tragedies. You have to be ready to slam on your breaks at any given second and we have had more than one close call.

The drive out of southern Turkey and into Syria was a crazy wild ride. For starters, the windshield got blown out by a passing truck. I thought we got shot at, and I still do. Dave was sure it was a stone kicked up by a passing truck. We had to break what was left of the windshield out because it was falling out anyway, and we did not want to be peppered by flying glass in

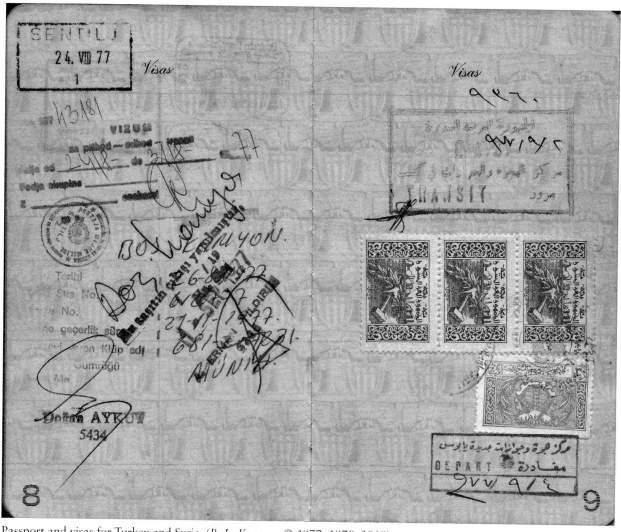

Passport and visas for Turkey and Syria. (*R. L. Kreamer © 1977, 1978, 2019*)

the face. Sammy was sure we did it on purpose when he saw the truck. When I said I thought we were shot at, he went quiet. We wrapped our faces in bandanas from the stinging sand and bugs smacking our faces. The look from other drivers as we roared passed said it all. The coastal road along the Mediterranean was spectacular. Like California Highway 101, only browner.

After crossing into Syria, I was happy to have that truck taken off my passport. Sammy wanted me to drive another truck. It was a big green thing with a large canvas top over the flatbed. "Hell yes," I said. It even had a windshield. After a few hours or so, I noticed a strange whapping sound. I pulled over and saw the tarp had come three quarters of the way off and I had been dragging it for miles. After cutting it free and stowing it away, I drove off knowing Sammy's look and howl would be coming my way.

The sun was setting, and I knew I was miles behind the convoy. I was the last in line and I was driving the thing as fast as it would go—about 52. I rounded some bend of the highway 20 miles from Damascus, and in the fading light, I saw a couple of dozen guys along the road and just a few cars and not many trucks. One guy had a stick with a flashlight taped to it and was waving it while standing in the road. A quick look was all I had time for and some of the guys had Andy of Mayberry-type uniforms on, but they were real phony looking. I thought they were bandits or something, I swear to God. I blew the horn and stomped on the gas. I screamed out the window "Ye haw" for a laugh. Lucky, I did not hit anyone, but I was counting on them diving out of the way, especially after I saw the look on the face of the guy with the stick when I stomped on the gas. The high beams lit up the whites of his eyes. Well, there I was, thinking I was home free. Surely that must be their tail lights up ahead. Then I noticed someone driving like hell to catch up to me. The flashing headlights caught my attention. They kept trying to play a high-speed, pull-alongside game of chicken and I was having none of it. After ten minutes of this game, I noticed one of the guys hanging out of the car waving and shaking his fist looked a lot like Sammy. It was hard to tell for sure in the fast fading twilight. The other guy hanging out of the same window, squeezed together with first guy, looked a lot like a real cop. Oh shit, oh shit, oh shit, was all I could think of and I stomped on the brakes and skidded to a halt while pulling off the road onto the dirt shoulder all at the same time. I kicked up a huge cloud of dust doing that. Of course, the other car had no way to anticipate that maneuver. The smoke from their skidding tires disappeared around the bend. I turned off the truck engine, lit up a cigarette, and waited. I was surrounded by the huge and slowly settling dust cloud I had just created. I sat there thinking. Maybe I was mistaken, and I should fire up this truck and go. Seconds later, the car pursuing me appeared back around the same bend it just disappeared around. Doors opened as it stopped in a cloud of dust nose to nose with my truck. I could recognize Sammy's shouting voice anywhere.

I could see cops and guns. I could see a huge amount of cash needed to save my ass. I could see the inside of a Syrian jail. A policeman pulled my door open and yanked me out. "Bandits, banditos, pirates!" The cop in charge looked cross and hurt. "We are not bandits," he quietly said to me in English. "Get in your truck and follow us." Sammy was swearing and turning beet red—just foaming with rage. I turned to Sammy and said, "I thought you guys were pirates, I was trying to save your truck." He looked at me sideways and kept on howling.

The cop who grabbed me slid into the passenger seat, and follow I did. As I drove, the cop started to search the stuff around him; my camera bag and my books were of particular interest to him. I offered him a cigarette and he said no. Damn, it was a police checkpoint after all. It seemed like it took forever, but we finally returned to the checkpoint and I soon knew how Crazy Joe had felt back in Graz. I went to the police chief and apologized to him in front of everyone, especially his men. Bowing and scraping, yes, I really knew how Crazy Joe felt. Later, I surmised being humble is what really saved me a lot of money. Gather round and watch; the Yankee is eating crow with a spoon. Dave could not stop laughing.

The convoy made its last trip under the cover of darkness into Damascus and we found a vacant lot somewhere near downtown. Sammy wanted us to sleep in the trucks and guard them. Early the next morning, I had the drivers pose for a picture in front of the trucks. Everyone gathered in front of the truck with no windshield. Sammy on top for the first photo, and then Crazy Joe on top for the second photo.

Damascus, Syria. Wow, made it to Damascus, the oldest continuously inhabited city on the planet—or so they say.

The next morning, the trucks were delivered, and then came the wad of money for Sammy and it was over. It was back to business and we filed past Sammy to collect our wages. Yo ho ho. I felt like a sailor putting into shore. I was shortchanged a little for the trouble I caused back at the last police checkpoint. Dave tried to get Sammy to change his mind. I took the money while looking Sammy in the eye. The last I saw of him, he was turning his face away and I said, "Good luck." We were paid in German Marks. I earned 375 DM. I almost felt nostalgic.

September 1. Hot and dry. So now we are in Damascus and it is weird. Even Dave feels self-conscious in his cut off shorts, which he has been wearing since it got hot. He will not stop wearing them. Some local cats are wearing bellbottomed trousers and semi-long hair. Still, lots of staring at us when we go walking around. The fact that Dave and Heino insist on wearing teeny-weenie shorts does not help us to blend in. As they walk around, I see local dudes nudging each other and pointing at their ass cheeks poking out of their shorts. Saw a bit of the old city and bazaars. Heard the wailing from the minaret calling all to prayer. The music blaring from the cafes is mesmerizing and exotic. The heat and dust of the day gives way to cool evenings, illuminated by neon and 100-Watt bulbs. Sent off a good selection of postcards. Made sure they were franked.

Everyone in the convoy crew is happy to have made it to the finish line in one piece to Damascus. (*R. L. Kreamer, Kodachrome 35-mm print film,* © *1977, 2019*)

Dave and Heino strolling through downtown Damascus, Syria in teeny-weeny shorts. (*R. L. Kreamer, Kodachrome 35-mm print film, © 1977, 2019*)

2

From Lebanon to the Holy Land

September 2. The days are hot. We found a great cafe that sells whole rotisserie chickens, and about the third time we stopped in the place, we noticed some dudes waiting outside and throwing up. They had sent their friend in to buy. We noticed a lot more people throwing up on the streets once we heard it was a symptom of cholera. We are now planning to get out of Damascus as fast as possible. We did not know anything about the epidemic for a day or so. No trucks anymore to jump into and split quickly. We are now on foot. We are going to Beirut and will try to get a boat to Cyprus— Dave's idea. It is the opposite direction I want to go, but it may be fun.

Went into a cafe and smoked a hookah. It was filled with tobacco, spices, and dried apples. It was weird but nice hanging with the old men watching the world go by. I had never seen women dressed in a burqa until now. They are few and far between, though, as most women dress like German housewives, and the men dress like rent-a-car counter salesman. True story. I was just commenting to Dave that I could not understand how anyone could see while wearing one of those, when we saw a burqa-clad figure trip and roll down about ten concrete steps outside a bank. I hope she is OK.

Met some locals whom seemed friendly. Dave asked them about buying some smoke. We were directed to some weird part of town and we got the creeps. Saw loads of cops and got freaked out and split quick. Dave thought we were set up to get busted, he was sure of it.

It seems a few days ago, one of the other drivers had tossed a huge tow bar on my backpack and twisted it out of shape. I tried to put it on, but it was hanging sideways and when I tried to twist the frame and bend

it back into shape, it broke. I was pissed off and furious about it. Dave told me to shut the fuck up because he did not want to hear about it, and it was my tough fucking luck and tough fucking shit to me, so fucking shut up. Yikes.

I searched the city and found the best backpack that I could find, and it turned out to be crappy. Cost way more than it should have. Canvas and nondescript, so at least I do not stand out much.

September 5. The days are dry and hot. Another wild ride. Went to some major taxi stand near a bus station and haggled for a cab ride from Damascus to Beirut. Cost was around 6 dollars U.S. The driver wanted a full load and he was not kidding: four people crammed in the back seat and four people crammed in the front. Luggage tied on top, stuffed into the trunk tied partially closed, and dudes up front with suitcases on their laps. I was surprised the taxi did not need a push to get started. Dave and I were in the back. The trip out of the city found us stuck in a traffic jam behind a garbage truck. The stench was so bad everyone was getting sick, so our fellow travelers had the bright idea to roll up the windows and light up cigs. No AC, so we almost passed out in the heat, driver included.

Border crossing into Lebanon was no problem. They just wanted the fee and for us to move on. Nice postage-type stamp in the passport. We heard there was a war on, but it is supposed to be over for now. Syrian troops everywhere at roadblocks and lots of marching around and showing off their guns. Things seemed normal at first, until we entered the outskirts of town and then we started seeing bullet holes everywhere, shattered buildings, shattered lives. Shit, I have never seen anything like it except in movies and newsreels.

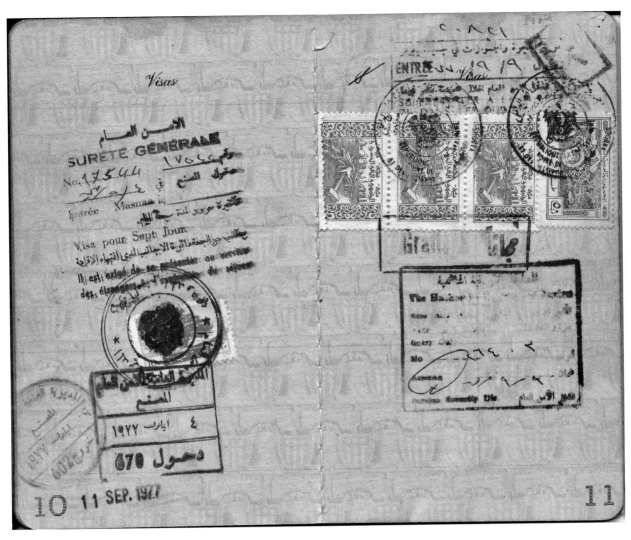

Passport and visas for Lebanon and Syria. (*R. L. Kreamer © 1977, 1978, 2019*)

Rolled into downtown as the sun was setting. We asked around and got directed to what was left of a hotel.

On the way, we encountered more and more troops on every intersection and on every street. All shouting at Dave and me to get off the streets. It was all guns until they saw a pair of scared tourists, then it was more shouts of "curfew" from the troops and shouts of "hotel" from us.

The hotel was once five stories tall, but only three are left in most places. The shower was on the third floor and that is now the roof. Small pipe sticking out of the wall with a trickle of water constantly running somewhere to the ruined nether reaches below. It is a very cold shower. Ceiling is open to the sky. The lobby is shot up and full of bullet holes. The hotel clerk is armed I think and had some armed backup as well. At night, we propped a chair against our hotel room door.

A few vendors are pushing carts around the streets. Some consumer goods, mostly deep-fried food stalls on wheels getting pushed quickly home before dark. Troops behind sandbagged intersections, with armored trucks and tanks backing them up. I guess it would be unwise to run a stop sign. Most of the locals looked calm, going about their business as usual. I guess either you are dead or you get on with life. As night fell, the city grew dark and quiet. No street lights and very little power to the remaining buildings. Lost track of the date.

Today, in the bright light of a September morning, the bombed-out city is a surreal backdrop to people going about their business. We have been walking around the city and whole areas are burned out and deserted— it is like a ghost town. Soldiers are everywhere, and they seem to outnumber the people on the streets two to one.

My first impression of all the militia being from Syria was wrong. A few other countries have troops here, and even the U.N. has a peacekeeping force—blue helmets

View from the hotel, Beirut, Lebanon. (*R. L. Kreamer, Kodachrome 35-mm print film*, © *1977, 2019*)

What was left of Victory Square, Beirut, Lebanon. (*R. L. Kreamer, Kodachrome 35-mm print film*, © *1977, 2018*)

Walking the streets of war-torn Beirut, Lebanon. (*R. L. Kreamer, Kodachrome 35-mm print film,* © *1977, 2018*)

hiding behind sandbags, sometimes peeking over the top. The barn door is now closed, but the horse did not bolt, it was shot. In the light of day, the immediate sense of danger seems to have lifted and replaced with a sense of tragedy. Beirut is like a once-beautiful actress ravaged by time. No, it is more like Montgomery Clift, ravaged by a car wreck. I had no idea there was a war on and I could take a taxi right to its door.

We have learned there is no regular ferry service to Cypress, but a boat may leave in three days. Maybe. The cost of a ticket is extreme. It seems that we are to leave by the route we traveled in on. We continue our wandering around the city and make plans to depart back through Syria.

In the hotel lobby appeared a woman. It was weird; she appeared out of nowhere like a spy or a ghost. She wanted to hang out with us. We got weird looks from the heavies in the hotel lobby. She walked through the streets with us and asked us a lot of questions about who we were and what we are doing here in the city. She seemed surprised at our answers. We are tourists, no more, no less. She found it hard to believe we were here for fun and travel, and to see the world. I wanted to ask her about her home and country, but Dave kept butting in with personal questions like he

was trying to get laid. She said she was from Baghdad. It turns out she is twenty-eight years old and never had a boyfriend. She told us if she had ever slept with a man before marriage, her family would kill her. Really kill her as in slit her throat kill her. She said in her country if an unmarried couple were found together, like in a parked car or something, they would go to jail. She said she planned on never getting married. The man had all the rights. The right to premarital sex was his alone. After marriage, the woman had to obey every command of her husband. She was getting a little pissed off as she spoke.

She told us her name was Máhá. She said in Arabic, it meant the pretty eyes of a deer or pretty eyes of a cow. When I told her my name was Bob, she said it meant door. I almost said "Knock, knock." She gave me her address and wrote it in my book. Máhá— Unknown Soldier State Organization for Engineering Industries—Baghdad," with a phone number. Máhá has been laughing her head off when she heard me trying out my feeble Arabic. I am trying to learn some words in Arabic. A lot of pleasure seems to be derived at constant corrections of my pronunciation by the locals.

After wandering around, dusk was falling and, like Cinderella, Máhá said she had to leave. The Syrian troops made her really uptight, and there is the curfew. Later, while I was buying cigarettes at a market stall, Dave and I were talking to a local guy. We asked him if he had any hash for sale. The look of fear soon left his face when he realized we were foreigners. He said if we were real tourists, we should visit Baalbek in the central highlands. He said they have famous Roman ruins and maybe we could find some smoke there. Dave wanted to hurry back to the hotel and pack, so we could leave right away—me too.

September 6. Blue skies and hot days. We made it to a place called Baalbek, Lebanon. Unbelievable, un-fucking-believable. I hope I can remember everything and write it down.

Dave and I caught a local bus from Victory Square in Beirut to Baalbek; it was a dusty and bumpy ride, with lots of checkpoints along the way. At one point, Syrian soldiers boarded the bus and walked the aisle looking everyone over. One soldier was leaning over me, and the barrel of his machine gun was poking my knee. I had visions of it going off and shattering more than my journey. I grabbed the barrel and moved it off my leg while saying, "Ouch." He looked up and laughed. The locals are cool and seem friendly. They are surprised to hear we are tourists.

By the time we rolled into Baalbek, there were very few people on the bus. A very young man made a beeline for the seat next to us and started talking and asking questions non-stop. What a chatterbox, he is worse than me. He said his name was T___. When we told him we were tourists, he invited us to stay with him. I had my doubts, but Dave had none, and as it turns out, Dave was right, and I am glad we did go with T___.

As we left the bus and started to follow him with our backpacks through the dusty streets, a wild-eyed demented man with bloodshot eyes ran up to us and started shouting. He screamed we should not go with this boy, he was no good and a thief and that he was always stealing his tourists. T___ exchanged a few words with this guy and we trudged on. At this point, I was wondering what kind of crazy scene we had wandered in to. When we got to his house, T___ started barking orders at his mother and his sisters. Later, we learned that after the death of his father, he was the man of the house. In this culture, despite being only fifteen years old, he was in charge, no questions asked. He told them to jump and they already knew how high. He ordered his older sisters and brother-in-law to bring Dave and me some tea. I found all this a bit

Our hosts in Baalbek, Lebanon. (*R. L. Kreamer, Kodachrome 35-mm print film, © 1977, 2019*)

embarrassing, especially after the women brought us a plate of cubed cold watermelon with all the seeds methodically picked out.

We asked about the Roman ruins and they all said they would make arrangements for us to see them. The family was well educated and spoke English as well as French perfectly.

T___ had a few of his friends drop by and it was like he was showing off a large fish he had just caught. T___ said we would hang out with his friends tomorrow and they left us to sit around while the women prepared dinner. When it was ready, a beautiful carpet was rolled out and we all sat in a circle with large plates of food set in the middle. We all ate with our hands, after washing first of course, and I received my first lesson in manners Middle Eastern style. Men take food first, and we are to use only the right hand for eating.

The main dish was lamb and spices, served with rice and vegetables. Some type of flat bread was passed around, each of us tearing off a piece. We were breaking bread with a family that had just opened their home and hearts to us. It was the best tasting meal I ever had. It was like love served on a dish. T___'s mother was happy and proud as we ate, and we were obviously really enjoying her cooking. At that moment, she reminded me of my own Italian mother, who also enjoyed giving hospitality and food to all and sundry who came to her door. My thick head opened a crack, and a trickle of universal truth managed to seep in.

Sleeping arrangements were being made for us, and when I found out T___'s pregnant sister and his brother in-law were giving me their room and bed, I tried to draw the line and insist I would sleep in the courtyard in my sleeping bag. They got truly insulted and huge arguments started, the gist of which was something like they must have done something wrong to make me turn the offer down. I finally said *"Daman, daman, teschhe kay ederem, teschhe kay ederem"* loud enough for them to hear me, and they all stopped and started laughing. Dave was getting someone else's room and bed. I did not sleep very well that night.

In the morning, when I saw T___'s pregnant sister holding her back like it was sore, I told them I had breathing problems and tonight I planned to sleep in the courtyard outside in the fresh air for my health. T___'s mother gave me a knowing smile. I cleared my backpack and sleeping bag out and stowed them in a corner of the courtyard. I think T___'s sister went right to bed.

After breakfast, we strolled out into Baalbek under blue skies and got a tour of T___'s world. When we wandered over to his friend's house and sat down, we were floored by the very next question we were asked. How many kilos of hash do you want to buy, 20, 30? Our jaws dropped as Dave and I immediately looked at each other. Then it was our turn to laugh. We said, "Hey man, we're tourists!" I was beginning to wonder what kind of gangster gang we got hooked up with. We explained we were really on our way to India, and no way could we carry 30 kilos of hash on us across those borders, let alone carry the extra weight. Then the shoe dropped for T___, we really were just tourists. The shoe dropped for Dave and I as well. We had wandered into something well beyond our control. We all had a good laugh, and this revelation did not seem to bother T___. After all, he still had his prize fish to show off and we were seen as some sort of celebrities having come a long, long way to stay with T___.

I had my map so I showed them where we came from and where we were going. They were fairly impressed with the idea we were on our way to India. The map is a good ice breaker. Still some of his buddies tried to make some sort of deal. They explained that with half the dough up front, they would deliver any amount, anywhere in the world, no problem. When we said no, really, we are just tourists, one of them handed Dave and I each a slab of hash the size of a deck of cards. I asked, "How much" and made like I was reaching for money, and they said, "No money, if you change your mind just let us know, remember us first, the J___ family, the best shit around." Now that's what I call a business card. They said the war had dried up the tourist trade and the major buyers were staying away. They had tons of hash left over from last year, let alone the stuff from this year. Prices are slashed, and everything must go. They were hoping for far more than we could deliver and if Dave and I represented the resurging tourist industry, this place was in trouble. Or we were in trouble because we didn't have a clue everyone was staying away.

They put some disco music on the stereo and then proceeded to roll up, Lebanese style. A Marlboro cigarette is emptied into the palm, and a chunk of blonde hash is added, and it is all mashed and mixed with the thumb. The thumb and palm are used like a portable and permanently attached mortar and pestle. All the mix is then reloaded into the empty cigarette cylinder and tapped tight. These guys could do this maneuver in less than a minute, without looking. Later, when I tried to duplicate this, it took me over half an hour.

Anyway, we sat around smoking this shit, though Dave, not being much of a tobacco smoker did not enjoy it much, but huff and puff he did. Man, this was some powerful smoke. Tripping and God is now talking to you powerful stuff. The disco music took a bit of the mystic edge off the experience, but it did not matter; they were trying to show us that they were hip, man, and I asked them if they had any Bob Dylan records. They said, "Yeah, Bob means door." After a while, I could not remember what we were talking about, but I remember we laughed and laughed. I remember they wanted to know what America was like and they were preoccupied with the concept of free love.

We must have wandered out of there because we ended up at the Roman ruins in the blazing afternoon sun with T___'s cousin. I had my camera with me. I was so stoned, it seemed to take me hours to set up, and some shots I fear may end up washed out in the noonday sun. I could not get the light meter to work, though it is OK now.

Dave and I wandered around, and T___ and his cousin looked bored and stayed in the shade smoking cigs. Deep blue sky overhead made the yellow and orange-colored ruins look fantastic and surreal. The scale of the ruins was impressive. They are huge. While

wandering to the ruins, we saw a straggly pot field near a garbage dump on the outskirts of town. I had the guys pose for a photo, and T___ hid behind the weeds.

Later, T___ took us to meet some of his uncles. After introducing us, T___ split, saying he had to be somewhere and he would be back. We ended up in a room with about a dozen guys, all much older than us. These cats are really old, and their ages seemed to range from forty-five to sixty-five years old. No one spoke English and, of course, we did not speak Arabic or French. Dave commented on us being on display. We agreed it was like being famous and I guess in a way we are famous around here. These guys were content with sitting around watching us like we were some sort of TV show. I was wondering what we should do when one of the old dudes said "Hubbly bubbly?"

We knew what water pipe meant. "*Daman*," came my reply. Everyone laughed. Out came a massive brass-inlayed water pipe with many hoses attached. It was like a work of art, covered with inlay and engravings. Out came a massive chunk of red hash. Wow, I had never seen anything like this before. The traditional clothes these guys were wearing, the water pipe, the

Walking around the outskirts Baalbek, Lebanon with T___'s cousin, Dave and T___ hiding behind the weeds. (*R. L. Kreamer, Kodachrome 35-mm print film, © 1977, 2019*)

The Temple of Jupiter, *c.* 60 CE, Roman ruins, Baalbek, Lebanon. (*R. L. Kreamer, Kodachrome 35-mm print film,* © *1977, 2019*)

Dave works on his tan with the city of Baalbek as a back drop. (*R. L. Kreamer, Kodachrome 35-mm print film,* © *1977, 2019*)

carpet, the house and décor, and garden outside with the glowing sun peeping through the window, it all seemed like a movie.

The old guy was filling the bowl of the pipe when he dropped a chunk of hash the size of your average goldfish on the carpet. He did not even bother to pick it up; he just rubbed it in with his foot like it was cigarette ash. We smoked until my throat was sore and my eyes were as red as the hash we were smoking. I could not keep up with these old guys. This stuff just keeps getting stronger and stronger. The old dude gave me a chunk as a keepsake.

After an hour of this smoking and choking, another one of these old dudes pulled out a huge glass jar of honey. They were passing it around and taking long swigs from it like Winnie the Pooh. I assumed the old dude was saying it was good for the throat as he passed the jar to me while speaking and rubbing his throat. I took a long drink. What a crazy scene. T___ finally returned to retrieve us.

On the way back to his house, we asked him where all this hash came from. He pointed to the nearby hills and said, "If you want, we can visit my uncle's farm" and we said, "Hell yes" in unison like we had been practicing.

Dave and I were sitting around the courtyard in the cool of the twilight with T___, his cousin, and his brother in-law. Dave and I were talking about what we saw in Beirut and so we started to ask them about the war that had destroyed the city and brought the occupying armies into Lebanon. T___ looked sad and did not say much, then he left.

T___'s cousin never says much anyway, so it was T___'s brother-in-law who spoke. He spoke in a soft voice. It was filled with sadness and regret, and it carried simplicity and directness, like a storyteller from a thousand years ago. All at once, I knew I had lived a sheltered and privileged life and these guys were living on the edge, and his story had barely begun. The world of chaos brought right to the doorstep. Their doorstep. He said the war had started as a power struggle between the politicians of the left wing and the politicians of the right-wing factions in a fight to control the state.

He said the press has simplified the start of the war incorrectly as a war between the Christians and the Muslims. He said in the beginning, although most of the left were Christian and most of the national right were Muslim, it was really a battle between the liberals who wanted a future with Europe and the rest of the world and the conservatives who wanted to be insular

and keep the West and its influences out. He said it got out of control, and since no one would back down, it is only going to get worse.

I mentioned the U.N. troops I saw and asked if a peace had not been worked out. He answered that this was just a lull in the war and both sides were using this time to rearm and to get ready. He said there are so many factions, it would make your head spin. What really troubled him was that the fundamental nationalists hated everyone and that they would sell out to the Syrians before they would let rival countrymen get a leg over on them. It seemed to move beyond politics. He said the irony is that now it seems to be turning into a religious struggle under the guise of a political struggle. The propaganda turns to truth. My head is spinning. Knowing I do not know anything about Middle East politics is all I know. I do not know if I wrote what was said. If I got that right or what. All I know is that I do not know what I thought I knew. He also filled us in on the real story around here. It appears Dave and I stumbled into a dope smoker's dream world fantasyland.

Everyone I have met in this little town just wants to try to keep all this madness away. It turns out the extra money from the hash industry earns enough bribe money to make that happen for now. They sure as hell are not spending the money on Rolls-Royces or huge mansions. Some people seem fashionably dressed, though, with lots of designer jeans and haircuts strolling around. Even the women are more Western-styled than in Syria, albeit modestly so. The cops and the military all have their hand out, and as long as something is put into it, the wolf is kept from the door. I guess that sometimes the greased palm has trouble catching hold of you. I hope they can keep this bubble of a dream around their lives and their town.

Turns out our host is just a young kid, really nice and a great guy. He is still in school. I wonder what he will be like in ten years. He is definitely not involved with what is going on around him, and he lives on its margins. His mother would not let him get involved.

This town is the major production center for blonde and red Lebanese hash. The whole scene is run by four families. T___ is related to someone in one of those families. I am glad we are low key.

The war has kept the tourists and all the big-time buyers away as well. No wonder everyone seems surprised to see us strolling around the town. But truth be told, hash or no hash, I am glad we came. The people are beautiful and kind. The ruins are beautiful and amazing, and the mountains and the deserts remind me of my hometown. The food is magic and T___ and his family are so cool that staying here forever is a gorgeous daydream. But, alas, I have miles to go before I reach India and Kathmandu, this current visa will expire, and I hope to see my ex-girlfriend again someday.

I must admit it is magic to spend the night, lying down and looking up at the millions of stars, just smoking and thinking and dreaming. Something about seeing so many stars makes for easy dreaming.

I have been thinking about my ex-girlfriend a lot lately. I guess she is my ex because we have not seen each other much. I cannot quite own up to the fact that she dumped me, or we just drifted apart—figuratively and literally. Drifting sounds better than dumped. If I am honest, I think I got dumped and I think I know I got dumped but cannot admit it. I think about her body and her skin. Her skin is like alabaster. It is soft and beautiful and seemingly flawless. She is even beautiful deep inside.

I find myself wondering about far too much, but for now, its cig and candle out, and time to pull this blanket of stars over me and sleep.

Strange, but I can clearly recall my father pointing out constellations and stars to me when I was a little boy, like it was yesterday. I could not see what he was pointing to until he handed me his glasses to try on.

Last night, as I slept in the courtyard under the stars, I dreamed that I was driving the trucks again. The trucks did not move, but the earth was spinning under our wheels. I knew I was dreaming and I felt as though I was being led. Cities that are now ancient ruins we saw being newly built in the distance. The cities seemed to gleam and shine in the full autumn sun under a cloudless blue sky. Other cities were burning as they spun past. We could not step out of the truck or we would be swept away, as if in a flood.

Today, when I woke up and was having a cup a tea and writing about my dream, T___ came to me very worried. It seems Dave was nowhere to be found. I was sure he was out strolling around, but T___ was really concerned, although he would not say why.

I was feeling the weight of all the political shit storm around me and a sense of the same dread that T___'s brother in law was dreading, like the coming flood. I was already having a spooky morning. I only knew two things: I should not have smoked hash for breakfast and I smoked too much hash for breakfast. I figured he was out somewhere, trying to get laid. After an hour or so of T___ pacing up and down, dashing out, and coming back, each time more uptight than

before, I started to get a bit freaked out too. Paranoia is contagious.

"Where's Dave, where's Dave?" T___ just kept repeating it over and over. He then told me he thought there were some "bad people" around and maybe he was in trouble. I really had no a clue what he could mean, but my wild imagination started to fill in the blanks. Holy shit, where was Dave? I did not even know if it was like him to split without a word or without telling anybody. I have known that cat for only a year or two. He is a nice guy and all, so what's going on?

Did the cops get him? Did some Syrian troops pick him up? Was he dead? Kidnapped, and a ransom was going to have to be paid? My mind played tricks on me, although I did not say anything. I wanted to know what "bad people" meant. T___ was not saying. We made the rounds and we kept asking "Where's Dave?"

It was like a bad pun to the old "Dave's not here" joke. Nevertheless, he finally did turn up, and just strolled in and was quite surprised at all the fuss.

He even started to blame me for all the concern for his wellbeing. I was surprised because it seemed he was only thinking of himself. He never seemed for a moment think of his host or how T___ felt. The funny part that he missed out on, and I did not bother to tell him, was word of us looking for him began to precede our search, and more than one old man mocked me with an embellished whine of "Where's Dave" before I had even said a word.

Dave just laughed at us and I think, in the end, T___ was sort of hurt. It turns out that Dave just went for a stroll and ran into some dudes and must have been hanging out and smoking or something. Pretty much how I called it from the start before getting wound up by T___. Dave thought we were fools for being worried.

September 9. The days are hot and sunny. Our visa expires in two days and I am sitting having tea and trying to recall the past few days for my journal. Strange days indeed. We are waiting to get the bus to Amman, Jordan. Tourist travelers read books while waiting. Locals mostly sit and watch. I scratch down all the stuff about stuff while waiting. Travel is a lot of waiting. We have taken our leave of T___ and family, and although they will be missed, they will never be forgotten.

A couple of days ago, Dave and I were dropped off at a farmhouse in the mountains near town. Only a couple of hours by car and a world away.

We camped out and had the run of the place. It had huge pot fields stretching down the slopes of the hill

At the farmhouse, Baalbek, Lebanon. (*R. L. Kreamer, Kodachrome 35-mm print film,* © *1977, 2019*)

where the farmhouse was situated. Acres and acres of ripe, perfect, and ready-for-picking buds. I went out into the middle of the field to take a dump, wiped my butt with a couple of buds, and tossed them aside.

One room of the house had a press used in making bricks of hash. Another room held sieves and screens used in processing the pollen from the plants. A third room held a pile of loose hash that was 4 or 5 feet tall and waiting to be pressed. T___ said it was last year's harvest, unsold because of the war. I walked up the pile, leaving deep footprints, and I made balls like snowballs and threw them at the walls where they stuck in place. Weird to think all this was lying around to rot. In the fields, the plants had huge 2-foot-long buds on them. Harvest time. The smell was heady. Later, we picked some of the larger purple buds and set them on the tin roof of the farmhouse. They dried in a couple of hours and Dave and I rolled huge joints like Rasta bats, and this horn of plenty was played until we could play no more. All I can remember is an unreal haze of wandering around the hills and fields all day in the sunshine. When our hosts had returned to pick us up and saw we had picked some buds for smoking, they got really upset. I offered to pay for the grass and they laughed. As it turned out, they were not

annoyed at us for picking the grass, but upset that we resorted to smoking "that shit, blah" and offered us some "proper" smoke.

It seems they thought we were crazy for smoking the grass before it was processed into hash. They offered us more free lumps of the stuff and implored us not to debase ourselves. We told them it was "American style," but they were definitely not impressed and gave us some puzzled looks and a ride back to town.

Dave and I realized we had not taken a stroll through the "downtown" area and we decided to have one last look around the town. So off we went exploring alone and on foot. The main drag was dusty and busy with traffic.

A traffic cop was strategically located in the middle of the busy main intersection, on a raised platform, fast asleep. He was oblivious to the horn-blowing chaos below, as drivers were left to figure out for themselves who had the right of way. The locals were happy to do their civic duty to keep the traffic flowing in some sort of fair, but a rather shuddering and jerking way and directed themselves through with shouts and hand gestures.

Very weird. We kept walking and were quickly approached by two policemen on foot. They started jabbering at us rapidly and all Dave and I could decipher was "Come with us." I thought of two things, how much hash I was holding and how much money I had on me for a bribe. They marched us to the police station and I really thought I was done for.

They started jabbering some more, and while Dave and I were looking at each other, wondering what was going on and what was going to happen, the guy in charge took a seat behind a big desk, opened a drawer, and pulled out a huge lump of hash the size of a baby's head. He proceeded to roll up a joint in the style we had become accustomed to. They said they had heard about us and were glad to finally meet us. Wow, we are famous, for not being afraid and just showing up.

The four of us could not stop laughing as we smoked and smoked. Smoking with the city's finest until my brain fell out and rolled across the floor—just when I thought I had seen it all. It seemed each of us had no idea what the other three were talking about, though it did not seem to matter at all. All that mattered was we were laughing and enjoying life.

September 10. The days are hot. Amman, Jordan. Traveled by local bus out of Lebanon. The border crossing was easy enough to be of no consequence. Staying at the Al-Farouk Hotel in Faisal Street across from the Arab Bank and it is costing 750 Phils a night.

The hotel stinks of grease and sweat. It is a cheap dive that is a real drag after the magic of Baalbek. The beds are 5 feet long, which is OK for Dave, but it is 1 foot too short for me. The walls next to the beds have huge grease stains where heads have rested. It is like someone was sitting up all night for months on end.

We have heard that we can get a visa at the main police station and the overland crossing into Israel is at a place along the Jordan River called the Allenby Bridge. People here seem all right and friendly, so we plan to hitchhike down the ancient Kings Highway.

September 11. The Palestine. On the border again. Visa to cross into "Occupied Palestine" obtained from the Jordanian police. It is a document separate from my passport. The deal at this border crossing is the issue of a visa on this separate bit of paper, so when I exit, the visa is removed without a stamp showing up on the passport. That will allow continued travel through Middle Eastern countries that would otherwise turn someone with the Israel visa away.

The Jordan side of the border is closed until morning. We spent the entire day with our thumbs out. We were the only ones on the highway going south trying to bum a ride.

We got to the city of Salt in two rides, and once there, we spent a while looking for water. Came down

Business card for the Al-Farouk Hotel, Aman, Jordan. (*R. L. Kreamer* © 1977, 1978, 2019)

out of the mountains to near sea level and ran out of water and we got plenty of stupid parched. Ended up deciding to go knocking on doors and were given a drink at the first house we stopped at. All the men came out and stared. A young man wanted to know where we were going, and we said Jerusalem and into Israel. He said he always wanted to know what it was like there. I told him if I returned this way, I would stop by and visit him again and tell him what it is like. I thanked him for his kindness and shook his hand. He said his name is Wada.

Dave wanted to toss a coin to see who was going to carry the stash. I said no way. Dave wants to keep our stash. I am a chicken shit and want to throw it away. Dave got his asshat on and we were revisiting the pool game again. He said we could split the stash fifty-fifty regardless who does the carry. I said no. After a long diatribe of how uncool I was being, I said OK and again immediately regretted it. I agreed knowing full well if I lost the toss, I was going to dump it when he was not looking. I almost told him as much but did not have to. He lost the toss and started to plan a hiding place. What a dope. I tried to talk him out of it, but he was determined.

I have a feeling this border crossing is going to be different from anything we have seen. Anyway, we made it from Salt to the Allenby Bridge and now must wait.

We have wandered around and now I am sitting against a rock and behind me is a pump house keeping a rhythmic pounding like a huge clock work, spewing water from the Jordan River into the parched desert fields and ditches that stretch into the sunset. Tiny houses dot the landscape. Lots of date palms.

Before leaving Germany, I wrote a letter to Mr. Korner at the Kibbutz Ami'ad, somewhere north of the Sea of Galilee. I did not get a reply, so I hope I can just show up. I have heard that one may not get to choose the Kibbutz, but it gets assigned. Our friends recommended this one because they were there, and they said it had a bar for the volunteers, run by the volunteers.

The sun is going down over the village and a soft wind is blowing from the west. People and a few tractors roll by as silhouettes, kicking up dust, illuminated and backlit. Dave and I are not the only ones waiting for the border to open. I am happy to sleep in the open tonight and under the stars again.

September 13. The days are hot and the nights are beginning to cool. Jerusalem. Staying in a youth hostel north of the Old City within easy walking distance of everything.

The city of Jericho, West Bank, Palestine. Archaeologists believe it to be one of the oldest inhabited cities in the world, dating back to 9000 BCE. (*R. L. Kreamer, Kodachrome 35-mm print film, © 1977, 2019*)

Heavy border crossing at the Jordan River. By dawn, a mass of people appeared out of nowhere to wait in line for the border to open. Dave spent the night trying to devise a way to bring our hash stash along. He decided to use my first aid kit and stuffed it into one of three bandage packs. Three identical packages but two packs weighed half an ounce and the third weighed half a pound. I thought for sure he was screwed. We split up and did not go through the line together. Later, I thought that must have looked weird.

They took my shoes to be X-rayed, my backpack was emptied on to a table, and everything was fingered, sniffed, and fingered again. Even pat down body searches by different soldiers in case they missed something. Every stitch of clothing turned inside out. Every book flipped through again and again.

Never ending questions about the visas from Lebanon, Syria, and Jordan asked over and over. Back to the fingering again. When it was almost all over, or nearing the end of the search, they asked me where I was going. I told them I was heading north to work as a volunteer on Kibbutz Ami'ad. The army dude said, "Well why the fuck didn't you say so?" He told me to pack up all my stuff and get going. I smiled and did just that. I got my visa stamped, and after passing through the gate, I found a spot to sit down and wait for Dave. And I waited some more. At last, I recognized his face and walk loping through the gate. He was nervous and almost shaking and he would not talk until we reached what he considered a safe distance from the border.

He said he waited until I started through and followed a bit behind. The intense search caught him by surprise, and he said the regret started right away, but it was too late as he had nowhere to dump the stash unseen. Dave said what saved his hide was some unknown stranger or soldier burned his arm with a cig. It was enough to distract the guard who was searching him. It happened at the crucial moment when they started to rummage through the first aid kit and they were busy watching Dave reach into the kit to put some ointment on the burn. Dave said while they were watching him, the guard picked up all three bandage packages at once and did not notice the weight difference. What a lucky fucker. Dave was still pretty shook up by the experience and vowed never to do that again. He wanted to find somewhere to light up before we set off hitchhiking to Jerusalem. While we were getting high, Dave announced that since he took all the risk, he was entitled to most of the stash. I was not even surprised that I was not surprised.

Hitchhiking has a whole new set of rules in this country. Lots of people do it and lots of people give rides. We had no clue to the pecking order though. The best roadside spots have loads of soldiers hanging around. None of them bother with sticking their thumb out if someone else is doing it. The second a vehicle stops, they shove the hitchhiker out of the way and climb in.

Dave got really annoyed when it first happened, and a huge argument started up. The soldiers left hanging around explained to us that this is the way it is done around here. The army has priority and right of way because there is a war on as far as they are concerned. They offered us a beer and they showed us how the sight on an AK-47 doubles as a bottle opener. It was all cool in the end. We now know not to hitchhike around the army, unless they are offering beer. You have to get in line.

Everybody is armed to the teeth. It is like the gunfight at the Jewish OK corral. Army dudes with guns are one thing, but every other civilian with a machine gun is making me nervous. I saw a well-armed old dude with a pistol in a holster and a machine gun around his neck, and he was wearing glasses with lenses as thick as the bottom of a coke bottle. Blind as a bat I bet, so what the fuck can he see to shoot at?

I am now afraid to make any sudden moves around some people. We got a ride as far as Jericho and decided to stop and find a cafe. After I had a falafel, we walked around town for a while. The first one I ever ate, by the way, and they are great and now I am living on them.

It was dusty and hot, and everyone seemed to be on a siesta. We were just getting ready to continue on to Jerusalem when we turned a corner and bumped into two Swiss girls.

They were drop dead cute and blonde, and visible for miles. I expected Dave to start howling like a coyote. We started to talk to them and Dave was just about shoving me out of the way as he was dominating the conversation. This shove your way in is a weird vibe. I did see a little of this from him in the bars of the Haupt Strasse and Untere Strasse. His drool could have turned this desert green.

It turned out they were on a little break from a kibbutz and it happened to be the very same kibbutz we were heading to: Ami'ad. I thought at first she was bullshitting me. What are the odds? The omen is good, even if Dave spoils the vibe. The really cute one that did all the talking said her name was Doris. Horn dog Dave would not let up and I stayed quiet and a little embarrassed. Dave's pestering amounted to "Where are you going, and can I go too?"

Doris said they were heading to the beach at the Dead Sea and they were running out of time and could not stick around, so see you on the kibbutz and bye bye. No room for ambiguity there. We watched in astonishment as they swaggered off, stuck out their thumbs and started hitchhiking, and a second later, a dozen cars came out of nowhere and immediately stopped to pick them up. The girls jumped in a new Mercedes and drove away and the dust started to settle, and Jericho returned to its siesta.

Dave looked at me and said, "Fuck Jerusalem, let's go to the Dead Sea!"

I said I wanted to spend a few days seeing the sights in Jerusalem before getting stuck on a kibbutz up north digging ditches or whatever it is they do on a kibbutz. These are ancient roads. Ancient towns. And I want to stop and look around. Dave was not to be deterred. Dave says I am a downer. I do not want to do what he wants to do.

He had picked up the scent and was straining on the leash. I said "let's split the stash and carry our own. Not all the eggs in one basket. I will see you up north." He was in such a rush to get on the trail of the blondes, he split the stash with no questions, no regret. The last time he was in a rush like this, he had to shit. He made a comment along the lines of what a fool I was, but I was spared a journey through his logic because he was in such a hurry.

A little while later, I watched as Dave was hoofing it down the road heading south with his thumb out. I walked out of Jericho heading west and started hitchhiking, and I was thinking about falafels and Doris and thinking maybe Dave was right.

I turned around, went back to the cafe, and had another falafel. I hung around the cafe and had another coffee and watched Jericho wake from its siesta. In the cafe, I was approached by a young dude, who was curious about who I was, where I had come from, and where I was going.

I gave him a brief rundown. American going to university part time in West Germany, driving the trucks out of Europe into Turkey to Damascus then on to Lebanon, Syria, Jordan, and now heading for Jerusalem. I said I was traveling to Kathmandu. He looked surprised. He said he was going to Jerusalem, but not Kathmandu.

I got my map out and showed him where I had been, where I was going, what I hoped to see. Having this map seems to help with communicating and just talking to people. The magic map. He offered me a ride. He knew the youth hostel I was looking for. On the way, I asked him about his world and he said he was Palestinian, going to some university, wanted to be a doctor or a lawyer or something so he could travel. He said he liked rock and roll but it was hard to find the good records around here. He was playing a Crosby, Stills and Nash tape on his car stereo. Great dude, really cool and would not take money for gas. He said we all have a duty to help each other in this life and to do so not for gain, but because it is the right thing to do.

He dropped me off and I checked into the hostel, showered off a couple days of worth of desert funkiness, and man was I stinky stinking. I pulled on some clean clothes, locked my bag up, got the camera loaded, and was ready to explore. I was leaving the men's dorm and was checking my pockets and camera bag and not looking where I was going, like a goof, and ran straight into some girl coming out of the women's dorm and I almost knocked us both over. I said sorry a bunch of times and looked up at her. It was Doris the Swiss girl, and she was on her own and she looked really wonderful. She asked, "Where's your friend?" I told her that he went to the Dead Sea. We looked at each other and started laughing.

September 16. The days are hot. Been in Jerusalem a couple of days now. Wandering around the ancient walled city, cheek to jowl with pilgrims, tourists, locals, police, U.N. troops, Israeli troops, shopkeepers, and touts.

Did a pretty good postcard mailing. My mom will like all the Holy Land stuff. Had to insist they frank the stamps and they were really annoyed. I spend my days walking everywhere. I seem to be able to walk around not noticed by most people. Seems like the off-season. Occasionally, the odd person seems to stop for a second and stare at me, before turning away and going back to whatever they were doing. Like I was a ghost. It is weird.

Walked up to the Dome of the Rock and Temple Mount by way of the church of Mary Magdalene and the side of Mount of Olives. Wandered amongst the thousands of graves along the hillside. When I reached the Dome of the Rock, some old man walked up to me and started telling me a story of when Jesus returns to Jerusalem, he will walk a tightrope stretched from the Dome of the Rock to the Golden Gate. The gate seems it has been long walled up. He asked me to take off my shoes and offered to escort me through the mosque. He showed me a slab of cut and polished marble on the wall, the natural strata outlining a man's face. He

U.N. troops put their blue berets back on, Jerusalem. (*R. L. Kreamer, Kodachrome 35-mm print film,* © *1977, 2019*)

The Jerusalem skyline from the Mount of Olives. (*R. L. Kreamer, Cibachrome 35-mm slide film,* © *1977, 2019*)

Doris, her friends, and the Henry Moore sculpture *Three Vertebrae* at the Israel Museum. (*R. L. Kreamer, Cibachrome 35-mm slide film,* © *1977, 2019*)

said it was the face of the prophet. And when we went outside, it suddenly occurred to me that he never asked if I spoke English and how did he know I did without having said a word to him, but he had disappeared, like the ghost I thought I was.

Climbed around some weird ruinous excavations below the Dung gate. No one was around, and I found bits of pots and tiles and could have had a souvenir or two if I felt so inclined. Did not feel a need to fill my pockets, just wanted to fill my mind.

Visited the Church of the Holy Sepulcher. Much smaller than I had imagined and very packed with people. Had to crawl to see the tomb. While I was there, I saw a horde of various Christian clergy get into a fight. Hats knocked of heads. Pushing and shoving and shouting. A punch thrown here and there, and more than one ruffled outfit and ego.

Any and everywhere I want to go, I seem to know the shortest and quickest way there. Found a few weird stairways on to the old wall, where I now sit and write.

Perfect place for a smoke and a think while watching the sunset, the dust settle, and the dusk stretch out. The Old City gets very quiet at night. People hurry home.

Dave showed up at the hostel. He said his trip to the Dead Sea was OK and he looks a little sunburnt. He said he went for a swim without sorting out where he could rinse off the salt. He still seemed annoyed about that.

I asked him if he ran into the blonde girls. He seemed to hesitate and then said no. I knew Doris and her friend split north to go back to the kibbutz. Dave did not believe me when I told him I ran into both of them at this hostel the day I arrived. I said I spent some time hanging out with them, sightseeing, and the occasional lunch. For the most part, we did our own thing though, and I realized early on they were not looking to hang out with me. At least not with a broke traveler like me. I wonder what Dave thinks I might get out of bullshitting him.

3

It is Hard Work if You Can Get It

September 18. Kibbutz Ami'ad. Arrived yesterday evening. Traveled north through Ramallah, the West Bank, Nazareth, Tiberius, and just past the Sea of Galilee.

Of course, the many soldiers hitchhiking get to step in front of you and take your lift. They make the rules on this stretch of the road.

After hitchhiking all day along the length of Lake Tiberius and many back-of-the-truck, hop-on, hop-off rides, we got dropped off at the bottom of a large hill. The only real green area of trees was up ahead. It seemed to be a very large oasis surrounded by a fence. Walked along a dirt driveway to a closed gate with a couple of casually dressed and armed young men on the other side of the gate, sitting in chairs under some trees. They asked us what we wanted. They were calm, bored, smoking cigarettes, and seemed sure of the answer while they asked it.

After explaining we were here to be volunteers and we had written letters, we were told to wait. Through the chain-link fence gate, I could see a row of half a dozen or so wooden houses. They would not seem out of place in a seaside town in New Jersey, but they seemed kind of small. Beyond I could see some larger buildings, trees, and cabins. One of the guys walked off towards the houses. We had to wait a while.

When the guy who was the guard returned, he was with an older, middle-aged man. He had the guards open the gate and he came out with one of the guards to speak to us. The man said he was Gabriel Korner. He said volunteers usually are assigned a kibbutz when they arrive at the airport in Tel Aviv. When we explained we arrived in Israel through Jordan, he looked very surprised. The guards then looked as though they did

not like the idea of that either, and one of them loudly asked, "You came from the West Bank?"

We hastily added we wrote a letter asking to volunteer and surely he must have received it by now. The kibbutz head of volunteers was this very Gabriel Korner and he said that he had not received my letter. He said taking in volunteers off the side of the road was not done. He added he did not like to be deceived. We were asked to show some IDs and after looking over our passports, everyone seem to relax a bit when they saw we were Americans. We explained we traveled from Germany where we were living. I also had a student I.D., which seemed to help. This was not unlike a border crossing.

Gabriel said he would consider the letter question and that they just had a few volunteers leave so it might be a possibility that we could stay. We were taken to an area that held a dozen or so small wooden cabins, and we were shown one in the middle of the row that was empty. We dumped our backpacks and followed Gabriel to the mess hall for the kibbutz.

He said we could get something to eat and he would see about assigning us some work in the morning. We walked in and I noticed seating for over fifty people. The mess hall was almost empty save for a group of people my age, some men mostly women, in grubby work clothes, huddled in a tight clique. They were clearly eyeing Dave and myself up and down like we were fresh meat just delivered.

September 20. The days are hot and the nights are warm, and indeed some work was found for us to do.

We traveled with a group down the highway to some cotton fields where we helped pack and load picked cotton for transport. The kibbutz loaned us volunteers

Dave and me and our Kibbutz cabin. (*R. L. Kreamer, Cibachrome 35-mm slide film,* © *1977, 2019*)

Kibbutz Ami'ad and the northern end of the Sea of Galilee. (*R. L. Kreamer, Kodachrome 35-mm print film,* © *1977, 2019*)

out to help another kibbutz with their harvest. They paired us up, boy-girl, boy-girl, and had us climb on to a flatbed trailer that was closed on all four sides with chain link making a kind of large box. As they started to dump the picked cotton into the container, we jumped up and down to pack it in tight and tried not to get buried. When one container was filled and packed, you climbed out and drank some water while it was towed away and waited for the next empty container to be brought up. There seemed to be twenty or so containers getting packed alongside a vast field. The girl I was paired with was from Germany. She said all the other kibbutz volunteers in the area know about Kibbutz Ami'ad because they are the only one where the volunteers have built themselves a bar.

We must have packed half a dozen of these cotton containers. We started out climbing up the chain link and jumping from the top. Four hours later, it is all we can do to keep from getting buried every time more cotton gets dumped in. The cotton seems to make it hotter, and we sweat like crazy, drink massive amounts of water, our shirts become soaked, and transparent and we have to hold each other up and take turns pulling each other up from under the cotton. Trying to pack the cotton down, we end up rolling around in a tangle of arms and legs, with our bodies constantly entwined. The day wears on and the process seems to become more and more erotic and charged, like the cotton is causing a static charge and it seems to be getting increasingly intimate despite being around so many people. No one cares how sweaty and wet everyone looks, and in fact, the women look sultry and like they have risen from the sea. This is the best job I have ever been asked to do and by far the best job in the world. Monika says she may come to Ami'ad and visit our bar if she has the chance. I watched her climb into the van with the other volunteers from her kibbutz and disappear in a cloud of dust when I realize I did not get her last name. I rode back to Ami'ad thinking about how badly I needed a cold shower.

September 22. Worked in the mess hall kitchen today. It was mostly run and staffed by much older men and women about my parent's age, doing the cooking. I washed a lot of pots and pans. I consider myself pretty good and fast at that job. I was a dish and pot washer in an Italian restaurant after school since the age of fourteen.

They asked me my name. I told them, and they said they wanted to know my last name. My family always pronounced the long "a", so it sounded like Kramer. One old guy said he did not like the Germans. I told

him I was American. Then a group of about five or six of these old folks gathered around me and rolled up their sleeves and showed me the tattoos of numbers on their wrists. They said they were survivors and they did not care for Germans. Later, an older woman from the kitchen crew came up to me and said I should not worry about what happened. She said they do that to everyone who comes to work in the kitchen. She said they always come around and warm up to everyone, even the Germans.

September 24. The days are hot. Been here for a week now and I find myself being assigned different jobs in various places around the kibbutz. Gabriel Korner told me it was a matter of working where needed to start and maybe later finding a niche to fill while I am here. He said he still had not decided if we could stay.

Dave and I are still roommates, but we are assigned to different parts of the kibbutz on different jobs. That is really a relief as I am starting to find my traveling partner a little tedious and annoying.

He has made it clear yet again that because he is older, by a couple of years, and he has more traveling experience than me, he is in fact wiser and knows more than me. He just keeps going on about it. It is like having another older brother who is a jerk. But I have to admit that it has made me see the way I treat my little brother, he is thirteen years old, and what a jerk I am to him sometimes. However, I have no need of a condescending big brother as I already have more than one of those.

Worked a day in the grapefruit groves, picking and hauling fruit for market. Got to use one of those lifts, like a cherry picker on wheels. Hard to drive fully extended, but loads of fun. The guy in charge had a race through the grove after work. It was crazy. I am meeting people from everywhere and most everyone is very cool. Do not think I will be taking my camera along to the work sites any more. Got back to the cabin to find Dave complaining and he kind of stank. He stank really bad. He said he did the chicken farm and he said it sucked. This job is known to the volunteers simply as "the chickens." Everyone has to pull at least one shift on the chicken farm every six weeks because no one wants to do it, so it has been made mandatory.

Dave said he had to push a wheelbarrow full of chicken shit down a dirt road to a composting site. He said he took a corner too fast and he dumped it all over the road, and down his legs, his socks, and his shoes. He said they made him shovel it all up. I told him he was stinking up the place and to take another shower and leave his socks and shoes and clothes outside. He got mad at me for telling him what to do. I left with the words "You fucking stink, dude" and asked him to leave the window open.

September 28. The days are hot. The amazing banana. Our friend the banana. I was asked if I wanted to help in the banana plantation, and I said yes. Had no idea what I was getting in to.

It is still dark. It is up and out of bed before four o'clock in the morning and hustle down to the gate for the van. You may find coffee in the mess hall, but it still way too early for the breakfast to be ready. The kitchen staff has yet to even get started. Then it is pile into the van, with the new guys crammed into the back. The van is crammed with about twelve people and we haul ass downhill towards the Sea of Galilee.

It is like Mr. Toad's Wild Ride, and I was sure we were going wreck on one of the hairpin curves. The banana plantation is about 300 yards off the west, north-west corner of the lake, and I am told it is near or below sea level.

The early start is because by noon the heat and humidity is so high no one could work. Not even mad dogs and Englishmen. We roll up to the work huts around 4.30 a.m., grab tools and water, and get to it. The first break is at 8.30 a.m. for breakfast at the breakfast hut, then it is pretty much work until it is too hot. The banana grove is quite large and divided into many acres with a checkerboard network of roads running throughout. In some places, there is a nice view of the lake. The first time I joined the crew, it was a harvest day.

Colored bands marked which trees are cut down and which of the banana bunch is removed. Each cutter had a gopher like me following the cutter through the grove. The various bands of different colors indicated the approximate month of harvest.

The cutter would chop the tree at the base just enough so it would start to fall and I would run under the 20-kilo bunch of bananas and catch it on my shoulder. The cutter would cut it free from the tree in one deft move so the weight transfer was soft and not jarring. I would hustle the bunch through the acre to the nearest road, lay it on the ground, and run back to where the cutter was making his way through the grove. By the time I arrived back, the old plant was chopped up, and he was waiting by the next tree and the process was repeated.

After breakfast, we harvested for a couple of hours. The sap from the banana tree runs clear until it hits the skin and dries, then it becomes a sticky brown film. When it came time to load the harvest, we followed a flatbed trailer pulled by a tractor up and down the roads amongst the acre of banana trees. The bunches weighed 15–25 kilos each. I had a lot of trouble raising them above my waist to get them on the flatbed. I was embarrassed at my lack of strength. I was told not to worry about it, but I did. I was told this harvest was a little over a ton. The ride back to the kibbutz was just as wild uphill as it was down. All the volunteers were still at their assigned tasks. Only the banana crew gets back early.

I dragged myself to the communal showers and looked in the mirror. My face and body was streaked in a brown mixture of dust and banana sap. To my surprise, I came clean in the hot water in minutes. I dragged myself back to the cabin and fell asleep in seconds. Dave woke me with some chatter about something I do not even remember. I told him I was beat and to wake me when dinner was served in the mess. He said dinner was served and almost over. I somehow made it in time to find something to eat.

The kibbutz member who ran the banana crew of volunteers approached me and asked if I wanted to do it again tomorrow. For some reason, I said, "sure, I'll see you at four." I told him I needed an alarm clock. He said he would be right back with one.

October 7. I have decided to stick with the banana plantation. It is hard work for sure. I am quickly getting into shape, and I can lift the 25-kilo bunches on to the flatbed without too much of a struggle.

The harvest days are about twice a week, or so I am told. In between harvests, we bag the banana bunches on the tree. The bagging tool is a long pole with a big horseshoe-shaped rod welded perpendicular to the end. Huge rubber bands are laced over the studs on the horseshoe and that secures the bag. From below, you shove the bag up and over the bunch and yank it away. If you get it right, the rubber band snaps over the bag and secures it to the stem of the bunch. It speeds up the ripening time. Paper bags for the plants on the outer trees of the grove and plastic for the shaded interior bunches.

October 8. Evening rolls in again, and I am finding myself on my own, so I will write. Had a little kibbutz picnic along the shores of the Sea of Galilee. Went along with six or seven people.

The guys acted like idiots and started playing catch with the watermelon while we were trying to hitchhike down to the lake. It ended up smashed and delayed us getting a ride. Nice lake to swim in. It was my turn to be an idiot when I decided to swim to a buoy in the middle of the lake. I ran out of gas over halfway there, but it was closer to keep going. After finally getting there, I was not sure about getting back. Hung on to the buoy for a while.

Later, the bearded long-haired German dude started telling me it was so uncool to travel with a camera and I should just remember it all in my mind.

October 9. The days are hot and the nights are cool. I have been told that Kibbutz Ami'ad invented their own water filtering system because the water they pump from the Sea of Galilee is heavy with silt. Part of the daily routine is to check and clean the filters on the water pumps.

October 10. The kibbutz is staffed with many young Israeli soldiers, both men and women. It is part of their military service to go and work on a kibbutz. Our proximity to the border of Lebanon makes for an unusually high number of soldiers assigned here.

The two dudes I met at the gate on the first day are friendlier with Dave and me than they were at first. I think they know we have a stash of hash and it is real hard to get some in Israel. However, its possession and use is a strict no-no. Getting caught would mean getting kicked out of the kibbutz and probably out of the country. Still, we caved in and got high with those dudes behind the kibbutz bar. They said they did not really smoke and proceeded to smoke and bogart the whole joint. They finally told me their names. Later that evening, Dave and I were telling them of our travel plans: how we were heading east overland first through places like Iran and Afghanistan and on to India and up to Nepal and Kathmandu. Then they related their travel dreams to us. They said they wanted to visit Petra in Jordan. They said it was the wish of many young Israelis. They told us stories of soldiers going on nighttime commando-type border crossings, followed by covert trekking through desert wastelands just to see the place. They spoke in a way that elevated Petra into legend and lore. They spoke as if was a magical and mystical place. They were quite blown away when Dave and I casually said we would visit the place on our way to India.

October 11. The days are warm. You can work five days a week and have Saturday and Sunday off, or you can work six days a week and save your owed day off and take up to a week off at a time. I am working six days a week on the banana plantation. Sunday through Friday.

My supervisor or boss man is named Ali. He is an old guy, about forty-five years old. He said he immigrated from Iraq. He said Jews in Iraq are treated quite badly, and anyway, he always had a dream of coming to

Israel to live and work. Ali said that years of doing this has made him good at what he does and he says he loves what he does. That is a good philosophy. He wanted to know if I realized how lucky I was to be born in America.

The plant puts all its nutrients into the bunch so that the cut tree offers nothing to replenish the soil. The dead and cut plants only litter the ground of the grove to slow the evaporation of water. Ali adds, "Even the useless is useful in the desert." Today, we picked 10 tons of bananas for export. It took eight of us five hours of backbreaking work. We worked as fast as possible without getting hurt.

On my way into the communal showers, I noticed three volunteers hanging around, which was weird for the time of day. I wondered if they were stealing stuff by the way they were acting. Everyone has got to pull their weight around here. Aimlessly laying around looks out of place or looks like burglary. One was a very, and I mean very, tall German blonde girl who looked around twenty-three, healthy type and funny face, standing there, hands on hips. She is taller than me and could easily kick my ass. The other two were scruffy, small dark-haired dudes, sitting with their backs to a wall, one asleep and the other dude looking annoyed—both looked about fourteen years old. They could not. I breezed around a corner and walked up on them fast, taking the two that were awake by surprise. The blonde girl was startled and jumped a bit and she was blocking the sidewalk, and I looked her in the eyes and said, "How's it going?" She looked shocked and said "hello," and the dude who was awake pulled his knees up and I stepped over the sleeping dude's legs and headed to the showers. I could not hear what the guy said but I did hear the girl say, "No, he wasn't."

I have been hanging out in the kibbutz bar most evenings. Got into a lively discussion and I found out that a few of my fellow volunteers think traveling with a camera is very uncool. Apparently, I should record everything with my mind only, according to the clutch of aggressively drunk Germans. I told them I only take photographs when I am sleepy. When my reply got a big laugh, it seemed to piss off the bearded German hippie.

October 12. Today, I got to drive a tractor around the plantation to move pipes and equipment around. After a quick driving lesson, I was off and running. Every day I seem to meet five new people, I cannot keep track. The soldier who showed me how to drive it said it was like driving a Russian tank. They laughed when I asked if I could drive it back to the kibbutz. I have been given more and more tasks that I have been able do with less and less supervision. On occasion, I work with James. He is moody. I have graduated from riding in the back of the van to the front seat.

I do not see much of Dave, so we are getting along much better. I see him in the bar or mess hall sometimes. He has a girlfriend from Australia named Kathy. He also informed me he has the best job on the kibbutz. He cleans the swimming pool and lays out in the sun all day.

October 15. Went on a hike around the kibbutz with some of my fellow volunteers. Susan from Canada came along. I really like her. We sometimes sit and talk in the bar or outside under the trees. We usually sit very close and she seems really interested in me, but whenever I think it is the right time and move in for a kiss, she pulls away. Maybe I smoke too much and my breath stinks. Maybe I am just misreading the situation or her feelings. Maybe I should quit smoking. Maybe I should wear my glasses more often so I can see what is actually going on.

We hiked the large hill to the west. It was covered with large, jagged, sharp, volcanic rock. Large boulders made for a tricky climb. Think I got a decent photo looking down on Kibbutz Ami'ad with the Golan Heights and the Sea of Galilee in the background.

Made it back to the kibbutz in time for an early evening of beers and conversation in the bar. It is well stocked with Gold Star beer, and Time and Airline non-filtered cigarettes. I smoke both brands. I opened a cig up and saw it was made from the whole tobacco plant, root and stem, with very little leaf. Hard to complain about it, though, at 10 cents a pack.

October 19. The days are hot and the nights are cool. Back on the plantation. Had to pull my shift at the "chickens" yesterday, and it was both weird and pretty fucked up.

It was Sunday at the church of the chicken. Had to rise at 3 a.m. and get to the chicken coop, which is really like a large hanger or barn with hundreds and hundreds of chickens in it. I could not get out of it; it was my turn. The member, who oversees the chickens, looks like a chicken, walks like a chicken, and jerks his head around like a chicken. He is really old—must be around fifty-five. He said it had to be early for this particular job because the chickens are pretty docile early in the morning.

The lights were low and it was quite dark inside and hard to see. The empty cages on the back of the trucks seemed a bit small for a chicken, but I really did not think much of it at the time. The hundreds of chickens were stirring and seemingly starting to wake

despite the lights being set down low. The noise they were making was unnerving. It was like hundreds of babies crying softly. The chicken man asked me and the other volunteer if we were right or left handed. We answered, and before we could ask why, the chicken man said we had to move fast and to follow him. We moved into the cavernous coop, and the chicken man told me to get ready and that he would hand me chickens by the feet. Five chickens in the right hand four in the left. I was told to run with the chickens to the guys by the trucks with the blue cages. I did. The guys grabbed them from me and started stuffing them six to a cage and yelling at me to hurry back for more. I ran back and noticed the other volunteer moving towards the truck with chickens flapping like crazy and she had a freaked out look on her face. She was one of the volunteers I had seen around, and I wanted to her meet for a long time. I knew in a split second I was forever tainted by this chicken round up and did not stand a chance. Blue plastic cages crammed with chickens, an eye here and a beak there, peeking out in random places. Chickens waking up to their own special chicken hell as the blue cages get stacked higher and higher. I stopped and watched those guys work as a cage got stuffed with live chickens and that was more than enough, and I wish I had not stopped to watch. I could not watch that again. And so on it went, on and on and on. The baby-like cries picked up in volume, and all the while, I struggled to hold the chickens far enough out to keep them from pecking at my legs. A half hour after that, the girl I wanted to meet could not take it anymore and left. I had not noticed until after she was gone that she was gone. All the while, the chicken man was running chickens to the cages as well. After another half an hour, I started dropping chickens and I could not hold but two chickens in my left hand and three in the right. Finished the job and I told the chicken man I was going to be late for my ride to the banana plantation and trotted off. I am not sure what ached more, my arms or my brain.

Had time to shower and change clothes. I caught a later, more relaxed ride to the plantation in a station wagon. After the chicken nightmare, Ali and the rest of the crew knew what the chicken shipment shift meant, and everyone was really cool about me having an easy day in the plantation. Ali told me while working in the grove to be on the lookout for Siamese bananas. I thought he was joking until he handed me one. One skin with two bananas in it. I have been eating a lot of bananas lately. He sent me out to bag bunches in an acre on the far edge of the plantation. It had been gone over before, so there would be very few to bag. After breakfast, I was sent to another far-flung corner to bag a few bunches, and I was told to show up for the ride back to the kibbutz. After bagging all the banana bunches I could find to bag, I sat under a banana tree. Say that three times fast.

My daydreaming was interrupted by the sound of trucks and machines rumbling through the plantation heading north. It turned out to be the Israeli army barreling along and whipping up a cloud of dust, with tanks, trucks, soldiers, and a lot of guns using the banana plantation as a shortcut to wherever they were going. I quickly made my way back to the kitchen hut and found a few of the Israeli workers hanging around nonchalantly drinking coffee. I was glad to see them calm and bored.

Apparently, it was not the end of the world. I asked if anyone knew what was going on and was told that of course they knew what was going on because they were in the army reserves and they said everyone calls everyone, so everyone is ready for anything. They said there was some sort of incident up on the border with Lebanon. A place they called the good fence. I was about to ask them why they used a shortcut through the plantation when one of the guys, must have been the mind reader of the group, said they were trying to use dirt roads so the tank treads did not chew up the asphalt highway.

October 20. Wow. My mind is blown. This kibbutz life is the best job I ever had. I had sex in the shower with the really tall girl who is a couple of years older than me. I really cannot believe it.

Came back to the kibbutz in the afternoon and found the volunteer's area quiet as usual. Stopped at the cabin Dave and I share to drop off my plantation tools and grab my towel, my wash kit, and grab clean clothes as usual. The place was deserted, like a ghost town, as usual. I am in the shower for like two minutes when I suddenly realize that I am not alone and into the shower stall walks the tall German girl naked. Not as usual.

It was my turn to be startled. She laughed at me and I think I mumbled "It's occupied" or something equally stupid. She asked if I minded. She was standing there looking at me and then I really noticed that her body was incredibly glorious. This was like something out of an Anaïs Nin story. Shit, I do not even know her name. I was all too happy to do whatever she wanted. I really cannot believe it.

We moved at the same time towards each other and we started making out and caressing each other. I had nowhere to hide an impossible to hide erection. She then stopped, and while looking me over, she said, "Finger me." I eagerly obliged her. Must have been a bit too eager I guess. She pointed out I was not stuffing the Christmas turkey and to please slow down. We laughed and then our caressing, kissing, and mutual stroking became smooth and slow. We were both getting really turned on and excited. She then said, "Fuck me," and she turned around and bent over. At first, she seemed a bit too tall for this, but she spread her legs and bent her knees and while reaching behind, she guided me in. I think she has done this before. The shower was still running, and the water was warm and the air was warm. She turned around and asked me to keep fucking her. I think we came together. I am liking this kibbutz more and more.

October 22. She is not really my girlfriend. She made that clear. I have only known her a couple of days. She said she is not very interested in hanging out with me, walking around holding hands, or sitting in the mess hall eating together. Nothing like that at all. It is like she makes a point of not making a point. But when I get back from the banana plantation, she shows up in the shower like clockwork and we ball and fuck like crazy. I think I am being used. She could have any guy here she wants and they all seem meaner or tougher than me.

Dave is talking about taking a trip to the down to the Sinai and burning our weeks' worth of days off. I told him I am not sure, there is a lot of work coming up on the plantation and I would think about it. He said I was crazy. All I was thinking or would be thinking about is my next after the plantation shift wash and shower. Normally I would be bragging and blabbing about fucking M___ in the shower. She said if I told anyone, it would stop and she would deny it. It is a no brainer. I would rather fuck M___ than brag about fucking M___. I have taken to hiding my journal.

We had a little sightseeing van trip north of the kibbutz for our day off. The vans were courtesy of the Kibbutz, which means courtesy of Gabriel. He is really a nice guy and looks after the volunteers. We went up to the hills west of the Jordan River and had nice views of the Golan Heights.

We did this little trip with the Australian girls. Kathy is Dave's girlfriend and is way, way older—twenty-five or twenty-six. She traveled to the kibbutz with Anne and Debbie. Anne is big and tall and looks like she could crush you like a grape, but is shy and sweet. Debbie has model magazine cover good looks, and she knows it. Everyone has tried it on with Debbie and got shot down, myself included. Debbie is not interested.

It was movie night at the kibbutz. They convert the dining hall into a cinema for the showing, and almost everyone shows up to watch. Someone got a hold of a scratchy and often-spliced 16-mm version of the film *Tommy* by The Who. I found the entire film vapid, boring, and stupid. The music was better left to one's imagination.

October 23. Back from the plantation and almost ran to the shower. After five minutes, I knew exactly what was going on but refused to accept it. I knew she had split. I even strolled by the pool to see if she was there.

I even braved the stench of the chicken farm and the noise of the plastic factory, and still I strolled on. Someone said they had heard she left the kibbutz on a bus heading to Tel Aviv to get her flight home. She must have known when she was going for a while now. Had I known, I probably would have blown it somehow anyway. Shit, I guess it is back to cold showers for me.

October 24. The days are hot. Over breakfast at the plantation this morning, I overheard the members talking about what they voted to spend the kibbutz profits on. The choice was everyone gets a television or an air conditioner. They voted for an air conditioner for every member's house.

The kibbutz members try to sustain the kibbutz in various ways. The moneymakers here are the cultivation and selling of bananas, grapefruit, and chickens. They grow vegetables. They have an injection mold plastic factory. They make irrigation filtration systems for water pumps. They irrigate the land.

They share the profits at the end of the year like a little insular socialist utopia, and they can do it all with free labor in the form of volunteers from around the world. That is the real moneymaker here, free labor. All you need to do is feed them and house them. The army even fills in labor shortages from the conscripts as part of their national service. Hell, the volunteers even pay their own travel fare to get here. Some as far away as America and Canada, but mostly Europe. The volunteers come for the work experience, the sunshine, maybe to escape some problem at home. They come for the travel and adventure. They come for the crazy casual sex. Just about everyone is on the prowl, especially the guys, but some of the girls are, too.

October 25. Pulled a very long overnight shift in the plastic factory making wheels for rolling overhead sprinklers for field crops. Repetitive, boring, and a real crap job. It ranks with the chickens in unpleasantness. I am deafened and tired.

4

The Road to Petra

November 1. Much has happened. We had our week holiday, and we are now off the kibbutz and back on the road. We had decided to bag the whole kibbutz scene and try to make it through the Khyber Pass before the winter makes it impossible. If we do not make a move soon, we may be stuck here for a long time.

We let the head of volunteers know of our plans and he seem surprised. For him, it was all very fast, and we had been here only a couple of months. He said he was getting ready to pair us up with a kibbutz family and get us out of the cabins, as they get cold in the winter. He said my letter arrived just a couple of days ago and he was pleased and happy and said he had been showing it around and we had been telling the truth. He showed it to us, and it was covered with odd stamps, misdirected address changes, and weird post office franks from god knows where. He wished us luck and said we were welcome back anytime, but please stay longer next time. When I told Ali I was leaving, he was sad and said he would miss me. He said he was happy, too, because I was going on my trip to Kathmandu.

We also had a little going away party on the lawn between the rows of cabins, and most of the volunteers and even a few of the soldiers showed up. Everyone still stayed in their little cliques and did not mingle much. When I thought about it, I was surprised how many people I knew and made friends with.

Hitchhiking from the kibbutz, we got to the southern end of Tiberias somewhere near Degania. Walked to the shore and camped. We stayed up late talking by the fire. We thought we saw some UFOs. I woke very early and watched the sunrise over the lake.

We left the next day for the Sinai, but it took us all day to get to Jerusalem. Got into Jerusalem very late. There was a half a dozen of us heading down to the beaches, but Dave and I were the only ones planning not to return to the kibbutz. The bus we wanted south was a morning bus from the Jerusalem bus station. It was cheap, but we heard it made every stop along the way and took most of the day.

We found a dive hotel in the old quarter of the city. The room was fantastic. A huge stone and brick room with a vaulted brick ceiling. It was a dorm-type setup. A few minutes later, something bit me on the leg. A second after that, it seemed everyone was swearing and saying "ouch" and the lights were flipped on. Bedbugs—lots and lots of bedbugs.

The girls were freaking out. I got the needle from the sewing kit out of my bag and turned my sleeping bag inside out. I found a few hidden in the seams. I skewered them like a kebab and had half a dozen on the needle like an insect collector would. Dave took it to the front desk and woke the clerk or owner up. Well done to Dave for raising hell with the guy and demanding our money back. Dave showed him the pin with the skewered bed bugs and he grabbed the bugs off the pin and said, "What bugs?" When Dave said we were going to call the police, the tone changed. The owner was still angry with being woken up, but we got our money back and shown different rooms. Most of our group wanted to leave, but I said I was going for it, and if I got bit, I would let them know. I was tired and at that point, I did not care. I checked my sleeping bag one last time and crawled into it, and fell asleep to the sounds of everyone else fussing and talking. The next morning, we split quick.

Israeli soldier gives me the finger on the Kibbutz lawn. (*R. L. Kreamer, Kodachrome 35-mm print film,* © *1977, 2019*)

Israeli soldier gives me the eye on the Kibbutz lawn. (*R. L. Kreamer, Kodachrome 35-mm print film,* © *1977, 2019*)

Sunrise on the southern shore of the Sea of Galilee. (*R. L. Kreamer, Cibachrome 35-mm slide film, © 1977, 2019*)

The miles and miles of deserted and pristine beaches at Dhahab, Sinai. The only part of Egypt located in Asia, the Sinai serves as a land bridge between Africa and Asia. (*R. L. Kreamer, Cibachrome 35-mm slide film, © 1977, 2019*)

The bus heading south turned out to be a clapped-out old American-style school bus painted green. We stopped at a street market for some travel food and water before we set off. For my store of supplies, I had included a kilo of dates. I started to munch a few and just kept going. They were amazing. By the time we got to the Gulf of Aqaba and the city of Eilat, I was as sick as a dog. I ate just about the entire kilo of dates. When we finally arrived at Nuweiba, I got off the bus with a massive stomach ache. The Israelis were calling the place Novoit. Surrounded by touts, people offering camel rides, cafes, impromptu beach shops, scuba diving trips, fishing excursions, camp grounds with tents set up, tourists, tours of the desert, soldiers, and Moses slept here, the first thing I noticed was a camel with its head in a tent eating a sleeping bag. The second thing was miles and miles of deserted, pristine beaches in the distance.

The first couple of days we spent around the beach area after finding a camping spot. We have been advised by some people to keep an eye on our stuff as there have been reports of tourists getting their stuff stolen off the beach and around the campgrounds.

November 5. The days are hot and the nights are cold. Approached by an Israeli tout offering rides out into the Sinai desert, with a visit to the monastery of Saint Catherine in his VW Bus. His set up is next to a group of Israeli soldiers and he says he is an ex-soldier. His price is low, and we said we would join his tour tomorrow. We are taking our backpacks because there is nowhere safe to stash them. He says the bus is full and will hold four in the front, four in the middle, and four in the back. Most are from our kibbutz group.

November 6. What a cluster fuck this ended up being. The next day, we departed late because the driver was hungover. He said not to worry, "let's go." We had spent the morning hanging around where he parked his van. We had a chance to look it over and it was a heap of junk. I should have walked away the very minute I saw the van. We piled in, a couple of dudes up front with the driver, Dave and myself in the middle with a fat girl between us and a couple of girls and a dude in the back, and everyone's shit piled on top and inside.

The van could barely move and we crept along, heading for the desert road. But we were on the move, and the van seemed to get up to around 40 miles an hour eventually. We were a couple of hours out and still a couple of hours from the monastery. There was a loud bang that signaled the death of one of the bald rear tires. After pulling over, the driver discovered something he already knew. Had no tire jack, never had a tire

jack, and there was not a tire jack within a 60-mile radius of where we were. We all lifted the back end as high as we could and secured it with a precarious pile of rocks. We then spent nearly an hour watching the driver trying to scratch a hole in the concrete like hardened desert dirt road under the flat tire with a sharp rock in hopes of making enough room to get the tire off the wheel. He finally succeeded, however, his self-congratulatory strutting around was all too soon as deflated as the tire he just pulled off, when he discovered the inflated spare required a deeper hole to have the clearance to fit back on the wheel. It was another hour before we were ready to roll. Dave and I had—about an hour before—agreed that he would probably forget to remove the improvised jack of jagged rocks and drive off and rip up the underside of his van beyond repair. We reminded him of what was under the van and still holding that side up. Dave said something about this being a pleasure tour, and not a work detail. One of the dudes with the driver said something about lazy Americans. I said something about doing enough volunteer work on the kibbutz. Of course, we pitched in with the old heave-ho while one of the girls pulled the rocks out from under the van. He got off light. We got underway with everyone in a sour mood. Of course, it took what seemed like forever and we arrived at the monastery after visiting hours and it was long shut and locked tight goodnight.

We had been there a half an hour and I watched a nun arriving at the large wooden door in the tall wall that was surrounding the monastery. She just walked up from the dirt road and must have been on foot for a long time as I heard no vehicle arrive or depart. Or maybe she was in a nearby building. She pulled the rope that rang the hanging bell over and over and pleaded with a voice I can still hear in my mind. "Hello, I'm Sister Margaret and I'm staying here, do you remember me? Please let me in." Over and over, she pleaded at that door and at that bell. It was like an old black and white film in color. Finally, the door opened a crack, she quickly squeezed in, and the door slammed shut. It seemed that all at once the desert fell into silence as the sun fell into early evening and the shadows grew long.

I climbed a nearby hill for a photo op. I think I got a couple of good ones with the lengthened shadows. Everyone pretty much at the same time realized it was time to go, and the sun was going to set in a couple of hours.

Most everyone showed up at the van at about the same time after their self-guided walking tours, except for the driver and some other dude from the front

The monastery of Saint Catherine, Sinai. The monastery contains the world's oldest continually operating library. (*R. L. Kreamer, Cibachrome 35-mm slide film, © 1977, 2019*)

seat—most likely behind a bush somewhere smoking some hash. Someone blew the horn on the van. I think it was Denise. The driver and his buddy showed up and we loaded up and rolled on down the road. Everyone was in a better mood because we were getting out of there and back to the beach. I even thought we would make it back just before dark. I was drifting off to sleep, falling in and out, for about twenty minutes.

There was a shout, and the moment I opened my eyes, I saw the driver struggling with the wheel and through the front windscreen a large boulder was looming up. It all took just a split second and we ran into the boulder with a bang while doing around 40 miles an hour. The driver did not even seem to try to use the brakes. All in the same split second as I was coming fully awake, a few people joined in together screaming and I could not brace myself and slammed face first into the metal seat back bar of the front seat. And it fucking hurt, almost knocking me out and breaking my glasses in two right off my face. The van rode up a foot or two onto the boulder, picking the front end up off the ground and stopped. The van rode up the boulder at just the most perfect distance.

Everything and everyone went silent. The van teetered on its new apex for a moment and then, like in slow motion, it rolled over on its side. Almost everyone was screaming and shouting again. I was on the side the van rolled on to. First, the fat girl fell on to me and knocked the wind out of me, followed by Dave. To add insult to injury, the crushing weight of screaming and yelling humans was immediately followed by everyone's luggage, years of dirt, bottles, garbage, and cigarette ends and just plain crap that had built up on the floor of the van like some geological strata from hell that was now raining down on me. And more luggage. Dave was the first out of the van and he helped the fat girl get out, but not before she used me as a step ladder to climb out. The people in the back seat took their cue from her and promptly did the same. Dave reached in and helped pull me out on to the side of the van. I staggered out past the scattered backpacks and sat down away from the van with a fucking almighty headache.

Dave was yelling at the driver for climbing out first and not helping anyone else out. Dave was also giving him shit for smoking dope and not paying attention to his driving. Later, when Dave tried to tell me what happened, he said, "It unfolded like," and then he was suddenly at a loss for words. I chimed in quickly with "Like a car crash!" We laughed. He said the driver and the dudes in the front seat were smoking a hash pipe and the driver was not paying attention to the road very much. When the driver turned to pass the pipe, he drifted just enough to his right to catch the front and back tires on the passenger side in the deep sandy part of the road on a corner. It pulled the van right off the road and into the boulder. The only boulder within miles and miles. The driver was too stoned to react fast enough on the brakes. It is now a couple of hours since the wreck and it is getting dark and it is really fucking cold in the desert in late October. Most of us were lucky enough to have our stuff with us, so we got cocooned in our sleeping bags well away from the road and the wrecked van lying on its side. We shared spare sweaters, shirts, and jackets with the unprepared. The driver and his stoner buddy were freezing their asses off trying to stay warm by sleeping in the van. No trees and bushes meant we did not have a fire for warmth or light. There is never a burning bush around when you need one. Some of us have flashlights, but we are using them sparingly. I had some bread, water, and crackers, and even some dates in my bag that I shared with everyone.

I fell asleep fast and had a weird dream. It was at night and I was alone, and it was very, very late and it was about to rain, and I was back at the monastery ringing the bell.

The next morning started cold, and a breakfast of recriminations was being served. Daylight revealed we have wrecked next to the only tree within 50 miles. What a trip.

Dave and a few of the others were having an argument with the driver and his stoner buddy. That is what woke me up. I had slept in my bag in my clothes. My face was sore; the deep-seated headache was going, but not gone. Looking around revealed we were in a really beautiful and isolated, one lone tree spot.

The driver was saying something about we could try to flip the van back over before we started trying to hitchhike out. The arguing started up again. I walked over to the van and looked in at the driver's side. I saw the brake and gas peddles were bent to fuck where the boulder came through the floor. Dave told him he just wanted to flip it back up, so he could have it towed,

The scene of the crash and the ride out of the desert, Sinai. (*R. L. Kreamer, Cibachrome 35-mm slide film, © 1977, 2019*)

it was his fault, so it was his problem. I knew that we would be lucky to get back before nightfall.

We spent a long time milling around as everyone grappled with the logistics of having to go to the toilet and having to go somewhere way out in the desert. Everyone started talking about the Bedouin camp a couple of people saw. Everyone came up with the notion of going over and checking it out, hoping to maybe find a ride out of the desert. A few people wanted to come along, then everyone tagged along.

As we approached the camp, it was obvious they had seen us coming. The van driver and a few other people started speaking at once over each other. Somehow, someone explained our predicament, the crash, and wanting to arrange a ride out of the desert. I saw him roll his eyes at the din of everyone talking at once.

He said they saw us, but thought we were some stupid tourists on a camping trip that wrecked their car. They were not sure what we were up to. He said not to worry, the Israeli army was always on patrol on this road and they would usually pass by in a couple of hours. We asked if they were making tea and if we could buy some. We were low on water and everyone was getting thirsty. They said sure and I sat myself down in front of a wizened old man tending a small twig fire with a teapot over it. I asked him if I could take his photograph and I was told, "yes, of course." The sun was up and getting warm. The old man closed his eyes and I took his photo.

Sure enough, a couple of hours after we returned, and our little group was clustered around the scene of our evening calamity, we heard machines in the distance. One sounded familiar to me. Into view came a bus being towed by a tractor. It was a Caterpillar D9 tractor, the same type I was driving on the banana plantation. It was like seeing an old friend. The tractor was setting the pace and a soldier was steering the bus being towed. Soon, a second tractor showed up with a bus slowly following behind. There was an Israeli soldier behind the wheel of each vehicle. When the tractor driver saw the wrecked VW van on its side, and all of us jumping up and down and waving and shouting like shipwrecked sailors on a raft adrift for months, he slowed to a full stop and shut off the engine.

Our idiot driver tout tour guide tried to take command of the show and started jabbering at the solider in Hebrew. Dave shouted him down and shut him up by yelling that this was the asshole who was smoking hash, crashed the van, and stranded us here, while pointing at him. Uh, oh, Dave dropped a dime on the dude.

The soldier just started shaking his head. I think it was Denise who stepped in and calmly explained the situation and asked if we could get a lift back to the beach. He said he had to ask, and they were busy and had to recover this broken-down army bus from the desert, but they need a break from driving anyway so they would wait and radio the commander of the area and find out what can be done. The D9 towing the bus was not waiting around and headed out.

Our tour guide driver tire repairman was in an animated conversation with the soldier tractor driver. Later, I found out he wanted them to use the tractor to right the van back on its wheels and he wanted to get a tow as well. The tractor driver soldier said no and no. He later changed his mind and righted the van while we were waiting. He then pushed the boulder way off the shoulder of the road. I used the time to hike out a way and took a photo. No one is going to believe this story.

We got the word from on high and we got a ride. We were piling into the running bus when our tour guide approached. He wanted to get paid. No one said a word, so Dave stepped up and gave him a good run down on what everyone was thinking but were too big a bunch of wussies to say. He was told that this was all his fuck up from the start. From a late start and no tire jack and being too late for a visit inside the monastery, to the crash and a cold night out with no food or water. He looked shocked. I said that he got some of the tour done, so I will pay some of the money and gave him a dollar. A few people followed suit, though most did not. Dave made it clear he was not happy about doing everyone's dirty work and telling the tour driver off. Cannot say that I blame him. The last I saw of our tour guide, he was gawking at the pittance in his palm. We rode off leaving him and his stoner buddy behind.

I asked the bus driver why the tour guide was left behind, and he said they promised him they were going to call his brother when they got to Novoit and he will get his van out. He said they gave him enough water and rations to wait a day or two. He did not want to leave the VW van unguarded because he was certain the Bedouin would strip it clean and make pots, pans, cups, knives, spoons, forks, and swords out of the metal, and use the engine to pump water from some desert well. I bet those van seats would furnish out one of those tents nicely. Like my old buddy Ali once said to me, "Even the useless is useful in the desert." This bus ride is free, but so slow. I have spent hours writing in my journal and we are only halfway there. No one is talking.

Tea with the Bedouin, Sinai. (*R. L. Kreamer, Cibachrome 35-mm slide film, © 1977, 2019*)

November 7. The days are hot and the nights are cold. Back in Jerusalem. After spending five or six days in the Sinai, we are getting ready to head to Jordan and then ever east. Bought some glasses frames and my old lenses popped right in. Got them from an optometrist shop in a weird part of Jerusalem. The neighborhood had posters plastered around saying in bold print "Notice to the Women of our Community." It went on to proclaim the dress code, dress length, sleeve length, and mandatory headscarves. What a bunch of uptight busybody meddlers. If you do not like what you see, then stop gawking at women. I had my glasses on and Dave laughed and called me "Woodsy the owl." Sent out a slew of postcards.

November 8. We headed for the Allenby Bridge by thumb at seven in the morning. Got there and found it closed for two days because of "military ceremonies." The army turned us away and directed us to an alternative route. We headed north to a place called the Adam Bridge—a lesser-known crossing in and out of the West Bank. The line was long as it was the only overland route open and it took two hours. However, once the officials were met and dealt with, we got through fast and our bags were touched by no one.

It took us two rides to get to the town of Salt. The road wound its way through the hills with an impressive view of the Sea of Galilee and the Jordan Valley below. I found the house where about two months before I had knocked on the door asking for water. We walked to the outskirts of town to start hitchhiking when a traditionally dressed man came up to us and greeted us like long lost, well loved, family members in a gentle voice and perfect English. He wanted to know if everything was all right, where were we going, and if there was anything he could do for us. We thanked him and said we were trying to get to Amman. He said he was sorry he did not have transportation, or he would take us there himself. He then said, "May God bless you on your journey, and may God bless the family you have left behind."

Hitched a ride to a deserted desert turn off along the highway to Amman. We found ourselves in a rapidly descending twilight and we knew it was getting more difficult for anyone to notice us alongside the road. We agreed a little camping would be all right.

Just then, a car pulled alongside and stopped. There was a family inside. The man said something in Arabic and we said something in English. "What are you doing?" he wanted to know. We said we were going camping. He was puzzled and did not know what we meant. We said we were going to sleep outside.

He said we could not do that. We asked why it was not allowed. He said, "Of course, the King of Jordan would allow you to sleep almost anywhere, but you can come home with us and stay with us." Before we could reply, a second car pulled off the road. The driver got out and, while looking us over, had a rapid and brief conversation with the first driver. I heard the word "Americans" in the middle of it all. The second driver said, "You can stay with me in my home and my wife will cook us dinner." The first driver did not take to the second driver pushing his way in. This started what seemed to be a heated argument when suddenly we were joined by a third car pulling off the road. It turned out to be another family with kids in the car. After a brief exchange with the first two drivers, the third driver declared, "It's settled, they can come with us and stay in my home." The first driver was now very unhappy with the third driver. He was motioning for us to climb into his already full car. Then the three drivers stood nose to nose in an animated almost full volume discussion about whom we were going home with.

About the same time the third driver had pulled up, we had put our backpacks back on, so while the three drivers were going at it, they did not notice we had slipped down a dry wash and up and over a small hill and disappeared right under their noses and into the night. We could hear their voices fading into the distance. Only one of the little kids in the back seat of the first car had noticed us slipping away. She just smiled at us and waved.

November 9. The days are hot. Back in Amman. We resolved two issues. We learned our visa request for Iraq got rejected. We discovered there had been a regime change of late, and apparently, the new boss does not like western backpackers. We got our tourist visas for Iran in two hours. We plan to leave Amman after lunch and hitchhike south to Petra.

November 10. We are in al-'Aqaba, Jordan, looking out across the border at the lights of Eilat, Israel. A little over a week ago, my former self was stuffing my face with dates while sitting on a bus passing through Eilat and heading south, a mere 10 miles from where I am standing.

Yesterday after hitchhiking within 20 miles of Petra, we camped in the desert overnight at the highway turnoff near the town of Maan. In the morning, I discovered I had lost my wallet and was sure I dropped it on the floor of the truck we got our last ride in. The driver wanted to know if we had a cigarette to give him, and I remember taking it out while rummaging through my bag to give him one and I was sure I

Dave hanging on to a ride while hitchhiking out of the Jordan Valley to Salt, Jordan. (*R. L. Kreamer, Cibachrome 35-mm slide film, © 1977, 2019*)

Me and Dave camping along the King's Highway on the road to Petra, Jordan. (*R. L. Kreamer, Cibachrome 35-mm slide film, © 1977, 2019*)

stuffed my shit back in my bag but must have missed it. Shit, I was not even stoned so I am not sure what happened.

I told Dave I was going to hitchhike down to the Gulf of Aqaba because that is where the driver said he was going with his delivery and I was sure I could find him. I said that Dave should carry on to Petra and I would catch up in a couple of days. I thought he was going to be a jerk about it, but he was really cool and said he was coming with me.

Got down to the port city in late afternoon, and I searched and hunted the rail depot, seaport, docks, and anywhere else that truck may have been. I searched twice. I knew what the truck looked like and eventually I knew my wallet was going, going, gone. I was not watching my shit like I should have. It was losing the student I.D. for cheap hotel and hostel rates and my international health vaccination card that is a major fuck up.

We sat on a hill in a newly started sub-division on the outskirts of El Aqaba, looking over at the north end of the gulf at the lights Eilat as the twilight unfolds. The place is so new up here the manholes do not have their covers on them yet and the sidewalks and roads are fresh and newly laid. The streetlights are not wired up either, and it is getting dark. Dave and I saw a dark figure fall into one of the open manholes. They caught themselves just in the nick of time.

We are at a place called the New Desert Highway, at the crossroad for Petra. The highway north was almost empty. This part is the "King's Highway." A lone car passes every hour or so in one direction or another. The road rolls under skies of dark clouds and skies heavy with the threat of rain and thunder. We got here in one ride from Aqaba in a truck laden with 20 tons of gas. The landscape is treeless, and void of life save for the odd camel in the distance or the proverbial lone lost sheep or goat. The only sign of life was the tarmac.

This truck driver told us that near the crossroads was a lone building that was a schoolhouse. One half is a classroom for Bedouin children and the teacher lives in the other half, alone. The truck driver said the teacher was a nice guy and very friendly and he may let us spend the night out of the rain. The driver is sure of the rain coming soon and I believe him. Once you have lived for a time in the desert, you can smell the rain coming for miles. We were dropped off at the crossroads at 8 p.m. and we walked down the road towards Petra, guided by a single light in the distant darkness. The teacher was wary of opening his door at night to strangers. He later told us this was only

because some people in the area do not approve of him teaching both boys and girls.

His name is Ali. The second Ali I have met on this trip so far. He was very curious about us and what we were doing. He wanted to look over my passport, so I let him. He wanted to look over my camera, so I let him. Ali said he was assigned to this school and he must do it for a while before he can teach somewhere else. He wants to teach at a large school in a large city. He says he will not find a wife out here. He seems a sad and lonely figure for sure.

We did nothing to cheer him up. On the contrary, the fact that we were free agents gallivanting to India on an overland road trip made him dislike his current plight even more. I showed him my map and the route we have taken and where we were planning to go. He studied the map for a very long time. He said we were welcome to stay. We were led outside to access the room from a separate entrance.

We thanked him for his hospitality and kindness and slept on the floor of the adjoining classroom. The wind had picked up and the smell of rain was still in the air.

November 11. Overcast and cool. We find ourselves down the road a piece from the schoolhouse. We got up this morning and I fired up my little camp stove. We had laid in a new store of canned goods and fuel in our bags in Amman, so we shared our breakfast with Ali. He has lots of water on store, so he said it was OK to fill up our water containers. That was good for us because we had no plan for water supply. He sadly said that was the only thing he had plenty of.

We are walking towards Petra and the traffic on this road is almost non-existent. Every couple of hours, a car or truck goes by. It is the same as the road from Aqaba. It is really no surprise; we are in the middle of nowhere. The landscape is dotted with a few more goats and camels and the odd herder watching over them. The looks we get from the herders and car drivers makes me think they are shocked to see us out here. I have lots and lots of time to sit on my bag and write and smoke. Last night, the rain never fell, it only passed close enough to leave its smell. Today is cooler and windy. The sand is getting whipped up over the hills and is backlit by the morning sun. There are storm clouds in the great distance and clear skies overhead.

November 13. Overcast. We are in Petra and its more incredible than the stories we were told. We walked in yesterday sometime in the afternoon. At long last, we got a lift and had been dropped off at what the driver said was the entrance to Petra.

The teacher Ali and Dave in front of the schoolhouse at the crossroads on the road to Petra, Jordan. (*R. L. Kreamer, Cibachrome 35-mm slide film, © 1977, 2019*)

He said the entrance was called the Siq, and indeed, that is what we do, we seek. I was beginning to doubt we had been steered in the right direction until we stumbled across a nondescript sign indicating that we were in fact heading in the right direction. We were told we had only a mile or so of a walk ahead of us. The dry sandy route in was diving between the rising hills that quickly rose into rock walls on either side. It narrowed even more to where, in places, the path seemed only 20-foot wide. A channel that had been carved into the rock wall at waist height made an appearance. We noticed weird runes and letters carved into the rock. The rock walls were now towering over us at an impressive height and we walked even faster. We commented to each other that we had no idea how far or for how long we had been walking. At the very instant we were wondering aloud about how we were losing any sense of time, we walked into the T-junction of a sandstone canyon, with the most imposing, amazing, mind-blowing, and beautiful building carved from solid rock I had ever seen instantly appearing before us.

The minute we walked into the canyon, we were approached by a little old man selling postcards. We had heard about this guy from other travelers. We were even given a head's up about him from people in Germany—I guess he is famous. He is one of the dudes that will point out a cave to sleep in, usually one of the lesser-known tombs. We laughed at ourselves for buying postcards of the very building we were standing in front of, and we asked him if we could camp here, but he seemed to know what we wanted. His name is Ali. Ali number three. He motioned for us to follow him and we did. The little old man pointed to a corner of the canyon where, on a low rocky hill, a derelict-looking building stood. There was a chair with a uniformed man sitting on it and he seemed asleep. The postcard seller said with a big toothless smile and a wave of his hand an obviously well-practiced line, as if he were in a play, "Thank you, bye, bye," he said. We were chattering and talking as we walked up to what now looked like a lone guard unhappy with being woken up. I did my overstated "Hello" and he immediately said the cafe was closed. We asked if he spoke English and could we camp overnight, and he said yes, he spoke English. He said we could camp if we were crazy enough to want to, but not in the open.

Above: The Siq and the way in, Petra, Jordan. (*R. L. Kreamer, Cibachrome 35-mm slide film,* © *1977, 2019*)

Right: The walls are closing in along the Siq and the way in, Petra, Jordan. (*R. L. Kreamer, Cibachrome 35-mm slide film,* © *1977, 2019*)

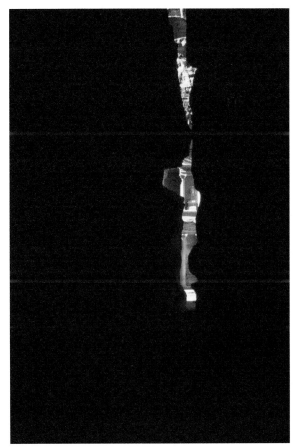

The Treasury, Petra, Jordan, the former capital of the Nabataean Kingdom and carved from solid rock sometime in the first century CE. (*R. L. Kreamer, Cibachrome 35-mm slide film, © 1977, 2019*)

He told to use one of the caves or tombs. He then said we were lucky and unlucky. We were lucky because soon using the caves would not be allowed when the hotel is built next year, and that the Bedouin who used these caves in the winter for their flocks of goats will be no longer given access. We were unlucky because the cafe has long been closed and is being removed and there is nowhere to buy food or drink. "If there were more tourists, there would be more postcard sellers and they sell sodas and water."

He said very few tourists come through here this time of year and he repeated that the government is planning to build a hotel here.

We walked back into the middle of the city of Petra and sat down for a rest in the sun. We then noticed the clouds were moving in again. We noticed Ali the postcard seller was gone.

Stark, steep, winding deep below the earth I walk. Canyons of time bite the earth, dead trees whisper, the stone will talk. You alone weigh its worth.

November 13. Rain and cold. The rain finally came and the first night in Petra was wet and cold. But we were dry. We found the cave we were told to use.

In truth, we made a guess and found one with the least amount of goat shit in it. A little funky smelling, but dry. The walls were blackened with countless fires. We set up the camp stove and cooked up what is advertised on the can as some sort of lamb stew. It was not quite dark, but I was tired and set up a place to crash out. I fell asleep looking out at the soft and steady rain. The sky was grey and seemed to be getting darker with each passing second.

The dawn came with a clear sky that seemed a much deeper blue when looking north, in the way only autumn or winter skies can be. Petra seems beyond what any imagining could conjure up, and the stories and the hype cannot even come close to describing its size and antiquity. The canyon walls are mostly towering, almost all vertical, sandstone and a mixture of yellows, reds, and dark browns. The dark browns are desert varnished from the years of exposure. The first building we saw, or any visitor sees from our route in, is called the Treasury. The ornate urn at the top is riddled and surrounded by bullet marks, because of the supposed treasure hidden inside and futile attempts to shatter it open—as legend tells it.

Dave inside the opening of the tomb we camped in, Petra, Jordan. (*R. L. Kreamer, Cibachrome 35-mm slide film, © 1977, 2019*)

In the morning, there were three or four tourists who appeared in the canyon, and they hung around the postcard seller and took photos of the Treasury, slowly wandering into the first few hundred yards of the wide and expansive main canyon. I thought I could hear them speaking German. I do not know, sometimes everything and everyone sounds German. Dave and I were still cleaning up and rolling up our bedrolls after breakfast as they wandered by. They were sticking to the wide-open sandy middle spaces of the main canyon and did not come up to the caves around us or the one we were occupying. I am sure they could see us, but they stayed about 60 yards away. I wondered if we appeared to be some sort of scary cave trolls. As they strolled by, I said to Dave, "You want to get high?" Dave was shocked. I was not really holding out on him, I just did not go through the Lebanese stuff we divided up long ago as quickly as he did. Dave looked at me as if he had seen a ghost. I knew what he must be thinking. Before he could say anything, I added, "Yeah, I didn't have all that time to kill hanging around the swimming pool." I added that I really did not have a lot left, but it was the good shit. I took out my pack of Marlboro's and took out one of my Baalbek specials.

Before we left the kibbutz, I remembered I had a few remaining bits of both the blonde and red. I mixed them together and had enough to repack three cigarettes and carefully placed them at the back of an almost full pack of smokes. Together with a couple of unopened packs, I stashed them at the bottom of my bag. I thought I would smoke them in the Sinai, but the timing was not right. I proceeded to light up. Took a deep drag and passed it to Dave. He said, "All right Bob!" I had forgotten all about them and even crossed a border with them, which is something I promised myself I would never do, ever. I was a bit shocked when I remembered and found them. Must be more careful. Before he even finished his first drag, I told him to quit bogarting. We had a laugh and quietly smoked and watched the tourists having what seemed like a timid look around.

About the time the hash started to take hold, I realized a couple of things. I was really, really, thirsty, and because I had not smoked in a while, I was really, really stoned. We made sure our bags were well hidden, checked my camera, and ventured from the cave. As we wandered around, we noticed that this was a tourist destination of long standing. The tombs and monuments had numbered plaques on small posts to help the visitor find their way round. Back when we were recently in Jerusalem, I looked over a few of the Middle East guidebooks in an Old City bookshop in anticipation of our visit. Aside from the fact that its existence has been known to the Bedouin for hundreds of years, it remained unknown to westerners until 1812. The western explorer who made a point of coming here was named Burckhardt and he came in disguise.

We found a path that wound its way above the tombs we are camping in. The vista looks down onto the Treasury and the threshold of the Siq. We climbed down and noticed the place seemed completely deserted. No guard, postcard seller, or tourists. We are completely alone and have the place to ourselves. We explored the main part of Petra, the tombs and caves within this part of the canyon. It seemed to take forever, but we were finished in a couple of hours. While climbing over the amphitheater, we took a seat and smoked another joint. Our cave was directly across from us. It looked weirdly fantastic in its eroded state. We sat and stared at it. I felt like I was tripping. I let Dave know that, after this, I had one joint left and today was our getting high day, I guess. It is a good day for it. We had noticed a sign directing the visitor to something called the high place.

It is paved in some places with worn blocks of stone. Stairs carved into the rock make for easy climbing. The sand that covers the way in a few places makes the path slippery. It is like walking on ball bearings. The first time this trip, I am aware of not wanting to break a leg.

We came across a monument that had been carved from a massive solid rock hillside. It jutted out and was almost freestanding. We could climb up the rock behind it and jump out on to its roof. The high place was just that. The path led to a large flat plateau with an altar like carved middle section. We thought we had been minutes climbing around the surrounding hills and canyons, but we noticed the day was starting to fade and we did not want to get caught in the dark without flashlights. On the climb down, we noticed people seemingly dwelling nearby in some sort of hut. One dude had a horse. There seemed to be a couple of huts in ruins. As we returned to the tomb where we had set up camp, we noticed we were not alone. A family of Bedouin were in the area near the Treasury and they watched us walk across the flat expanse from the amphitheater. Dave mentioned that he hoped they had not gone through our stuff. I had not thought of that possibility and found myself getting a little paranoid. It was getting dark in our cave, but the twilight outside was still bright. Lit the candle stub and placed it on a rock in the back of the cave and I gathered up my camp

Above the tomb where we camped, Petra, Jordan. (*R. L. Kreamer, Cibachrome 35-mm slide film, © 1977, 2019*)

The climb to the High Place, Petra, Jordan. (*R. L. Kreamer, Cibachrome 35-mm slide film, © 1977, 2019*)

Dave on top of a monument, Petra, Jordan. (*R. L. Kreamer, Cibachrome 35-mm slide film,* © *1977, 2019*)

stove and pan and grabbed a tin of the stew I had in my stash. I set the stove up near the entrance to take advantage of the remaining twilight. Dave was messing around with a flashlight and going through his stuff. I sat down and lit a cigarette. I am sure it looked like we were in residence here.

I noticed the group of people were on the move, walking south where the expanse of the canyon floor widens out. They walked past the amphitheater and then I noticed they were heading towards another small group of people who were already camped inside of a cave on the far side of Petra. They had a small fire going. There were children and goats as well.

We were approached in the gathering darkness by a young man from the group of Bedouin. He spoke perfect English and asked if we wanted to buy some bread. He said his grandmother sent him over to ask us, and his mother was making it. We said yes. We watched her cook the bread on a convex metal bowl. It was like a grill placed on rocks suspended over the fire. The little children chased each other around laughing. The grandmother came over to the fire and picked up three red hot coals, one at a time, neither fast nor slow, and placed them in a tin can. It was like she was picking up paper. She said something to us and her grandson translated. She wanted to know where we were from. After we told her, she said she was glad some Americans were normal and did not always need a house or a hotel. She was pleased to know we could camp outside and appreciate and enjoy it. I did not have the heart to mention I would not mind a hot shower, a sink to wash my smelly clothes in, and a nice bed to lie in.

The woman making the bread was finished and wanted her money. I think it was around 50 cents U.S. for four huge steaming hot fresh flatbreads. We could see the faint glow of the candle when we got about halfway back. The stars are out, and the Milky Way arches over Petra. We had our supper and Dave offered to carry the camp stove and gas occasionally—to take turns and share the load he said. I said thanks and I will take him up on it. I added I was planning on smoking my last joint with him tonight anyway, so no need for the bribe. With the white noise of the camp stove silenced, we sat out under the stars and smoked. We can hear the children laugh in the distance

5

Burgers, Fries, and Cokes, But No Boat

November 15. Sunny and warm. Hitchhiked after walking out of Petra in the early morning. Walking out seemed hard going at first, as if Petra was pulling on us like extra gravity. We were back in the Al-Farouk hotel again around lunchtime. It is almost like coming home.

We dropped off our passports at the Saudi embassy. We have decided to swing south and avoid a return to Syria and to avoid Turkey. Well Dave has, and I am going along with it—I am not so sure. We could be through Syria and Turkey in no time. Dave thought it would be too uptight and expensive of a country to go tramping through. I am knocked back losing the 70 bucks and my wallet. We return to the embassy tomorrow at one in the afternoon to get our passports back.

Nice to be in a hotel, even if it is a bit of a dive—as long as it is only a couple of nights. Time to clean up, sleep, eat, catch up in my journal, and stock up on local cigarettes, travel food, and supplies—we need white gas for the stove.

Amman is crowed and dirty. The noise from the street traffic and car horns is constant and deafening. I am feeling nostalgic for some reason. Nostalgic for Petra and the kibbutz. Nostalgic for my hometown and my ex-girlfriend, for my family and friends.

November 16. Clear skies. Hitched north to the Syria–Jordan border. Staying on the Jordan side and we are fairly sure of getting a quick ride once the border opens. Took all day and we got here just as the border closed at seven. The truck drivers we spoke to are waiting for their agents to bring the visas for Saudi. Mad scenes at the Saudi embassy in Amman earlier.

The gates were mobbed by hundreds of people trying to get visas before the embassy shut for ten days due to upcoming holidays. At this point, we just assumed we got the visas because they got the money they wanted for them. There was no "Excuse me," and "Sorry but they are expecting us" polite squeeze to the front of the mob. After about a half an hour, we realized we had to strong arm and push our way through. It seemed to get worse and worse as we got deeper into the crowd, and it ended up being a real tussle and shoving match, with a lot of elbows thrown—and those elbows were not mine. It was a just as much of a challenge to be heard over the yelling and shouting din of the crowd and get the attention of the guards. We got their attention all right when we started to climb the gates and when we started to shout at them in English and then they took our papers. Most everyone else at the gates were just trying to get in, shouting, pushing, and clutching and waving papers. It seemed one or two would be let in every ten minutes or so. The ones trying to get out had it worse, if you could believe it. The guards gave them a little nudge as they tried to squeeze past the crowd that would not give way. In fact, when the gate opened for any reason, the crowd pushed forward a little harder. We hung on to the gates and finally were let inside and given our receipts and told to retrieve our passports. What a fucking madhouse. We were given transit visas, so the clock starts ticking the minute we cross the border.

Dave and I had another discussion about our route. His idea is for us to also try to enter Kuwait and he thinks we can get a visa at the border. I pointed out that, according to the map, this route seems to have around 800 or so extra desert-full-of-nothing miles before the coast. He got annoyed and insisted this was the best option money and time wise.

Spent the night sleeping in the back of an empty British lorry. I woke up early and saw about a dozen local guys next to the lorry taking a shit. They had small brass pots to wash their ass with—no toilet paper. Later, when I mentioned it to the English driver, he said he hated that and had to learn quickly to watch where he was stepping when climbing out of his truck in the morning. He said because it is an exposed, treeless place, people use the trucks as cover. He said he sometimes got his kicks waking up early, and if a bunch of guys were using his truck as cover for the morning shit, he would fire up his truck and pull forward, honking the horn to expose them to all and sundry. What a jerk. Later in the morning, we did not get a straight-through ride into Saudi. Still, we covered the 200 miles across Jordan with Greek truckers hauling eggs, and we got dropped at the Jordan side of the border.

I have walked your earth and breathed your sky and your empty deserts found me alone. The measure of my worth before I die is found within my home.

November 17. Hot and clear days and cold nights. We crossed the 7-mile-wide no-man's-land between the Jordan–Saudi border yesterday with ease. But before that, we tried to clear the border with Jordan.

The Jordanian police said our visas expired over two months ago when we entered the West Bank. He could not fathom how or why we were let back in. He said our exit visas cost 4 dinars each—that is 10 bucks each please. Dave mentions to the policeman that this was expensive, and we were very poor. The policeman looked us over and said he was very sorry and that he would not charge us for the exit visas. We did not expect that.

However, now we seem stuck. The cars we have seen all day long are stuffed with belongings and people. No room for a couple of backpackers.

The road in this no-man's-land is lined with dozens and dozens of shacks, trailers, and cabins. Most are import companies, clearance, and haulage firms. Loads of trucks are parked everywhere. There are a few tea and restaurant shacks with water, crackers, sodas, and such for sale. Up the road a few hundred yards is the Saudi police checkpoint and the border. We bide our time sitting along the side of the road hitchhiking and taking turns wandering around looking at everything and everyone. As usual, I have lots of time to sit, write, and smoke.

It seems the police at this checkpoint say that even if we get a ride, and they doubt we will, we are recorded on the driver's passport. Even if we hire a taxi, it is the same. Passengers are not allowed transit in trucks. We tried to bluff our way with our international driver's licenses, but no dice—we must be hired and driving a truck when we show up to cross the border. Apparently, we need to be escorted in and out of this country. We found this out when we tried to walk through the checkpoint and into the desert to start hitchhiking. They do not like the idea of us doing that and they do not seem to like us either. I tell Dave I want to bale now and head to Turkey. In this no-man's-land, they will take a few different currencies and even barter a little in the small shops scattered around. It is like a Wild West-type boomtown. Really more a mild west. No booze out in the open.

Dave is off somewhere trying to sell his wares. Before we left Germany, a few seasoned travelers recommended that we take some type of items or wares with us that we could later sell for a profit and for extra travel coin. Many suggestions were offered. I decided to take blue jeans. Yeah, a little heavy in the old backpack, but in great demand. I sold one pair already.

Dave decided to take *Playboy* magazines. He returned from his foray a bit annoyed and shocked. I asked him what happened, and he said that after the old dude in the shop had looked them over, he said they were too tame. Dave reported the man said he wanted pictures of men and women fucking. I told him I did not know why he toted them way the hell out here anyway and to just throw them away. I recalled and recited one of the stories Heino told us when we were driving those trucks to Syria. He said someone had porno mags in his truck and border guards in Syria found them. They were to be burned on the spot, but to ensure the guy burning them would not see them, another guard covered the dude's eyes with his hands and turned his head away. The guy doing the burning, unable to see, kept burning his hands.

Our hanging around has not gone unnoticed. People come up to speak to us and to find out what we are doing here. Kind of fun the first thirty times, but it is starting to wear thin, especially on Dave. He said his name was Faissall. He wrote it on the back of a business card and gave it to me. He said he was working for his uncle and he had to live out here pretty much all the time, working seven days a week. His last name matches the last name on the card. That must be his uncle he is referring to. He is one of about a dozen kids that seem to be about thirteen or seventeen years old and living and working here on their own.

It was a typical Middle Eastern meal of mutton stew, rice, and flatbread, and it was good. There never seems to be much in the way of vegetables or salad around.

On the Jordan–Saudi Arabia border, hanging out with the working kids. Dave is on the far left. (*R. L. Kreamer, Cibachrome 35-mm slide film, © 1977, 2019*)

Hard and expensive to grow in the desert I guess. They should try to promote more trade with the Israelis. Having just come off a kibbutz, I have seen with my own eyes the Israeli knowhow at work. They can grow bananas in an old shoe if they want to. With the Israeli knowhow and the Arab oil money, this would be the breadbasket of the world—the new Eden. But that is not going to happen. Over the meal, we were asked where we had been. We ran down the list of countries, and when we got to Israel, the murmurs and tsk-tsk noises started up. Stories of atrocities against holy sites, people, and mistrust were traded, and I am sure some were true and some exaggerated or made up or both. But it was exactly the same stories I heard in Israel about the very people I was breaking bread with. I told them that, but it did not seem to go down well. Both sides do not get the irony either. Nothing will change until everyone decides to forgive and forget, and that is not going to happen either—that would take a miracle.

We went back to the road to hitchhike but nothing was stopping for us. The border closed at seven and that was it. We were lucky to be offered a place to crash in Faissall's back room. It is where he slept like an indentured servant. It had a heater and he insisted Dave and I took the places closest to it. Just before I fell into sleep, a weird thought popped into my head, so I write this: if mankind falls, who will care to measure the distance?

November 18. Night is falling and the border is closing. Here all day again and no ride. Dave has gotten a bit worked up over being stuck here. He is a bit better now, but I feel his mood has not helped endear us to potential rides. His latest idea was to dress as Arabs to blend in. We were invited to eat and sleep at Faissall's place again so that was good news. The desert is getting very cold at night. Faissall seemed in a great mood; I asked him why, and he said that if we ended up stuck here, we could go to work for him. Had another weird dream last night. I have had a lot of them lately. This one was about a young kid we encountered on the drive at a gas station in Graz. He had been wandering from vehicle to vehicle asking for a ride to Istanbul. We turned him down at the time. In my dream I encountered him in Petra wandering around, still asking for a ride to Istanbul.

November 19. Well there is the good news and then there is the bad news. First the good news: we got a ride to Kuwait in one ride, and it was a hell-for-leather fast and crazy through the day and into the night and on to the next day kind of ride you only read about in books.

Before Faissall was even half-awake, we were packed and out the door. I said thank you and I hope we meet again, but we are going to try to find a ride now. He said, "OK, bye," almost like he expected to see us again at lunch. We got lucky real fast. A dozen or so cars were already in line, mixed with trucks large and small, all waiting for the border to open in an hour or so. The dawn was still far on the horizon and we were still in the cold and dark. It was a slightly older model Chevy Impala—a big American road boat sent from heaven to way out here. One guy in the front seat and no one in the back. He rolled down his window and said, "Kuwait?" He said his English was not good, but his friend was coming and to wait. It turns out they wanted help with the driving. Dave and I ran back, grabbed our bags, and ran to the car. His buddy had showed up and they were in an animated conversation. The guy outside the car turned to us and asked if we were going to Kuwait and could we help them with the driving. We said yes. We showed him our international licenses, and after briefly looking them over, told us, "OK, get in." We went to put our bags in the trunk, but we were told there was no room. We piled them in the center of the back seat and floor and piled in on either side. Dave behind the driver and me behind the passenger.

It turns out these guys have done this drive before, a few times at least. They were visiting family in Jordan and now they were going back to their jobs in Kuwait. One did oilfield work and the other one was a teacher. Well, the guy who spoke English said so.

They asked about the usual stuff: America, living in West Germany, where are we going and why. We had not gone a hundred miles and we started running out of things to say, but it did not matter. The radio was blasting, and we were doing 70 alongside the trans-Arabian pipeline. No seat belts and no cares.

The road is elevated around 10 feet off the desert floor because of blowing sand, which makes it less likely for the road to get buried. It is a two-lane black top with wide shoulders. Shoulders that turn into a gradual gradient to the desert floor. The road is straight as hell and, according to the map, has a slight bend every 300 miles or so. Just like the death roads we drove down on from Europe, only straighter. Drift

just a bit or lose your concentration for a second and it is a head-on smash up highway to the pearly gates. There is not much in the way of civilization out here in this stretch of desert. A small settlement built around a gas station or an airstrip, and every couple of hundred miles or so the odd wrecked car or truck in the desert left to rot.

Every so often we pass a car broken down on the shoulder, with someone under the hood or changing a tire. Sometimes it is a breakdown with a family clustered together off the shoulder looking concerned. There are no phones for hundreds of miles and we pass no tow trucks. The traffic is moving slower and so are we. The hours drag on. We smoke cigarettes and stop to change drivers or to piss. We stop every couple of hundred miles to gas up and get water and sodas. There is no beer around here and Al is not selling whiskey. We kick in some money for gas, but it is not necessary—it is cheaper than water. Before one of the gas stops, I noticed the tracks of a truck that had pulled off the highway, drove down the embankment, and carried on way out into the desert. The tracks ran straight and disappeared on the flat horizon. A while later, I noticed more tracks all heading out into the empty desert, appearing to converge at some unseen point. Miles up ahead I see a dirt turnoff, heavy with traffic coming and going and with traffic waiting to merge back on to the highway. The tracks I saw earlier were drivers creating their own cut-off route to this road, miles and miles ahead of time.

As we turn off, the driver says we are stopping for gas. A few miles down the dirt road, we came to a haphazard parking lot next to what looks like a miniature refinery and gas station. It looks like the border crossing into Turkey, with a chaotic line of cars and trucks trying to get to the gas pumps. The desert floor is one huge oil and gas stain carpeting the entire area. We join the line and eventually pull up to the pumps. The pumps only display the amount of fuel dispensed and not the price. After refueling, the driver haggles over the money owed. It turns out that a tank of gas costs less than a dollar.

We pull away and park near a makeshift bazaar. A cluster of shacks and trucks are selling rugs, pots and pans, clothes, and bric-a-brac. There are a few food stalls scattered around, porta toilets, and outdoor sinks nearby. We pile out and the driver leaves the car unlocked and the windows down. I ask the driver if he is going to lock the car and he laughs and tell me not to worry. He says anyone caught stealing gets their right hand chopped off.

As we stroll around, the first thing I notice is how grubby and unfashionable Dave and I must look. We are dressed in our grubby jeans and old kibbutz work shirts. The young dudes are sporting designer jeans, nice leather jackets, hip haircuts from 1969, and the occasional moustache—though some are clean-shaven. The women are modestly dressed in full covering and a headscarf. There is the occasional hijab being worn and then a few women wearing burqas— but not that many.

The old dudes sport beards and most are in traditional long shirts with a keffiyeh on their heads. We take our time to use the toilets and wash in some outdoor sinks. I stock up on cigs and we grab something to eat before we hit the road again. The sun is going down.

We drink lots of coffee. The oncoming traffic becomes less and less after sunset and as the night wears on. A lot of time is spent overtaking slower trucks and heavily over-packed cars. They tend to cluster in a chain, five or six vehicles long—sometimes more. Sometimes, it is rather slow going, and it takes a long time to pass safely. A few times, we charged up to the back of a slow-moving vehicle with no taillights, hidden until the last minute.

The road is so flat and straight that approaching headlights seem to be a permanent part of the vista out ahead, hypnotic and seemingly never getting closer, until all at once, the car is filled with blinding light, and then with a roar we are left in darkness again. The play of the headlights repeats over and over, in a slow dance far into the distance, and over time, it becomes more drawn out, more mesmerizing. Whomever is not driving is sleeping. The radio picks up no station. We are deep into the desert.

We are couple of hundred miles from our last gas stop and I know we are running low. Right on cue, the engine knocks a little then dies. The gas gauge is way below E. We coast on to the far side of the shoulder in the dead of night and we all climb out of the car into the cold desert air. The road is empty save for the far-off distant dance of headlights ahead and behind.

The driver moves towards the trunk and we all follow. Inside are four gas cans holding 5 gallons each. We all help with emptying the gas into the car and rinse the gas from our hands on the side of the road with a water bottle, all the while, the distant traffic has yet to catch up. The driver wants Dave to drive.

We all pile back into the car. The two dudes grab the back seat and say they want to sleep. Dave gets behind the wheel and I am riding shotgun. It is like the old days of three months ago, charging south through Europe.

I start messing with the radio and find a station and a far-off exotic lament comes through the speakers. I turn around and ask the dudes in the back if it was OK. "Yeah, sure, sure," came the reply with a wave of a hand.

We have a little more than a couple of hundred miles until the turn off for the Kuwait border at a town called Hafar Al-Batin. I heard one of the dudes mention it, and I looked it up on my map. I mentioned that to Dave and it seemed to perk him up a bit. The dudes in the back were fast asleep now. Hell, I forgot their names the minute they told me—Dave probably remembers. All the while Dave has upped his speed, little at a time. We started at 60, and after the first half hour, Dave's doing 65. Dave wants another cig and now we are doing 75 and creeping up to 80. For the last hour, Dave had the old Chevy doing 85 and the car was running smooth. We were facing east and could see a streak of dawn in the sky. Not much traffic. I caught a glimpse of the sign for our turn and I warned Dave.

It was a T-junction and Dave had to go just a little heavy on the brakes. It woke the dudes up and Dave said, "We're here at the turnoff." He pulled over and I hopped out and stretched. The guy who did most of the driving and owned this car got out and looked around. He looked at his watch and looked around some more. Dave got out and the guy was looking his car over like Dave had broken it. Dave said something about maybe driving a little fast. The guy just shook his head and took over driving. After our last pit stop for gas with these guys, we were at the border in a couple of hours. Our hosts were glad to have us accounted for and have us off the driver's passport. Our two-week transit visa to Saudi was dutifully stamped and cancelled, and we were marked as exited.

The plan was that we would be dropped off at some hotel in Al Kuwait and we would be on our way. The no-man's-land between border checkpoints was 20 kilometers wide and we were the only travelers on that stretch of road that morning. We rolled up to the Kuwait checkpoint and they had us get out of the car for the usual checks. The two dudes we were with were cool; we were not. There was a lot of back and forth with the driver and the guards. The driver turned to us and explained we did not have a visa and we were being denied entry. Dave said something about only wanting a transit visa. The driver's buddy got our bags out of the back of the car.

A guard who spoke English approached us and explained that without a visa obtained beforehand, they were under instructions not to let anyone in. He said they did not even have the forms available, all they had were entry and exit stamps. All this bad news took under five minutes. The dudes wished us luck and shook our hands and gave a shrug before driving off in that sweet Chevy. Dave and I were taken aback, and we just stared at the border guards going about their business and then back at each other.

I was fishing out a cig and Dave went back to pleading with the border guards. No dice, they told us to go back to Saudi Arabia while waving their hands. I shouldered my bag and started the 20-kilometre hike.

We finally got a ride back to the Saudi border. When we got there, the guards were very surprised to see us. I think they recognized us. They asked what we were doing here. They said we should not be here and to go back. They told us our passports are stamped exit, the visa is now finished. We explained that is just what the guards at the Kuwait border said. The guards got on the phone and called someone of a higher rank. Much discussion followed, our passports examined again and again, another call made, and the boss's boss showed up. Again, there was much discussion, our passports again as if something new would appear. We were shown an empty office and asked to wait—and wait. Dave is not happy. I realize no one knows where we are and I would not know who to call for help anyway. The American embassy, I suppose. We are a little further out than the middle of nowhere. We were in that room for hours, but it seemed like days; long enough for the imagination to run wild. Then the door flies open and we are summoned into the head honcho's office. There are a couple of extra border guards with him and our passports are on the desk in front of him. We are told we are going to be given a thirty-six-hour transit visa. We are told if there is any overstay, we could be jailed. After much bowing and scraping on our part, we had our passports stamped, our packs on our backs, and we were outside the gate trudging down the road with our thumbs out.

November 21. Clear days and cold nights and not a cloud in the sky. We had a rough time hitchhiking. Finally got a ride to ad-Dammām, on the gulf. Arrived at night and we had trouble finding our way around. I went into a kiosk and bought some cigarettes and postcards. Saw a number of religious items for sale. Something caught my eye. I asked the man behind the counter what the hand with the eyeball on the palm meant; he said it means god is always watching. It is a sticker for your car or something. It now adorns the cover of my journal.

Getting here ate up a lot of the time on the visa. There are no boats going to where we want to go, or none that will take us. We are trying to get to the airport and hope for a cheap standby flight. I want to fly on to Iran from here; take the gulf in one jump. Dave wants to make a short hop to Bahrain and find a boat. He is fixated on taking a boat across the gulf. Maybe it is a boat thing with him, maybe a dream of being a sailor or pirate. I think Dave's Disneyland boat ride, ticket fantasy is going to cost us in money and time. The Saudi transit visa is running out.

I think we have gone from the frying pan and into the fire. We had to go and go we did, in a small plane for big money. Packed in tight for a twenty-minute flight. The minute we left the runway and before the wheels were up, drinks were being served to the booze-starved passengers who were forbidden drinks on the ground.

Custom and passport control was lax for a change. We walked into the main lobby of the Bahrain International Airport, we dropped our bags in the middle of the great entry hall, on the floor, and we just walked out the main doors with all the flare of a cheesy actor. We had heard from somewhere or someone that there was a U.S. military base somewhere on the island. It is not a secret base, but its presence is not loudly advertised. We walked to the nearby main road and started hitchhiking to where we heard this base was. We found the base with ease. It is more a compound really, and we walked right in. We were sort of challenged at the gate by a couple of G.I.'s. At first, they were not paying attention and then were startled we were already inside, strolling past them. When they finally clamped eyes on us, I smiled and waved. We told them we are Americans far from home, kind of homesick, and we wanted to get some decent hamburgers from the mess hall. We showed them our passports and I showed them my PX card from working at a PX in Germany. They saw the complete logic and necessity of our request, waved us through, and pointed us in the direction of the mess hall. We stuffed our faces with burgers, fries, and cokes, and we were charged a dollar each. The grill cook said he was proud to be a Puerto Rican from NYC. I hit the PX and took advantage of the cheap cigarettes and stocked up. I told Dave he should trash the girlie mags and sell some cartons of cigs in Afghanistan. When we got back to the airport a couple of hours later, no one had touched our bags and the janitor was sweeping around them. I asked him why they were not moved, and he said in broken English that stealing could get your hand cut off and made a chopping motion on his wrist. We grabbed our bags and headed for the docks and our possible boat ride. Did not do the homework and went on a hunch based on a rumor that was not a reality. Beautiful wooden sailboats from another century called Dhows. I can see why Dave is chasing this fantasy. The crews are weather-beaten men, seemingly of different nationalities, and looking tougher than nails and bricks. After walking around and talking to some of the captains, it became clear that any ride across the gulf in one of these was going to cost big bucks. Dave was rather dumbfounded. I was relieved. I had visions of being dumped overboard in the dead of night for our possessions and money.

I gave up, sat down, watched the sunset, and took in the incredible beauty of the scene. The poetry of these boats. I left it to Dave to keep asking, keep searching. I got the vibe right away that these cats were not interested in taking some unknown white guys anywhere. Truth be told, we were probably seen as more trouble than we were worth. Dave returned flabbergasted; he just could not get over that the going price was $300 U.S. per person. A standby flight to Iran was going to cost us $160 each. Two tops. It was getting dark and I realized I should have taken a photo of those wooden ships in the golden sunset. I was happy just to have it in my mind's eye.

It is getting cold on the docks and we have nowhere to go. The hotel prices are as crazy as the boat passenger prices, and within the first few hours of our arrival to Bahrain, we rejected any notion of a $400 a night hotel or a $50 a night fleabag hotel. We decided to crash somewhere near the docks and found cover behind a parking lot filled with buses.

Today we are hanging around the airport. Got some time to kill. Had a wash in the airport restroom. We found a place outside under a stairwell to nap and let some of the stuff I washed dry out. The cops showed up and were surprised to hear us speaking English. They wanted to know what we were doing. We told them we were waiting around ten hours for our flight. They told us we should stay in a hotel. We said they we too expensive for us. They said they did not like poor people hanging around like beggars and they were glad we would be leaving.

We decided to change some money for Iran. The moneychanger was in a corner of the airport, standing in the middle of a round, low desk-like counter. At his feet and clearly visible were a dozen boxes. Large cardboard boxes of dollars, yen, marks and Middle Eastern currencies, unsorted denominations stuffed to the brim. He acted frantic and busy, and we were the only people at his counter.

We met some Germans who were flying to Bombay and we killed some more time playing cards. I was a little envious of them for doing a big leap into India.

November 22. The flight was not even half-full, just like my pockets. In just a couple of hours, we had cleared the gulf and had started the descent into the city of Shiraz. Looking down on the blue gulf waters from 20,000 feet, I could see tiny boats plying their way and I imagined they were Dhows under sail.

While clearing customs and passport control, we were asked for our health certificates with the proof of vaccinations. I told them I lost mine, but I had all my shots. They prepared a new health card for me, compliments of the Imperial Government of Iran. The cholera shot I got in Germany was a small scratch made by a button with five little pins on it. I was thinking this was no big deal and rolled up my sleeve for the doctor. He picked up a glass vial and a stonking great syringe. He dipped the needle in the vial and attempted to duplicate the five pins by rapidly jabbing the fuck out of my arm. About the seventh or eighth deep jab, I grabbed his arm to stop him while I yelped like a kicked dog. He said, "That's good," and turned to his next victim. I left with a sore arm and not feeling very well. We got to our dive hotel somewhere downtown and I was definitely not feeling very well. After seeing the doctor, I think I need to see a doctor. Dave was chomping at the bit and wanted to go here, there, and everywhere right now. I told him I was not well and fell on the bed and slept in my clothes for sixteen hours.

The usual touts and hustlers are to be found around the tourist sites, but everyone seems very friendly. It is a noticeably better and more relaxed vibe we are getting from the locals compared to the last couple of countries. Our route heads almost straight north to the Caspian Sea before turning east.

November 24. The days are warm and clear and the nights are getting cold. Hitchhiked out of Shiraz and headed to the ruins of Persepolis. Before we accepted the lift, we kept saying "No taxi" over and over while shaking a finger at this guy. He was an old dude, about fifty years old. We were warned about this sort of scam by some western travelers we met in Shiraz. Maybe this was the same guy. He repeated what we had said again and again. "No taxi," he kept repeating and we put our stuff in his open trunk.

When we arrived, he jumped out of his car and refused to open his trunk until we forked over the fare he just announced we owed him. A huge shouting match followed, and we soon attracted a crowd of Iranian tourists. I thought Dave was going to punch the

The interior of The Mirrored Mosque, Shiraz, Iran. (*R. L. Kreamer, Cibachrome 35-mm slide film, © 1977, 2019*)

Shah Cheragh, also known as The Mirrored Mosque, Shiraz, Iran. Built in 1130 CE and remodelled in 1350 CE. Repaired over many centuries due to continuous earth quake damage, it had a replacement dome of iron fixed in place in the 1950s. (*R. L. Kreamer, Cibachrome 35-mm slide film, © 1977, 2019*)

guy. A few university students interceded on our behalf, but we had to pay a couple of dollars to get our bags from his car. That was the negotiated settlement. Both the driver and Dave left feeling cheated. For having a scam run on us, and stupidly going along with it, I thought we got off light. The ruins are amazing. I think Dave felt let down by them. I guess we were spoiled by Petra. Did not hang around long enough for me though. We started hitchhiking out before noon.

We got a lift from a South Korean who was traveling to Esfahan. He was mystified at our repeated questions of "Are you a taxi?" He assured us he was not, and he wanted to know why we kept asking him. It is quite a distance to Esfahan and a rather deserted highway, so we knew we were in for a long day when he had a blowout. We were in the middle of nowhere, 30 miles from the nearest town. We helped him remove the flat tire and, luckily, he had a jack; unluckily, he had no spare. The towns we have gone past so far are so sparse he will be lucky to find a shade tree mechanic to fix his tire. He asked if we would watch the car. He said he would take the tire to the nearest town to be

fixed. We said yes, and then we watched him disappear around a bend, rolling the flat tire out ahead of him as he walked.

About twenty minutes after the driver left, a truck driver stopped and asked what was wrong. We explained the situation. He said he would keep an eye out for the guy with the tire and give him a lift. The driver returned two hours later with his tire fixed and we helped him put it on.

It was late at night when we reached the outskirts of the city. The driver said this was as far as he was going and wished us luck. As he drove off, we had no idea of where he dropped us off, all we knew was it was freezing cold. We decided to move off the road and into what we thought was a field to crash out for the night. The frost-covered morning revealed we had camped in someone's vegetable patch near a house. We quickly got up, packed, got to the road, and started walking towards the city.

We had not gone far when we were approached by a young man about our age, who wanted to know who we were and what we were doing. After telling him

Persepolis, Iran. The ceremonial capital of the Achaemenid Empire, *c. 550–330 BCE. (R. L. Kreamer, Kodachrome 35-mm print film, © 1977, 2019)*

our tale, he said he would drive us into the city, and after gathering up a couple of his friends, we all piled into his car and roared off. He drove around Esfahan like a demented tour guide in a rush, albeit a nice one. Racing around the city streets, he would gesture and point out the windows in various directions. The museum, the park, the university, the mosque, the other mosque, the cinema where couples go to hold hands all flew by in a blur. He went on and on about how much they liked American culture—the movies, books, rock and roll, and fashion. They expressed a desire to be the kind of person they wanted to be in relation to their culture, themselves, and the world, and to live in peace and respect for others. Quite a tall order and I told them that is exactly the very thing I wanted and was hoping to discover out in the world. After lunch, they wanted to exchange a couple of our U.S. dollars for a couple of their Iranian banknotes. They signed theirs and they wanted us to sign the dollars as if we were famous. Counting faces along the way. Highways full of millions standing alone. Buses roll into the night. A ribbon of lights and a ribbon of eyes. Straining for a glimpse of the distance.

November 26. In Tehran and we are getting our visa for Afghanistan. We travelled from Esfahan by bus. It was cheap and fast. We are staying at the Aisa Hotel near Amir Kabir in Fardowsi Street. The nights are getting colder and we no longer relish the idea of getting stuck overnight on the road while hitchhiking. We will probably stick to using buses. We met a young man named James from Panama; he said he was robbed of his suitcase and all his money in Istanbul, although he did not say it, he wrote it down because he has indicated to us that he is deaf and mute. He is wearing bellbottoms and a blue velvet jacket. He says all he has is his passport, a toothbrush, and £3 U.S. The toothbrush he keeps in the breast pocket of his jacket like a pen.

America has just given the Panama Canal back to Panama with great fanfare and boasting of continued international cooperation. I am sure we can get him some sort of help. We are going to pay for a phone call for him to make in hopes of him getting some assistance from the Panamanian embassy or maybe he can get in touch with his family for support. We will do the talking for him. Dave knows some Spanish. I gave

James and Dave in downtown Tehran, Iran. (*R. L. Kreamer, Kodachrome 35-mm print film,* © *1977, 2019*)

James $10 U.S., which is a fair amount of money in Tehran and should keep him going for a short while. I gave him my gas camping stove to try and sell, and told him he could keep the money. He said he got $7 U.S. for it. We have seen him around the tourist sites and cafes panhandling for money, so for now, he seems to be doing all right.

Got my passport back, with my tourist visa for Afghanistan paid for, stamped, and approved. I noticed I was running out of space for visas so planned to visit the American embassy to get some extra pages added. Dave wanted to tag along, so we were going to bring James along to see about a phone call. At one of the bus stations, we asked about getting a bus to the American embassy. From a group of old guys, we were given careful and detailed directions. First, such and such bus to such and such road and then this numbered bus to that specific road and so on. We followed their directions and wound up on the outskirts of town near a junkyard. Very funny. I bet they were howling with laughter as our first bus pulled away with us on it. Sure, we failed to see the funny side of that joke, but it did make us keenly aware that while the young

Iranians were friendly and cool, the old dudes were uptight and sour.

We finally arrived at the American embassy and I waited in line until I was called to the service window. I was greeted by a very crabby thirty-five-year-old American man and his even crabbier thirty-five-year-old co-worker. After explaining that I was running out of pages in my passport, the first old dude hissed that extra pages were not free and this service cost $5. I said, "Sure," and handed him a $5 bill. For some reason, that seemed to piss him off even more. I watched as he snatched the money from my hand, rummaged around in a drawer while getting angrier, and glued some accordion folded pages to my passport. He then slid his handiwork along the new paper seam into an embossing hand stamp and achieved the indicium by smashing his fist down on to it, twice. He tossed my passport back to me. After thanking him, I said excuse me, but I need some help. He rolled his eyes and asked, "What is it now?" This seemed to pique his crony as well and they both listened as I explained my request. I told him my friend from Panama was robbed and left stranded: "Could I pay for a phone call to the Panamanian embassy in India, so he could get some help?" That instantly cheered them up and, as his colleague laughed, the other dude jabbed a finger at me and said, "There is no way in hell I would want to help your friend." For good measure, in a low, almost menacing tone, he added, "In fact, if you were in trouble, I wouldn't help you either." He then looked past me and yelled, "Next!" and before I could even drop my jaw on the floor, I was getting elbowed out of the service window by their next unsuspecting victim.

Dave had watched the whole exchange and could only shake his head and say, "Damn dude!" I told James what happened and that I was sorry. He seemed to take the news better than I did.

November 28. The days are cooler and the nights are cold. We are on the Silk Road. Tehran to the Afghan border is a little over 600 miles by road—by this road. It has been three weeks since we left Jerusalem, and despite some setbacks, we have momentum and intention driving us on. That and money keeps us moving.

The crowded cities, empty deserts, and the thousand faces that pass before me fill my mind with wonder and a sense of a shared destiny. We are all on the human journey, and the differences of cultures, color, and beliefs are just a random throw of the dice. Who among us believes they picked their birth mother, picked their families, and the skin they wake every morning in?

The road we travel on is not always a luxury we get to choose; the heart we take along is our only real indulgence. The dust and heat of the day and the cool of the evening becomes part of a rhythm. The faces, dialects, and rituals like the taking of tea, the crush of humanity rushing for trains or buses all gets under the skin. Physical and spiritual relief comes and goes like the tide, sometimes knocking us over, and sometimes just out of reach. Like the sun and the moon, the road is always there, even when we are not.

We ride buses towards the border, passing cities with names like Aradan, Damghan, and Mayamey. Passengers climb aboard and disembark into the night. We stop at cafes and we stop at gas stations, taking on more travelers and letting more off. Men, women, and children traveling alone and in groups fill and then empty the seats in a slow game of musical chairs as we travel on.

The passengers that straddle the central aisle involuntarily lean into the empty space of the gangway, eyes straining for a glimpse of the distance. It is as though by keeping a watchful eye on the road, they ensure their arrival.

Somewhere ahead in the darkness is our current destination, the city of Mashhad, and 200 miles further on is the border. In Mashhad, we overnight for the morning bus to the frontier. We put up for the night at the Naderi Hotel on Game Street. It is near the mosque.

6

An Audience with the Great Buddha

December 4. Overcast and cold. We have been in a small city in the southern desert of Afghanistan called Kandahar for a couple of days now.

After the ritual of waiting in line and presenting one's self to a government official, watching your papers and paltry possessions being pawed over and inspected by persons at the ready to pass judgement on your worthiness to join the local rabble, we crossed the border.

As we travel east, the going gets slower. The traffic is slower and the less expensive buses are older, slower, and make more stops. The interiors of these buses are retrofitted with smaller and tightly packed bench seats to maximize capacity. Our backpacks are stowed on the roof, along with all manner of the quantifiable goods of human existence. Sacks of grain, building materials, auto parts, furniture, luggage, carpets, live chickens and goats, and the odd humans are all tied down and clinging on for dear life.

We crossed the border into Afghanistan at night. There are no buses heading to Herat until the next day, so all the western travelers are put up for the night in a sort of combination cafe and hotel, all in one large room. However, buses to and from some of the nearby towns roll in from the border throughout the night.

About a dozen of us westerners heading east are shown a raised wooden platform to sleep on. It takes up the back portion of the dining hall, and the tables, chairs, and Afghani patrons crowd into the sleeping area. Through the night, I could hear the coming and going of hungry travelers stopping for a bite to eat before moving on to their destinations. More than once I peeked out from my cocoon to see someone smiling and dribbling rice on to the foot of my sleeping bag.

The next morning, we got our transport to Herat. A huge adobe, mudbrick fort looms over the town. Small compounds and farms hidden behind adobe walls are dotted around the suburbs. Massive adobe minarets. The suburbs are laced with irrigation ditches, trickling water to gardens and fields. I saw an ancient-looking mudbrick minaret, leaning slightly with age. I can feel a change in the seasons, too. Winter is coming. The central part of the town has wide streets and a crowded, chaotic hustle vibe hangs in the dusty air. We stick out like sore thumbs, as everyone is in native dress—young and old alike. A noticeable increase in burqas and men wearing a sort of turban. Some men sport a rather striking hat that resembles a fourteenth-century Christopher Columbus-type hat.

I am getting more and more cautious about taking out my camera and taking photos. It garners even more hostile looks and gathers far too much attention. We caught our bus to Kandahar and found a room in the Peace Hotel. This is a larger city than Herat and it has a few young people in western dress. Some of the younger women have a more modern European style as well that would look right at home in 1950s America. The young dudes are more disco fashion with hip leather jackets, but still, nothing too loud. A lot of the Afghani men love to spit. They spit on buses, in restaurants, on the street and sidewalks. I even saw a guy spit on his own shoe.

Got the low down from some western travelers: what hotels to avoid in Kabul and such. Learned the going price for hash is 3–5 Afs a gram, or about 20 cents depending on quality, but keep its use to the hotels and restaurants that serve it on their menus—no walking around smoking. That advice is kind of like the rules

Passport and visas for Afghanistan and Pakistan. (*R. L. Kreamer* © 1977, 1978, 2019)

The wide and dusty streets of Herat, Afghanistan. (*R. L. Kreamer, Kodachrome 35-mm print film,* © 1977, 2019)

The Old Fort, also known as the Citadel of Herat, has been in use for 2,000 years and has been destroyed and rebuilt many times over the centuries. Herat, Afghanistan. (*R. L. Kreamer, Kodachrome 35-mm print film, © 1977, 2018*)

anywhere really. Met some more travelers going west after a few months in India. They look kind of rough, malnourished, spaced, and drugged out. A good early lesson: beware of what lies ahead.

Took a bus south to the village of Lashkargāh—it is sort of a village; a cluster of small adobe houses along a dirt road junction, 30 miles south of Kandahar and surrounded by fields. A large irrigation canal meets up with and runs alongside the road in a few places. It is marked as an ancient site on my map. We walked a few miles south to another marked ancient site called Bost. The entire 6-mile walk took us through the site of adobe walls, houses, mosques, and buildings all in ruin. A few of the ruins look like forts or compounds. There was an occasional dwelling that showed signs of habitation. Goats, children, and maybe the odd horse, very few people around, and cultivated fields on either side of the waterway. Beyond the fields stretched an empty, arid, and treeless high desert.

As the traces of habitation and ruins were becoming few and far between, and it looked like a dead end, we were approached by what looked like two farmers. This weatherworn duo looked a little older than us, but not by much. They did not speak English, but we knew they had something to show us and they motioned

us to follow. We were joined by a third local who spoke English, who told us they wanted to show us an ancient site and it would cost us 5 Afs each. They were pointing to an old corrugated tin building that seemed like an old barn. I thought it was some sort of scam and told them as much. In fact, I got really huffy and loud with them, and I called them rip-offs and said, "What kind of stupid tourist do you think I am?" Turns out I did not know what I was thinking or talking about. Turns out, I did not know shit. The three local guys looked like I had really hurt their feelings. Dave said, "What's your problem, man?" I was kind of embarrassed but still thought I was right. I said, "Ok, I'll look," and marched over to the huge shed to look through the already opened door. I looked in and said, "Holy shit!" Dave was asking me, "What is it?" I walked back, while digging into my pockets to pay the local guys the pittance they had asked for. I started digging into my soul, ashamed of the lack of a meagre amount of patience and respect that was asked for and that I failed to show these strangers. Hell, I am the stranger. After all, I am trespassing into their world. I handed over the fee and said I was sorry to each one of them. I had trouble looking them in the eye, but I forced myself. Everyone shrugged it off, but when I saw what an asshole I was, it was ugly, and I did not like it.

We all went back and had a good look. Not sure what I was looking at or what it was built for, but it was astonishing. It may have been a well. It was a 30 or 40-foot-wide hole in the earth. It seemed to be five stories deep, or more. There was a lit oil lantern about three stories down. The locals had flashlights. It took a while for or eyes to adjust, and as they did, this hole in the earth, this underground structure, appeared even more amazing. The walls were lined in stone, staircases marched downwards on one side, and archways led to passages on every level like spokes on a wheel. The stairs seemed to be 6 feet wide and hugged one side of the excavation. It was like an M. C. Escher drawing, albeit one drawn in a proper perspective. Each level became an architectural copy of the one above it. You could take the stairs or jump into empty space and fall a couple of stories. On the lower levels, we could see the tools being used to excavate the structure. Picks, shovels, lamps, and wheelbarrows could be seen about four stories down. The third and fourth level were still half buried in dirt and some rubble.

As we were leaving, I saw Dave haggling with one of the local dudes who had shown us the underground structure. He had some small items in his hands and Dave was saying something about it being too much money and no way was he paying that much. Dave turned his back on the guy and walked away. I walked up and he showed me what was in his hand. He said they all split the money and it was found in the ruin where we had just been. It was four very old, weird-looking coins and a small carved head in black stone about the size of a thumb nail. I was still feeling really guilty about my initial encounter with these dudes, so I saw a chance to redeem myself in some small way to them. I said I would buy them and gladly forked over the money he was asking for. It turned out to be double what Dave had counter offered, but at the time, I did not know that. I could ill afford the financial cost to my pocket, but I was more concerned about the cost to my karma and I thought I could buy back some of my dignity as well. Five bucks. A dollar an item. I did not even want to haggle. Dave immediately marched over as I merrily stuffed the trinkets into my camera bag, and he started yelling about how I had fucked up his deal, and this guy was going to drop his price and I am such an asshole and I was out to fuck him over and blah, blah, blah. For fuck's sake. I cannot catch a break.

We hiked back towards Lashkargah to get our bus back to Kandahar. We did not have to wait long, and we waved a passing bus down and climbed the back ladder onto the roof. There were five people on the roof when we climbed on. By the time we got to the paved highway, there were twenty-eight people sitting up there. As we passed through the suburbs, the bus driver ran over a goat. We all heard a weird very loud pop and looking over the edge of the roof at the road as it rolled out from under the bus, we saw the entrails followed by a perfectly flat goat. The bus had to roll to a stop, and in no time the goat was a beloved pet, and the owner of the goat wanted a lot of money and had a little girl crying in his arms. He said the goat belonged to his little daughter.

We have spent two days in Kandahar staying at the Peace Hotel. The city is hot and dusty during the day, even this time of year. There seems to be a plague of flies. They are everywhere and on everything, inside and outside. We are sharing our room with a French dude to help cut costs. He is playing his flute while I write in my journal. He is not very good. Toilet paper is getting hard to find and it is getting a bit pricey too. The locals just use water and their left hand. The shoe has just dropped as to why I was told by the janitor at the airport in Bahrain that thieves have their right hands cut off. They have to spend the rest of their days eating with the hand they wipe with.

We ran into James from Panama. He has been given money by some tourists and seems to be doing a lot better than he was when we saw him last. He deserves to have a rich patron. I would like one, too. Waiting to get a bus. If not waiting, I am moving. At the very least, most everyone I know sees the same moon I am looking at.

December 7. In Kabul and staying at the Faruk Hotel. What a scene this hotel is. Packed full of western tourists, all on their way to somewhere or on their way to nowhere but here.

Kabul is a very popular destination for Europe's hardcore dopers or Europe's hardcore travelers. The hippie trail passes through Kabul.

If it gets too cold for the dope heads, there is always Goa in India. If you do not cause any trouble and always pay your bill, a blind eye is turned for the hash smokers and the junkies alike. There is a fair number of opium and heroin users around, and most of the infrequent and rare stealing of travelers' cameras and money is down to them and not the locals. The law of common sense prevails, and you just need to watch your shit around some people.

This hotel has a cafe, and every night, the master of ceremonies puts on a show. He is a very old man and he wanders into the cafe at random times during the night. He is a little chubby and he gets up on a little

The northern suburbs of Kabul, Afghanistan. (*R. L. Kreamer, Kodachrome 35-mm print film,* © *1977, 2018*)

The market at the lower end of Chicken Street, Kabul, Afghanistan. (*R. L. Kreamer, Kodachrome 35-mm print film,* © *1977, 2019*)

stage that sits in one corner of the cafe, with a big lump of hash he is rolling around in his mouth, and he sits down and stares at everyone for some time. At some point, he takes the hash ball out of his mouth and loads up a massive and ornate water pipe. He then takes a live red-hot coal from the wood-burning stove and places it on the bowl of the pipe. He then puffs and puffs until he disappears under a cloud of smoke. He huffs and puffs some more until he falls into a fit of choking and coughing like a two-pack-a-day, seventy-year-old cigarette smoker. After a few minutes of this, he recovers enough to begin this opening act of his show all over again. At some point, he calls out to huge a Danish guy I have seen in the cafe before. The old man yells out, "Martin, water pipe is good?"

The old man then picks up a two-string instrument, and while being accompanied by a kid playing a drum, he begins playing a hypnotic drone, slowly at first and then building into a frenzied climax over the course

of an hour. When his performance finally comes to its feverish end, he stops, he stares, and then slowly stands and wanders away. He returns in a couple of hours and does it all over again. It is utterly spellbinding, even without the hash. I wrote down what I heard.

I needed a few extra I.D. photos for visas and permits. I have run out of the few I brought along, so I went searching for somewhere to get photos done. Dave came along. He said he needed some too, so it became a joint mission.

On Chicken Street, I found a local man doing photographs for I.D.s. He was a little old man with a traveling photography and darkroom service. His camera was a hundred-year-old pinhole camera on a large wooden tripod. A real camera obscura. He had me sit very still, loaded the camera, and then he removed the lens cap, counted to six, and put the lens cap back on.

He said come back in one hour. I asked if I could watch and wait. As I waited, he processed the first

Above left: The author in Kabul. Camera obscura photograph, unknown photographer, Kabul, Afghanistan. (*R. L. Kreamer* © *1977, 1978, 2019*)

Above right: Dave in Kabul. Camera obscura photograph, unknown photographer, Kabul, Afghanistan. (*R. L. Kreamer* © *1977, 1978, 2019*)

print, which was a negative on paper. He then used this to make four small portrait prints by photographing the negative. His darkroom was the back end of his large box camera. I waited an hour for the prints to dry. It turned out to be the best souvenir of my trip so far.

December 10. Snow followed by clear skies. It snowed two nights in a row and this morning I was roused into a world dusted white. It was more than that though. A deep blue sky, bright sunlight, bright yellow orange sandstone distilled on ice more than that.

The hotel has no heat and the room was so cold I could see my breath when I looked from under my sleeping bag. Orange light illuminates my breath. The clear dawn lit up the great Buddha and lit up the cliffs outside my window and the color orange flooded my room, waking me with its weird light long before I thought I wanted to. It seemed like the Buddha woke me.

I stumbled from my room at the Marco Polo Hotel to the outdoor cafe to sit in the warm winter sun. As I write and watch the town, I can catch up on this journal after being snowed in and unable to explore much.

The past twenty-four hours have been a matter of finding some sort of open cafe or hotel with a lounge and a communal fire, trying to stay warm enough, have something to eat, and then a plucky return through snowy howling day and night to the unheated hotel room for sleep.

Dave and I arrived by bus with a plan to see Bamiyan and then pushed on through the high pass to the lakes of Band-i-Amir. The recent snowfall has made the trip through the pass impossible. The 8,000-foot above sea level Bamiyan valley is as far as we can go until the snow clears from the roads. After that, travel along this stretch of the Silk Road will be possible when the mud refreezes enough for rolling tires. The passing Russian-built tour buses from Kabul slowly grind by as the morning wears on. I slowly thaw out as well. The buses are belching out smoke and a few tourists at every hotel and cafe stop along the main road through town.

The face of the Buddha looks like it was sawn off. Erosion, cannon fire, and bullet holes have left their mark. The vandalism to the Buddha now seems as antique and natural as the effigy itself. It has looked over this valley for nearly a thousand years. The attempt to disfigure it has rendered it weirdly beautiful. Cannon fire to the kneecaps. The somewhat smaller Buddha is about a mile to the east, also carved out

The Great Buddha of Bamiyan, Afghanistan, from the Marco Polo Hotel. (*R. L. Kreamer, Kodachrome 35-mm print film,* © *1977, 2019*)

Kevin and Dave in Bamiyan, Afghanistan. (*R. L. Kreamer, Kodachrome 35-mm print film,* © *1977, 2019*)

The author in Bamiyan, Afghanistan. (*R. L. Kreamer, Kodachrome 35-mm print film,* © *1977, 2019*)

of the cliff face. I hope the sun stays warm, the good weather holds out, not too many tourists show up, and the locals do not object to my wanderings.

December 11. Warm days and cold, cold nights. This hotel is really, really funky. The showers are ice cold, but for a fee, you can have a bucket of hot water to wash with. The communal toilets have been clogged and overflowing for days. To have a successful crap, one must balance on the rim of the toilet in a squatting position, ignore the stench, and hope one can dismount without an unfortunate slip. The management is kind enough to provide a pot of warm tea to wash one's butt with. I do not drink the tea at their cafe any more. The morning ablution is now akin to some sort of mad yoga work out, and this is one of the better hotels in town. There is no toilet paper, and the hotel refuses to supply any. They do, however, have an endless supply of hashish and are offering that at cut-rate prices: two for the price of one. They hotel staff are genuinely puzzled that I am not simply overjoyed at this replacement offer.

The past two days have been extraordinary and surreal. I wandered around the valley for hours and hours yesterday, crisscrossing it for some distance. I photographed some amazing views. Adobe walls and building dot the landscape. The faceless Buddha added a nice surreal touch to the wandering. Yeah, a real sense of place, ancient place memory, like the memory of fire or a mother that belongs to everyone.

The locals that deal with the tourists are nice enough for the most part. They are used to dealing with a vast array of foreigners and their bullshit. The rest of the locals seem to go about their business seemingly trying to avoid contact with the travelers.

Dave and I did some palling around, looking at the Buddha and some of the village when we first arrived. He said he wanted to have a little talk and he came out with this view of me being some sort of burden on him and holding him back from having the great time that he is sure he can have if I was not always around. I just answered that we had an original plan to watch each other's back on this trip. If that is no longer possible for him, that is fine. I said that for whatever reason, if it is now a burden to him, well he could grab a bus whenever to wherever he wanted to go.

What appears to be the main entrance at the Buddha's feet is more like a false entry, leading into a main or great room, with a few passage openings at the back of the room that lead on to smaller rooms

The Vale of Bamiyan, Afghanistan. (*R. L. Kreamer, Kodachrome 35-mm print film,* © *1977, 2019*)

The Great Buddha of Bamiyan, Afghanistan. In 1221, Genghis Khan and his armies swept through the Vale of Bamiyan and killed thousands of Buddhist monks but spared the statues. In the fifteenth and eighteenth centuries, various attempts to destroy the statues were made by using cannon and artillery fire. Built in 554 CE, it was destroyed in 2001 by the Taliban leader Mohammed Omar. (*R. L. Kreamer, Kodachrome 35-mm print film, © 1977, 2019*)

and eventually dead ends after leading one on for 30 or 40 yards. These rooms are impressive enough on their own, but it is one way in and the same way out. The only real clue from the outside to the modern visitor as to a false ingress is the lack of official guides at this entry offering their services. The passage to the top of the Buddha is gained through a cave on the right, 50 feet or so to the side of the Buddha.

It is a nondescript low door that requires one to crouch or crawl. The guide that led me through the labyrinth of rooms and stairs was momentarily lost at times himself. There were numbers, runes, Roman numerals, and other symbols as well, marked above and on the side of doorways and at the foot of stairs. I was led from room to room, through a combination of low doors and openings carved from the sandstone. I climbed deeper into this warren of caves, all the while climbing upward on worn stairs that were carved into the rock. Some rooms still held traces of plaster frescos, though they held on to the walls with a tenuous grasp at best. Some sandstone staircases were completely worn and replaced with wooden flights of stairs or ladders. The guide would pause now and again to study the runes and symbols, and as it turned out, we did have to backtrack more than once. I would watch him pause and stroke his beard in thought while we passed through some of the rooms that offered more than one choice of a passage. On occasion, we would pass through a cave that presented a windblown window onto the valley below. After crawling through yet another low doorway, we emerged at the head of the Buddha. The gap between the opening in the wall of the cliff, and the head itself, was about 5 feet across, but it looked like 20. It was a 35-foot drop down to just the top of the shoulders. The Buddha was not free standing, it was still attached to the cliff starting just below the shoulders and going all the way down the back to the ground below. My guide said people were not allowed out on to the head. Earlier in the day, from below, I had seen and photographed Dave out on the head, so I knew it was possible, I just did not know how much of a bribe it was going to cost me. Before my guide, or myself for that matter, had a chance to think about it, I just threw myself across to the head.

I should have thought about it, though, as I nearly slipped off, and then I nearly dropped my camera over the edge while trying to regain my footing. My trip almost ended right there. I thought about some luckless tourist looking up at the Buddha, only to end with up with more than a look of wonder on their face. The word "Minolta" embossed on the forehead in mirror image would indeed be an unfortunate souvenir to take away from the Great Buddha. After taking a photo and looking around, it became hard to act casual and ignore the shouting of my guide. His anger turned into singsong happiness when I reached in to my pocket and pulled out a couple of Afghan banknotes and waved them like a passport.

He promised to catch me when I jumped back. I wonder how Dave got away with jumping out on to the head. He is way too cheap to bribe the guide, but he can be charming when he wants to be.

December 12. Dave is very singsong chirpy and in a good mood today. He is being really nice. We were sitting outside at one of the cafes with an American dude we met named Kevin. We have been traveling with him—or him with us—since Iran. Dave is saying that since buses to Band-i-Amir cannot get through because of the snow, we should try to get to a place he has heard about nearby. After the last snowfall, I am concerned that I could get stuck in Afghanistan for the winter. I cannot afford another plane ticket out of a travel jam. Turns out, it was a little farther out, and we should have walked the 15 miles one way. We never got to a hot spring. The road was very muddy and there were a few stuck cars and a couple of trucks on the move. I think Dave thought it would be like the old times, hitchhiking through the Holy Lands and Iran. Once we got dropped off a few miles down the road, it took us a very long time to get a lift the last dozen miles. There were no hot springs to be found, and what locals we encountered had no idea what we were talking about. The Silk Road was muddy, and the air was cold. The driver of our last outbound lift dropped us at a crossroad and he said this was Red City. We meandered around a little bit and noticed a few tumbledown forts on the hillsides. The sun was going down and clouds were moving in, so it seemed to get darker and colder faster than usual. We started to hitchhike back to Bamiyan and Dave seemed disappointed with the outing. He was freezing cold. I was kind of enjoying it and I was glad we did this little day trip. With the night coming on, I felt I was really out in the world, with no luggage, cold feet, and hitchhiking along the road. I felt that this would be something I would remember when I was an old man. The way the night was coming on was like poetry, and I was in a wild place in a foreign land. The faceless Buddha watches the snows melt, the roads turn to mud, and the rivers run deep and wild.

December 13. Clear and cold. Made it back to Kabul and staying at the Faruk Hotel again. The old man

View from the head of the Great Buddha, Bamiyan, Afghanistan. (*R. L. Kreamer, Kodachrome 35-mm print film,* © *1977, 2019*)

and his water pipe are gone and replaced with a new group of musicians. Traditional Afghan stuff. Young guys my age. I had a nice chat with the singer; he is a young guy who wants to go to America or France.

December 14. Dave and I spent our last full day in Kabul exploring and wandering around the less tourist tramped areas. I have already completed the usual route of march I do when in a new city. The fee to get into galleries, museums, and ancient sites that I have visited on this trip so far have cost me a fortune. There were two soldiers lounging around the Kabul Museum entrance. When I was leaving, one of them called me over and wanted to sell me his Afghani Army belt buckle. He wanted $20 for it. I thanked him and said I was too poor to afford it and walked away. Dave thinks I should have haggled him down and bought it. Wandered around a few suburbs and

neighborhoods. We visited an Afghani writer we met and saw his house. He was a cool dude. His house was like a garden bungalow from upstate New York. I think he found us boring. Posted my last batch of postcards from Kabul. We climbed a hill that had parts of the old city wall in places. Saw what was left of something called the noon gun. The streets and roads were thick with black mud. Little children who were very excited to see us were following us around. They were laughing and shouting, and at one point, some of the boys started chucking the occasional rock. Must have been a dozen of them. Dave and I quietly counted to three and suddenly turned around and roared at them like monsters. They all squealed and laughed with delight. They wanted us to do this over and over. Tomorrow we leave for the Khyber Pass.

7

On the Silk Road through the Khyber Pass to the Golden Temple

December 15. Part cloudy and dry. Bus ride to Jalalabad was packed full and took the better part of the day. Mostly locals on board. We are traveling with the dude from California—Kevin—and an Irish guy—Brian. The four of us made a conscious decision to band together for this leg of the journey through the Khyber. Slow going ride with many stops and twisting road following the Kabul River through the mountains and the Kabul Gorge. Absolutely spectacular. The mountains are dusted with snow, but the road is clear. Every vehicle seems crammed full. No wasted space or solo drivers. We are spending the night in Jalalabad and getting a bus for the Pakistan border in the morning.

December 17. Dave and I are sitting in the third-class car of a train taking us from Peshawar to Taxila. I am still buzzing from the road and I can tell Dave is too. We have been constantly on the move for two days.

The first leg of the journey was to the border by bus. It was about 60 miles and took a little over two hours. The gorge got a little wider in this stretch of road, so the traffic moved a bit quicker than it had the first day out of Kabul. The bus dropped us at the border, and after the Afghani police check and customs, it was on to the Pakistani version of the same routine. In Kabul, I bought a stupid souvenir. It was a plastic Afghani passport cover. In the chaos that is sometimes a border crossing, the passport control mixes up passports. This time, it happened to me. He gave my passport to an Afghani dude and I was given his. We did not even look all that much alike. We were both searching around frantically for our doppelganger, and we ended up only recognizing what we were each holding in our hands. Dave thought it was the funniest thing he had seen in a long time. He kept saying, "You should have seen the look on your face!"

We then had to find and haggle for the price of our taxi through the Khyber Pass and on to the town of Laṇḍī Kōtal. We found two brothers who were running a type of shuttle service and they ran the gauntlet together. Each drove a late 1950s Ford pickup truck packed tight. Four or five people on the front bench seat, three to five people seated on a luggage type rack bolted to the roof of the cab, and up to nine or so people standing in the bed. No set schedule of departures and arrivals. They would head out when the trucks were full and come back when they were full.

We were crossing tribal lands under very little government control. We were warned: do not leave the road and do not take photos of the tribesmen. Lollygagging or not paying attention to the rules has been known to end badly. This is where at one time the mightiest empire in the world was cut down to size. I saw a lot of dudes carrying old Enfield rifles. It was time to take it all in, cause we are not stopping.

It was an hour of switchbacks climbing up steeply to the Khyber Pass. We were driven to Laṇḍī Kōtal and this place is like a Wild West town: dusty streets lined with wooden buildings and shacks, a few hotels and eateries, and a lot of tribesmen walking around with rifles and guns. We did not stop long. We are still deep in tribal-ruled lands. We found our bus heading to Peshawar and paid our fare and climbed on to the roof with a couple of westerners, lots of locals, and a few dudes sporting rifles. We rode the entire way on the roof of the bus, and the four of us were very stoked when we arrived without a hitch. There is something about riding a long way on the roof of a bus, you feel you see everything.

Taxi ride in a Ford pickup truck through the Khyber Pass, Afghanistan. The 1842 British retreat from the city of Kabul through the Khyber Pass ended with the deaths 4,500 British troops and the deaths of the 12,000 civilians that were accompanying them from attacks by the local tribesmen and the severe winter. Only one man is said to have made it out alive. (*R. L. Kreamer, Kodachrome 35-mm print film,* © *1977, 2018*)

Hoping on a bus in the dusty town of Landi Kotal, Pakistan. (*R. L. Kreamer, Kodachrome 35-mm print film,* © *1977, 2019*)

Riding on the roof of the bus to Peshawar, Pakistan. (*R. L. Kreamer, Kodachrome 35-mm print film,* © *1977, 2019*)

In Peshawar, we stayed at the New Mehran hotel. It cost us 10 rupees a night. Cold showers. Peshawar is a real trip. Crowed and dust and smog filled, it is teeming with horse-drawn carts, pedestrians, bicycles, Cushman three wheelers as mini taxis, narrow streets packed with shops and people where no cars dare drive, and bazaars. The background roar of traffic, trains, honking horns, people, and donkeys at every turn is crazy. Brian has decided to hang around Peshawar an extra day or two and Kevin grabbed a train to Lahore the minute we arrived. He was not interested in spending a minute in Peshawar.

Dave and I are spending the night sleeping on the lobby floor of the Tourist Rest House. We seem to have grabbed the wrong train. It took all day and made every stop along the way. It seemed to stop every 6 miles. The same journey by bus would have taken two hours.

December 18. Express train to Lahore took a few hours with one stop on a siding to let the mail train pass. The railway men are extremely friendly and are talkative, courteous, and ask a lot of questions about who we are and who our parents are. I have been give given the name and address of more than one railway worker who came up to me and introduced himself to me in hopes of being his friend and coming home with him to meet the family.

From other travelers, we hear that India is tightening up their entry rules. Seems that if you do not have what they think is enough money, they will refuse you entry. They simply do not want a bunch of broke hippies to contend with. We had heard about this early on and it simply entails going to the nearest American Express office and reporting your traveler's checks stolen. They cancel the old checks, issue new ones, and you suddenly appear to have twice the amount of money you really have if you hang on to the canceled checks. You just need to remember which are which, and not be stupid and try to cash the canceled checks in the future. We have heard of travelers using canceled checks as a hand over to pay corrupt police and other crooked officials demanding extortion and bribes.

I am noticing more and more children on the streets as I travel east. Lots and lots of stray dogs and stray children—lots of children. Not playing, but working; pushing wagons, at market stalls, herding goats, feeding chickens, hauling water, begging, selling trinkets, and sweeping up. Most the same age as my little brother or younger, though none with the future opportunities that he or myself will enjoy. I feel like I am being swept along in a fast-moving river. Spent the day running around Lahore, sent some postcards, and got our visas for India while we were in Kabul, so we saved ourselves a lot of time and hassle. We have noticed a little more of a hostile and harsh vibe from the locals. Nothing too heavy, but there is an edge to it. Dave is sensibly dressed, so that is not it. There is no section of youth dressed in western clothes and hip haircuts, at least not that I have seen. It all seems oppressed, dour, and run by a bunch of shouting sour old dudes who apparently think they know what is best for everyone. Everyone seems harassed by somebody else. We did meet a few nice people, though. The train dudes are groovy. We stopped at the American Express office and did our business. We did a trip to the Lahore Museum and I saw a few interesting things. I saw a human-sized statue of a Buddha titled "The Fasting Siddhartha."

I took a photo of it and the guards came out of nowhere and shouted at me. The guy in charge had a stick, and for a second, I thought he was going to hit me with it. I wandered down to the basement and came across a massive statue of Queen Victoria. It seems that there is no way for it to fit down the stairs, but there it is, at the bottom of the stairs. It is like they built the building around it. The electric lights in the basement are off and most of the rooms are in darkness as if the basement is closed. Light filters down the stairwell, but there is no sign or guard that says it is closed. The space is shared with a painter or two, whose works were stacked against the walls. Some of the paintings appear to be by the same hand of the muralist who adorned the entry walls of the museum. In the dim light, I could tell they were painted in blues and blacks. They were beautiful and spooky. The paintings looked like a couple of different artists.

December 19. On the train after passport control and customs. Out of Pakistan and into India. The train ride from Lahore to Amritsar is supposed to be short and quick, and the people who work on the Pakistani railway are incredibly friendly; it has been that way since entering the country.

I ask Dave if he wants to split and I point out that now is a good time. We made it to India and it is a big place, with lots to see and visit, and we can make plans to meet up anywhere, anytime. I tell him that this country is big enough for the both of us. He got the joke and laughed. He said things were cool and he wanted to see the Golden Temple and head up to Kashmir, and that traveling together was cool.

December 21. Clear skies and cool nights. The first couple of days in India have been eye watering: the smell of spices and the smell of rot. It has been nothing like I imagined it could be. Dusty. Damn, this place is crowed with people, cows, every mode of transport ever invented (made and used in the past 200 years), farm animals, stray dogs, feral orphaned children, beggars, and lepers. Every country as I head east seems a little more crowded, chaotic, and crazed than the one previous.

When we arrived in Amritsar, we made tracks for the Sikh's Golden Temple. They have a hostel-type hotel, and they will put up any traveler of any race, country, or creed for up to five days. It is a dorm-like setting and a nominal fee is charged, but after five days, you must move on. We have heard about this place from other travelers in Afghanistan and we wanted to check it out. They also feed anyone in need for free, and they do two meals per day. The masses are fed in a couple of large rooms that have long wicker mats that are like runners across the length of the room, which act as tables. Asian and Persian carpets for everyone to sit on. We all sit in neat rows. One room for men and one room for women and children. Rows and rows of the hungry sit cross-legged on the floor in front of the mats. They have this service down like a well-oiled machine. Once all the diners are shepherded into the room and properly seated, an army of people hand out hundreds of tin plates and cups, and behind them water bearers fill the cups. Behind them follow half a dozen guys with clean steel buckets and ladles. Some buckets are filled with rice and others are filled with dahl. One chapatti is given to each person as well. They start the clearing of plates and cups right away and wash and rinse them for immediate reuse. Feed, rinse and repeat, feed, rinse and repeat, feed, rinse and repeat. Dave and I, after getting a place in the dorm, getting showered and clean, and being fed, stashed our bags and went to the Temple.

With our shoes off and heads covered, we could wander freely around the site. I walked out to the Golden Temple for a closer look and ended up in a line of devotees inside the temple. A crush of people prevented me from backing out and I was swept forward and found myself in front of the crowd facing a holy man with his priests and followers surrounding him. One of the priests had a brass bowl with a white grain paste-like porridge in it. The holy man took a scoop from the bowl with his fingers and offered it to me with a gesture of the hand. I did think about turning and trying to run away for a second. I smiled and moved forward with my hand out and he shoved it in my mouth. The crowd murmured its approval, and I then got some kind of blessing and was ushered out of the interior with a shove.

The Fasting Siddhartha, Lahore, Pakistan. (*R. L. Kreamer, Kodachrome 35-mm print film, © 1977, 2019*)

Above: Rail ticket from Pakistan to India. (*R. L. Kreamer © 1977, 1978, 2019*)

Below: Passport and visas for India and Sri Lanka. (*R. L. Kreamer © 1977, 1978, 2019*)

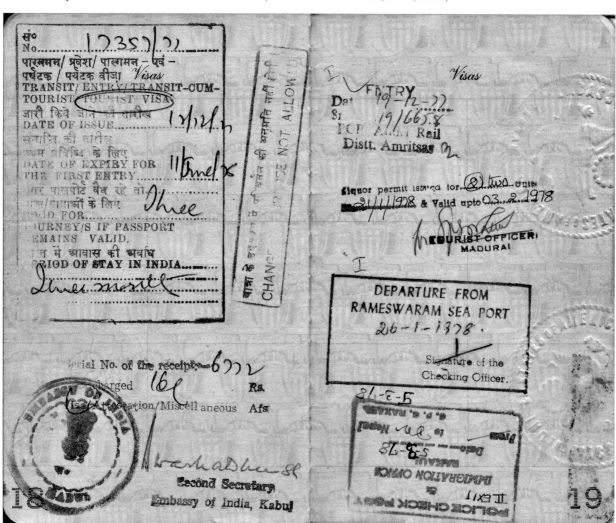

Dave at the Sikh's Golden Temple, Amritsar, India. (*R. L. Kreamer, Kodachrome 35-mm print film, © 1977, 2019*)

Walking around town, we were approached by a group of young schoolboys. They wanted to know where we were from and where we were going—the usual twenty questions. We tried to be nice and talked with them for a long time. One young man asked me if I had anything to trade with him as he offered me his school pin. He held it up with a grin on his face and all his buddies watched and waited to see what I would do. I had nothing I thought worth offering. I held up my red cowboy bandana I been wearing and carrying. He seemed really happy with the trade as he walked away. I think Dave may have made a trade as well.

8

India

December 22. Overcast. Got the train from Amritsar to Jammu. This is our jumping-off point for Kashmir. The train journey was nine hours, and it started with no seats available and we sat on huge rolls of burlap piled near the door of the carriage and toilet. The first three hours were really comfy until the burlap was offloaded at a station and we had to find proper seats. We are traveling to the north with a dude from England named John. We decided to split the cost of renting a houseboat three ways to save money.

December 24. The bus ride from Jammu to Srinagar was a spectacular climb into the mountains. The road wound its way through the Vale of Kashmir, past terraced fields and farms with the ever-present backdrop of the Pangi Range of the western Himalayas. The mountains around Srinagar are like the little cousins of the Himalayas at 16,000 and 17,000 feet. The road was a seemingly never-ending series of hair-raising hairpin corners and sheer drops into the valley below.

I read his business card. He was the houseboat tout we decided on because he was not pushy.

December 25. Frozen fog. Night falls and we are camped in the front room of our houseboat. This floating hotel is beautifully hand built and hand carved. Filled with Kashmiri carpets and ornate brass things, it is real luxury. We each have our own bedrooms with windows that look out over the lake. The houseboat is so cold that we sleep around the only wood stove we can afford to keep going day and night in the living room.

Christmas caught me by surprise. The lifetime of adverts and pressure to buy gifts and crap people do not need, for people who do not deserve them anyway, was not there this year. No Christmas songs played in cafes.

Late into the night on Christmas Eve, while on the houseboat, John read the story of the birth of the Christ child from the bible he carries around. The snow was falling over Srinagar. It was like a movie. At the moment he was reading aloud, his voice faded and this houseboat melted away and I was transported back to when my father would gather up my mother, my siblings, and myself, and on Christmas Eve read to us the very same passage in the low, quiet, assured voice that is my father's alone. Christmas day was filled with the three of us trekking around town. The town is much larger than it first seems. Ghosts of colonial Britain are in the architecture and streets.

Dave has, at last, got himself some more winter-type wear. He got a cloak, and I do not have the heart to tell him he looks like Julie Andrews and the Von Trapp family from *The Sound of Music* in that thing. He got the local wicker basket with the ceramic pot inside to go with it. It is a pretty cool local get up with a heater, and it is filled with hot coals and carried under the cloak for portable warmth. I guess he will have to constantly borrow coals from other people's fires.

We went to a boatyard and watched the craftsmen building and carving new houseboats without a power tool in sight.

Our hosts took us to a Kashmir carpet seller and showroom always in hopes of us buying something and our host would be happy to receive a commission. I think it has finally dawned on the proprietor that we are not seeking luxuries. We were taken to a carpet workshop where little children were put to work weaving. Their young and keen eyesight exploited until

REGD BY TOURISM DEPTT, J. & K. GOVT.
G. R. SHALA & BROTHER
PROP. DELUXE CLASS HOUSEBOAT
ALZIRA & YOUNG ALZIRA
WITH TAP WATER AVAILABLE
DAL LAKE, (NEHRU PARK)
SRINAGAR - KASHMIR.
SUPPLIERS OF :-
Luxurious & Economic Class House Boats,
Modern Amenities, Excellent Vegetarian Non-Vegetarian
Food & Service.
ARRANGEMENTS MADE FOR :-
Camping, Trekking, Fishing, Big & Small Games
Sight - Seeing Etc, Etc,

Business card for Mr. Shala. (*R. L. Kreamer © 1977, 1978, 2018*)

Floating shopkeeper, Dal Lake, Srinagar, Kashmir, India. (*R. L. Kreamer, Cibachrome 35-mm slide film, © 1977, 2019*)

The frozen fog on Dal Lake. (*R. L. Kreamer, Cibachrome 35-mm slide film,* © *1977, 2019*)

Child carpet weavers, Srinagar, Kashmir, India. (*R. L. Kreamer, Kodachrome 35-mm print film,* © *1977, 2019*)

Houseboat builders, Srinagar, Kashmir, India. (*R. L. Kreamer, Kodachrome 35-mm print film,* © *1977, 2019*)

they could no longer see the detailed work and then they would be given the boot. I can no longer walk on or see a fine Kashmiri rug without thinking of the some-kids-lost-forever-childhood cost of owning one.

The clouds briefly lifted to reveal the surrounding snowcapped peaks. Dave and I got hold of a small boat and went out on the lake—amazingly clear water and not that deep in most places. The boat was designed to be paddled like a canoe. I was in front, Dave in the back. Dave insisted he was in charge and I was to paddle as instructed. I pointed out I do not have eyes in the back of my head and he needs to counter stroke the opposite side from me or get in the front because the guy in front sets the pace. Then all was made clear as he insisted that he was not going to follow my lead because he is older and in charge. I think he knew he was being a dope. We were paddling in metaphorical and actual circles. I turned around and laughed at him and took his picture. I am hoping that sheepish look on his face comes out. I stowed my paddle, lit up a joint, and told him he could row any way he wants to because I am done rowing. I was laughing when I asked him to drop me off at the houseboat since we are going by. He asked why, was I having a tantrum? I could not stop laughing. He asked what I was laughing at; I said, "No, look at your feet

dipshit, the boat's leaking and filling with water and we're going to sink." Laurel and Hardy.

December 26. Took some photos of the houseboat owner and his family. For some reason, he posed holding a big chunk of snow. Got talked into going skiing at a nearby former British colonial resort up in the hills. Big fucking mistake. The binding was set too tight. They set the skis up and two barefoot guys then carried me in a chair up the hill and set my feet into the boots, so I did not have to step in the snow. It was embarrassing and funny at the same time. I was coming in way too fast and being a mediocre skier at best, my turn to avoid the wall turned into a crash and burn. The skis that should have come off stayed on, and I twisted the shit out of my knee. The barefoot servants ran out into the snow, picked me up, carried me into the lodge, and plunked me down in front of the empty and unlit stone-cold fireplace. The manager and staff disappeared like ghosts, and I was left on my own to get out of my ski boots and into my boots and hobble on out of there.

December 27. Clear and cold. Bus ride from Srinagar was as spectacular as the ride in.
We had a couple of delays with landslides blocking the road. When our bus joined the queue waiting for

John, Mr. Shala, Dave, and the Shala family, Dal Lake. (*R. L. Kreamer, Cibachrome 35-mm slide film*, © *1977, 2019*)

The fog lifts from Dal Lake. (*R. L. Kreamer, Cibachrome 35-mm slide film*, © *1977, 2019*)

Dave paddles the boat, Dal Lake. (*R. L. Kreamer, Cibachrome 35-mm slide film,* © *1977, 2019*)

the road to be cleared, the earthmovers were already there working on moving some huge boulders. It was freezing cold in the unheated bus. Dave's portable fire went out an hour ago, and he got very cold. He was not the only guy allowed on the bus with a basket of fire. My feet got so cold I unpacked my sleeping bag and got my legs into it to stay warm. Football-sized rocks were still occasionally bouncing from the cliff side and across the road when our bus driver tried to make a break for it.

When we got back to Jammu, we were too late for our train so we slept on the floor of the second-class waiting room along with a dozen other locals and tourists all waiting for the morning. Stashing our bags at the left luggage room, we had plenty of time for a wander around the city of Jammu. We went inside a Hindu temple and it was really ornate and painted in a riot of colors. Most of the roads are muddy and cows are wandering in and out of traffic. The train to Delhi leaves at nine at night and takes twelve hours. We have a lot of time to kill, but at least Dave is glad the temperature is warmer. We were drinking tea at the rail station tearoom and a constant parade of people came up to us asking basically the same three questions. What is your name? Where are you going? What does your father do for a living? Funny at first, bothersome after a dozen times, really annoying after an hour. It became funny again after we started giving outrageous and unbelievable answers to their questions. Still, we were always nice about it. It became a competition with us seeing who could come up with the funniest name for themselves and the craziest backstory. Time started to fly by. It obviously did not matter what we answered, but how we answered. People just wanted a look at us and hear us speak and for us to acknowledge their presence in front of us.

December 28. Arrived into the New Delhi station at ten in the morning. We rode the Srinagar Express from Jammu in the third tier, second-class sleeper. There was an armed guard in each railcar the entire way. Apparently, there had been a lot of trouble and strife in Kashmir over the issues with the separatist movement. We were fortunate not to be involved in any of the trouble and wandered around blissfully unaware.

We had breakfast at the train station and it was a real extravagance of eggs and toast and coffee. It was very cheap. We hit the streets in search of our hotel. In Germany, I was given a list of hotels scattered along the road to Kathmandu. In New Delhi, a hotel called Mrs. Calico was recommended as being near the train station, a good bargain, and relatively clean. We found it and got into a dorm-type room. Lots of beggars, stray children, and stray dogs outside the hotel's front door.

I remembered when I announced to my parents that I was planning this trip, they were not very happy about it at all, but then again, they did not say no way or try to stand in my way. I was twenty. I said I was going to take a break from school to do this trip and briefly outlined the planned journey: drive to the Middle East, work on a kibbutz, hitchhike east to Kathmandu. I said I had been saving my money. I said I was going with my buddy Dave and we planned to look out for each other. My father said, "Where do you want us to send the body?" My mother cried. My little thirteen-year-old brother Joe looked alarmed and asked my father, "I don't have to go, do I?" My father chuckled and I was relieved the tension was broken.

In the quiet twilight, I row my father's boat, and like my father and all the fathers before, a young man casts from the shore and upon the water.

December 30. I saw a dead guy today. This is the first dead guy I ever saw. Other than a grandmother, grandfather, or an ancient uncle or aunt from my past all dressed, made up, and carefully presented for viewing by a funeral home in a nice silk-lined box at a well-attended funeral, complete with music, a priest saying mass, and a handout card with a photo of the deceased in better times. This was different. This was out in the world. This was an anonymous death in a place with limited resources to quickly remove the body from the street. I was shocked but acted like I was not. I retrieved my letters from the embassy. I was sent two letters, one from my mother and one from my old flame, and I was elated and buzzing at having in my possession artifacts from the life I had many miles from here. I was crossing one of the circular roads of Connaught Place. I was in my own little world of errands, concerns, and plans for doing this and seeing that. It was like I had made a beeline and just walked right up on him.

It looked like he fell after stepping off the curb and was face down in the road. It appeared this had happened a while ago. His face was slightly turned, and vomit had come from his mouth and formed a puddle under his head. His eyes were open, but you could tell they saw nothing. His face was a strange color. People were stepping over and around him. I saw a policeman up the street. I went over to him and told him what I saw and pointed down the road where the man's body could be seen. The cop asked if I knew who the dead man was. I said no. He said he knows he is there and the man will be removed soon. Later in the day, towards sundown, I was heading back to my hotel and I could see from across the street that he was still there and had not been moved or touched. The only difference was the people stepping around or over him were holding their noses. The image I saw early this morning when I first saw him, I am sure to carry for a long time.

This has to be the busiest city I have ever seen—people and traffic all day and most of the night. There are always so many people on the street all the time. Went to the usual tourist sites around New Delhi. Went to the Qutub Minar and the Iskcon Temple with Dave.

At the Iron Pillar, there were a couple of dudes hanging around helping people get their wish. The story is that if you can stand with your back to the pillar, wrap your arms behind you and around the pillar, and touch your hands together, your wish comes true. If these guys saw anyone struggling with the task at the Iron Pillar, they would run up, uninvited, and grabbing the hands of their now hapless victim and force the person's hands together. It was like some public service medieval torture device.

December 31. We saw some fairly crazy shit out on the streets tonight on the last day of 1977. We were wandering around after having something to eat. It was me, Dave, and a couple of dudes from our hotel. As the evening wore on, we noticed clusters of young local dudes hanging around corners and on the streets in Delhi's hotel, shopping, and cafe district near Connaught Place. They were drunk, loud, and in greater numbers than we had seen before. When they saw us, they were saying Happy New Year and some other drunken stuff we could not understand. We were not sure what was going on, but we all started to comment to each other that something was up. Hundreds of dudes in their little groups and cliques on every street and on every corner. I thought it was going to be like Times Square with a big countdown to the New Year in a few hours, followed by a big sing along of "Auld Lang Syne." Later, I heard it referred to by a local guy as a New Year tradition on the streets of Delhi called "teasing." What a bunch of fucking drunk assholes, who did not see anything wrong with what they were doing or anything wrong with what was going on. It was anything but teasing. It was groping and sexual assault on a mass scale. We saw a commotion up ahead of us on the sidewalk. A pack of a dozen or so of these drunk fuckers mobbed a tourist couple. She started screaming as they started groping her and working on tearing her clothes, grabbing her all over her body. The dude she was with was struggling with a few

other dudes who were keeping him occupied while their buddies did the dirty work. Dave and I waded into the crowd pulling people off and out of the way. Some started shoving us. I did not come all the way to India with the intention of getting into a fistfight, but that is what happened. The quest for peace and love and spiritual enlightenment would have to wait. I think Dave started it, but I did back him up. The Swiss dudes we were with hung back and did some pushing and shoving but really did not help much. The mob backed off, but they were still surrounding us. We were attracting an even bigger crowd and they were getting really pissed off that their fun was spoiled. Dave and I grabbed the dude and his girlfriend and hustled them into a nearby cafe. She was crying and yelling and just plain pissed off. We pushed the couple into the cafe and backed in after them. Dave and I held the door shut. The boyfriend was really freaked out and really not much help at all. We were followed to the cafe by a bunch of now-angry shouting locals who were not happy at seeing their blonde and easy prey being spirited away. The cafe owner was aghast at what he saw and was very apologetic about his fellow countrymen. We asked him to call the police, but he did not want them involved. He said his brother owned a cab and he called him instead to give the couple a ride back to their hotel. When the cab came, Dave and I hustled them out the door and into the cab. We made fake lunges at the crowd of dudes with our fists raised to get them to back off. When they all flinched in unison in a really exaggerated manner, Dave and I looked at each other and started laughing. I mean, we are outnumbered, but it does not seem to matter. I have always liked the fact that like me, Dave can see the funny side to a shit situation. We got back to our hotel and related our story to anyone who would listen. A few of the tourists we told just shrugged it off like they did not believe us and went on their merry way out into the night. We were jabbering like we were on speed. Must have scared them about the wrong thing. We were in the hotel before midnight not wanting to venture out and get in a fight.

January 2. First of all, I got sick and I am ill as fuck. After our New Year's Eve fistfight, we stayed put and hunkered down at the hotel. Weird scene where one of the traveler tourist dudes in the hotel was going room to room selling Thai stick. Powerful grass and famous for its potency. Dave was keen to buy some and wanted me to split the cost. He was sure it was a done deal. He was already picking out the buds he wanted to buy. I had a sinking feeling my current budget was not quite

The Iron Pillar, New Delhi, India. Thought to have been made in 402 CE. The high phosphorus content iron has an even layer of crystalline iron hydrogen phosphate hydrate on its surface. In its 1,500 years of existence, it has never shown any signs of rust. (*R. L. Kreamer, Cibachrome 35-mm slide film, © 1977, 2019*)

Hindu Temple, New Delhi, India. (*R. L. Kreamer, Cibachrome 35-mm slide film, © 1977, 2019*)

enough to see me through to the end. Actually, I knew it already, but I was still trying to kid myself. Anyway, I said no, I do not want it, cost too much money, and it is too much weed to carry around. Dave went nuts; he got pissed off and would not believe that I could not afford it. He hissed in my face "You fucking asshole, you're just trying to look cool and fuck me over." I did not know what to say except "Whatever dude." He bought a reduced stash, rolled up a joint, and said I could not have any. He said it was all his. He had a scowl on his face as he started smoking it. I went to bed hoping I was not coming down with something.

I slept late, and when I woke, I looked around and noticed Dave and the other roommates were out, but all their stuff was still there. I was feeling a little queasy. I noticed I needed the bathroom and as I rolled out of my bed, I shit myself uncontrollably. My gut felt like I had been stabbed. I gathered my sleeping bag and hurried to the communal showers. Thank god no one was around. I spent an hour washing and scrubbing my sleeping bag, clothes and myself. It took a long time and a lot of soap. I went back to the room and hung everything by the window to dry. I noticed I had to go, again, and again. I spent a couple of hours with the foulest smelling shit coming out of one end of me and bile and vomit coming out of the other end. I was in agony. After an hour, I tried drinking some water and the flow of sewage out of me started up again. I had to shower again. I felt weak and unable to stand. I tried lying down. Five minutes later, I was yet again crawling on my hands and knees for the bathroom. Fuck, I should never have left Germany.

Late in the afternoon, Dave showed up. He looked at me in bed, laughed, and said, "What's your problem?" I told him I have been sick all day and I think I need to see a doctor. He grabbed some of his stash, rolled a joint, and asked me if I needed anything. I said I think I need to see a doctor and he said I could not have any of his weed and then he split. I spent the rest of the day and night the way the morning started. I tried to drink some water again. I think it did not help much.

The next morning, I woke to find Dave standing over me. He had packed his stuff and was wearing his backpack. He must have been trying to wake me up for a while. He had a ridiculous grin on his face and a clay pot in his hand. He said he hoped I felt better, and he was going to leave now. He thrust the clay pot in my face and said, "Here, I got you some yogurt." When he saw I was not reaching for it he set it down on a shelf and made a little speech. It was something about not wanting to be burdened by my problems,

and my illness was my fault and so it was my problem to deal with and not his. I said, "Dude, I'm sick, I think I need a doctor." With a shrug and a smirk, he walked out. All I could do was fall asleep. When I woke up again, I could tell by the light it was late in the day. I looked at the shelf where he had set down the clay pot of yogurt. The porous bottom let all the water seep out and it had run down the wall like an abstract painting. The weirdly poetic stain.

January 3. You know it is time to leave when the hotel owner says that you may be better off at the YMCA. I told her I was leaving tomorrow morning for Agra and settled my bill. Saw a doctor earlier. It was all I could do to get to his office, doubling over in pain and having to stop and sit down wherever I found myself. I had to wait outside so I was sprawled on the ground and the locals found it very amusing to see me like that. They laughed as they stepped over me.

The doctor thinks I have amoebic dysentery. Travelers have nicknamed this the dreaded Delhi belly. Ironic because the doctor says it takes three weeks to germinate into its full-blown symptoms. Which for me is more like Kabul belly, or Amritsar belly. Whatever it is, it sucks. He gave me some tablets to get the shits under control. He said antibiotics in India are useless, overpriced, and impossible to find and to beware of fake medications. He said I would be better off going back to Germany and getting them there. I told him I had a couple of months of traveling to do before going home. He said things should calm down soon, but I could find my stomach swelling up along with some discomfort every couple of weeks or so. I am still unbelievably weak and the occasional pain my guts still causes me to double up. While using the toilets at the hotel, I saw some graffiti on the wall I had not noticed before. It said, "If the bottom falls out of your world, eat at the Peshawar Cafe and watch the world fall out of your bottom."

9

Going South

January 4. Clear skies and hot days and still sick. Boarded the Agra Express at seven in the morning and arrived at Agra by 10 a.m. at the Cantonment Station. Checked into the Kailash Hotel, stashed my bag and headed to the Taj Mahal.

I asked directions and got on a public bus.

Around the entry were some lepers. I never saw someone infected with the disease before. Only depicted in films. It is more gruesome and heartbreaking in real life. Fingers, noses, and ears seem to be rotting and melting off the tragic victims of poverty and lack of medical help. Victims of someone's indifferent god or government. I gave them what coins I had and went to the gate and paid my entry with paper money. I felt ashamed of my life of privilege and luck.

The reflection pool had been drained for repairs. Tourists from everywhere were milling around in small groups taking in the awesome sight. A hippie traveler was playing a flute in the main part of the mausoleum and the sound the huge vaulted tomb echoed back was beautiful. Although the building was large and imposing, its setting in this small park, backing on to the river, made it appear at the same time small and stunted at first. A caricature of itself. Walking towards and around it revealed its true colossal appearance. All in all, it was as trippy as I had imagined it would be. The more I wandered around and looked, the more beautiful it seemed. I went off to the side lawn and smoked and watched the people come and go. There were a couple of peacocks strutting around. I watched the large black crows perch on the white marble of the Taj. I fell asleep for an hour or so and was woken up by a gardener. He said he had to clean and there was no camping allowed. I was about to protest that I was

not camping, but I let it go. I was in such a peaceful beautiful setting that I felt nothing could bother me. I stayed a while longer and found myself amongst Indian tourists. Not a westerner in sight. It was a very slow day at the Taj.

A sign indicated that moonlight visits were canceled until further notice. I asked the gardener why the night visits had been stopped, and he said it was because of all the hippies making a mess and a nuisance of themselves.

In the time I had been there, I noticed the marble of the Taj reflected the change of the light depending on the time of day. In the afternoon light on my arrival, the Taj Mahal was bright blue white. When the evening was creeping in, the marble was a vague shade of pink. I left around 5 p.m. and walked back to my hotel. I made it back with few gut cramps and clean underwear.

January 5. Taking out my camera still causes a lot of unwanted attention. Did some more walking around town, and in a park I saw an old man under a tree, and he waved me over. He turned out to be a Sadhu and he was begging. He was smoking weed and he wanted a rupee. I sat down hoping he would share his weed. He seemed pleased to have me sitting there watching, though. I gave him a few coins. More than a few coins. I took out a joint and started smoking it. After a few puffs, I offered it to him. He smiled and took it and smoked it all without passing it back. It was then I jumped out of my skin. I noticed something out of the corner of my eye. Sort of noticed it all along without really noticing. A man was tied by his feet and hanging upside down. He was breathing all right. It was some sort of yoga or meditation or something I guess. The old man thought it was hilarious the way I

The Taj Mahal, Agra, India. Built in 1643 CE as a tomb. (*R. L. Kreamer, Kodachrome 35-mm print film*, © *1978, 2019*)

The Taj Mahal, Agra, India. (*R. L. Kreamer, Kodachrome 35-mm print film, © 1978, 2018*)

jumped when I noticed the dude hanging behind me. He laughed and laughed and could not stop laughing and laughed himself into a coughing fit. As I wandered away, I could still hear him laughing in the distance.

Went to the train station and got some travel info. I bought a rather thick paperback book titled *India Railway Abstract Time Tables* printed on cheap thin newsprint-like paper complete with a fold out railway map of India. Leaving the station, I was approached by an army of taxi touts, all knowing the best hotels and offering the best service at the best price. They know the best carpet sellers, the best restaurants, best gem dealers, all for the best price and usually owned and operated by an uncle, father, or brother. For most tourists, it is this experience of the hustle these touts and shopkeepers engage in that make up their view of locals. There is a constant barrage of "One pen, one rupee," from children. The constant outstretched hand of a beggar or a leper dressed in rags. I do not have enough money to give everyone a coin, a pen, or one rupee. If I lived to be a hundred and was the richest man alive and handed it out one rupee at a time, it would never be enough.

After running the gauntlet of taxis and rickshaws, I noticed the poorer-looking drivers were kept at the end of the rank. Like anywhere, there was an obvious pecking order with the fatter and better-dressed guys to the front. One young dude at the very end of the line looked at me and said he could be my driver for the day at a cheap price. It struck me that having my own driver for the day could lessen, even halt the constant badgering from taxi drivers. We quickly settled on a price. I made a halfhearted attempt at haggling the price down. I know it is the done thing not to settle on the asking price of anything the first time; however, weeks of watching Dave and other western tourists brow beat and humiliate a poverty-stricken rickshaw driver, shopkeeper, or fruit seller over five fucking cents always sickened me. It is always justified with the whine of "You'll ruin it for the next tourist if you cave in at the first price." No, sorry asshole tourists, your white master routine has ruined it for me in the here and now. The drivers name was Sha. He was upfront with information about drivers and the way to earn extra money by bringing tourists into shops for a kickback. He said he had a guru who ran a gem business and did I want to see some gems. He said his guru smoked a lot of ganja and at least we could get high.

Of course, I said of course. I told him to peddle as slow as he liked, and I did not want to spend much time with his guru. I said I wanted to see the Red Fort and the Taj Mahal today. The gem shop was not very far away, and we rolled up much sooner than I had expected. I was ushered in and the "guru" shuffled through a pile of paperwork and letters to prove how trustworthy and legitimate he was. He made himself look busy and barely looked up at me. Letters to and from clients in Europe and America and orders sent to and from the same, and piles of letters of recommendations. Letters of recommendation are very popular and a big deal in India.

During all this time, he made up a pipe full of hash, weed, and some tobacco. I suspected that part of the razzle-dazzle was getting the buyer stoned. As we got high, he started to take out bags and bags of gems. Sapphires, rubies, garnets, and all manner of precious and semi-precious stones. Before he started his show and tell routine, I told him I had little to no money, and if I was going to buy, it would be for a keepsake and not for investment. That did not seem to deter or dismiss his zeal for his spiel. We got very stoned and for almost next to nothing, I bought a ring with a black star stone and three semi-precious stones. I think I spent two bucks. Everyone seemed happy. I did not even haggle. Yeah, I guess the ganja worked. I wanted to buy some weed, but he was not selling. He assured me that in my travels, I would come across a government-sponsored seller, as ganja was still legal and sold in a few Indian states. Then the gemstone seller guru gave me some sage advice about the use of ganja by a tourist in India.

I realized this was Sha's business guru. He said that he hoped one day to be his apprentice. I wanted to go to the Red Fort and we set off slowly through the city. Navigating the crazy chaos of trucks, cars, bikes, rickshaws, taxis, people, and cows through the crowded city of Agra seemed nothing short of a miracle or magic. The Red Fort had amazing views downriver of the Taj in the distance. I spent a while wandering around taking some photographs. When I walked out, I was besieged by taxi drivers. The words, "I have a driver" made the sea of tout's part and immediately melt away. I found Sha perched on the back of his rickshaw having a nap. I almost hated to wake him.

I found a place to photograph the outer walls of the Red Fort and I had to change film.   When I finished, I saw Sha watching me. When I walked over, he said I had a nice camera. I knew he also meant, "I see you're wealthy." He said he wanted to take me to his house and have some lunch and tea. His home was a one-room mud hut down a dirt alley way in a jam-packed intercity part of town. I guess it was a slum. He seemed to have eight kids and very little else and his wife seemed happy to see us. She dished us out some food and I explained to Sha that I had been ill and had stomach trouble. He translated this into Hindi to his wife and I insisted on a very small portion of food and one cup of tea. They were obviously very, very poor.

He pulled out his book of hand-written references from people he has ferried around and he wanted me to add to it. I read a few of the notes written by Germans, Swiss, Americans, and other tourists from around the world. It was all good stuff. He said he was lucky to live in a city that attracted so many people from around the world and the living it provided him. He said if he ever became rich, he would buy his wife a new house and then travel to all the places that his clients were from. His book of references was like his travel wish list. I added my recommendation, my name, and where I was from, but instead of Germany, I used my old hometown of Tucson for my address. Maybe he will make it to Tucson.

I had Sha peddle me back to the Taj Mahal. It was getting late in the afternoon and I said I was going to be an hour or two and then he could return me to hotel. He was surprised that his day was going to be less peddling than he thought it would be.

At the Taj, it seemed an even more awesome sight than it was yesterday. Saw a very well-dressed group of tourists trying to get into the entry gate. The ladies were wearing pearls and the men were wearing suits and ties. I looked like a vagabond next to them. They were middle-aged, and I could hear that they were French. They were pretending they could not see a couple of lepers in rags, crawling on the ground, and begging at their feet. I was still stoned, and I marched up to their little group and said "Pardon." They looked startled and shuffled aside. I knew that to get out of my way, they would have to look at the beggars so they did not trip over them. I gave the lepers some coins and walked away without looking back. I thought I could hear them swear at me.

I watched an Indian photographer taking roll after roll of photographs of an unbelievably beautiful Indian woman striking different poses with the Taj Mahal as her backdrop. I watched the tourists come and go and pose for their own photo op in front of the Taj. I watched the large black crows take up their perch on the Taj for a time and then fly away.

I watched the crows and tourists repeat their visits like a prearranged and well-rehearsed play. I watched the marble of the Taj change its hue as the afternoon turned to evening. Just as it did before I arrived, and as it will after I am gone.

I found Sha having another nap. As for myself, I was slapped awake by the harsh reality of the gritty traffic and journey and what lies ahead would be harder for some. Stacked deck. I called his name and he opened

The Red Fort, Agra, India. Built in the fifteenth century CE. (*R. L. Kreamer, Cibachrome 35-mm slide film, © 1978, 2019*)

The Taj Mahal from the Red Fort, Agra, India. (*R. L. Kreamer, Kodachrome 35-mm print film, © 1978, 2019*)

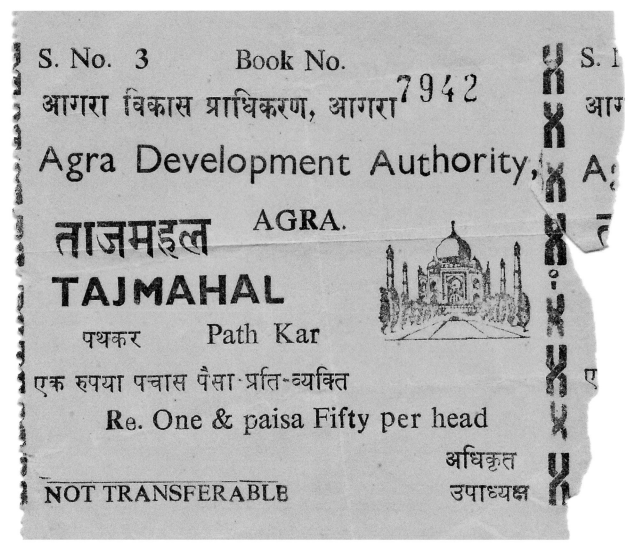

Taj Mahal day ticket, Agra, India. (*R. L. Kreamer* © *1977, 1978, 2019*)

an eye. I told him I was ready to go back to my hotel. For me, the ride was a typically crazy journey through the chaotic streets of India. For Sha, it was just the end of another day at work.

At the hotel, I settled the fare for the agreed price and I added a decent tip. He seemed pleased with the payment. I told him I had a present for him and to wait. When I ran back from my room I handed over my last pair of new Levi 501 jeans complete with the tags still on them. He seemed very pleased and I said he could sell them for money or wear them and that they should last a couple of years. I shook his hand, said that I hope to meet again someday, and walked away. I knew that I most likely would not. I was happy that my backpack would be lighter, and so my burden.

January 6. Left Agra this morning for a place called Khajuraho. I have heard a few things about this site, but still have no idea what I will find.

At the station, I met a guy named Hubert and discovered we were heading to the same place. The random meeting of travelers and the immediate sense of camaraderie, albeit fleeting, makes this journey endlessly interesting. If you put yourself out there, it could be that the world is for the curious and the world is for the finding.

The train is rumbling towards the city of Jhansi. From there, it is a long and rough bus journey to the temples of Khajuraho. Thank god, the third-class railcars have a toilet.

Arrived in Jhansi at one in the morning. Hubert is not keen on roughing it and wanted to find a hotel. I mentioned that for me it was not worth it for just a few hours. I asked around and found where the buses were departing for Khajuraho. The first bus leaves at seven. I found the men's waiting room and told Hubert that I was going to sleep here, and I guess I would see him later on the bus. It was sort of crowded and noisy. I found a corner and got into my sleeping bag, tied my backpack to it, and used my camera bag as my pillow. I saw that Hubert found an empty chair instead of a hotel. While finishing these journal entries, I saw out of the corner of my eye he was still wide awake and watching. I am going to sleep with an anxious-looking Hubert keeping watch.

January 7. The bus ride was rough, but I made it without shitting myself somehow. It was a close call. The ride took the better part of the day. The whole gut trouble thing is a drag. Found lodging at a cheap hotel close to the temple grounds. I have heard there are cheaper cafes and hotels in the small town nearby but cannot be bothered to move just yet. I am not planning to stay very long anyway.

A few hours of daylight meant I had time to see some of the temples. I was not expecting what I saw, but then again, it is blindingly obvious why they are called the erotic temples. It is the unpublished volume two, three, and four of the *Kama Sutra*.

The rectangular floor plan of the temples give rise to a tall dildo and shaped like a cock tower on one side, and an entrance and entry way shaped like a vagina on the other side. The walls were split with a meter-wide horizontal slit running the length of the temple, which at some angles created the illusion of the upper part of the temple was floating. The exterior walls were covered in sculptures of gloriously adorned and supple-bodied men and women engaged in every sexual act and position you could and could not imagine.

Twosomes, threesomes, foursomes, and on and on somes in a seemingly endless parade of groupings of men and women in diverse and numerous combinations of sexual partners and positions. It is enough to baffle a mathematician or a gymnast and outrage a prude. Some of the men and women depicted seemed to be applying makeup like mascara or just pleasuring themselves. Dotted around the temple steps were larger standalone sculptures of a women submitting herself to a tiger. Each depicting a different stage of either submitting, being devoured, or pleasuring the tiger.

A separate small open-sided temple held a life-sized bronze sculpture of a large bull sitting down, his great big bollocks protruding out from under him from behind. I watched the Hindu devotees visiting this temple circle the bull and rub its bronze balls in hopes of gaining fertility. At another temple, I was told that rubbing the sculpture of a cock attached to a man fucking a donkey would bring luck.

The half a dozen or so temples I saw were in a park-like setting with mowed lawns, peacocks strutting around, clumps of trees on the periphery, and large ponds or lakes in the distance. Tour guides offer to guide all under blue skies.

I was taking a break from the temples at a cafe and having tea. I should have rubbed that cock for luck because I ran into Dave. In fact, I was glad to see him, and my first reaction was to greet him like a long-lost brother, even though it had been barely a week since I last saw him. I was a little floored when he did not respond to me, or ask if I was feeling better or seen a doctor, or even say, "Hey man how's it going?" He turned to the people he was with and said, "Here's the guy I told you about who's been following me around for months." His little group was amused and as he started to say something else, I gave him the finger. I turned to walk away, but in that moment, I just lost it with his big brother act. I spun around and said, "Fuck you Dave, you're always waiting for me to show up, so you can mooch and borrow money."

After that, I kind of lost it again and laid into him about being a shit friend who only pretends to be a friend because he only wants money and thinks he is better than everyone. I know that is not completely true, but that was just the start. I told him he is the one who fucked everything up, with the Kuwait shit costing a lot more travel money than the simple northern route. I said he either did it on purpose or was stupid. I must have been foaming at the mouth. The people he was with looked at me like I was crazy and backed off. I guess I was crazy. I ended with something like fuck off to Goa, shoot up some smack, and fucking die motherfucker. I think I added for good measure that he could go fuck himself, fuck his friends, and fuck the horse he rode in on. Keeping with the theme of the erotic temples was not my intention. I finished by spitting on the ground and walking away.

I do not know where that outburst came from, but it was out of my mouth from some ugly place and now, as I recount that moment, I feel bad. Yeah, hurt feelings all round. Maybe I hurt his feelings as much as I hurt mine by saying something like that. Now as I recount and write these events down, I am feeling a shame that burns with a stark harsh light, like the bare ceiling bulb in my unadorned and grubby hotel room. I find myself wishing I could unsay words.

January 9. Spent another full day in Khajuraho. Half expected to run into Dave again but was relieved I did not. Almost decided to split north to Kathmandu and forget the rest of India. My rail map shows that the

The Erotic Temples of Khajuraho, India. (*R. L. Kreamer, Kodachrome 35-mm print film, © 1978, 2018*)

The Erotic Temples of Khajuraho, India. (*R. L. Kreamer, Kodachrome 35-mm print film, © 1978, 2019*)

The Erotic Temples of Khajuraho, India. (*R. L. Kreamer, Kodachrome 35-mm print film,* © *1978, 2019*)

The Erotic Temples of Khajuraho, India. (*R. L. Kreamer, Kodachrome 35-mm print film,* © *1978, 2018*)

The Erotic Temples
of Khajuraho,
India. Built over
a 100-year period
between 950
and 1050 CE.
(*R. L. Kreamer,*
Kodachrome
35-mm print film,
© *1978, 2019*)

major rail network lines of India are like a massive figure eight superimposed on the shape of the Indian subcontinent. Branch rail lines radiate like veins and spider webs from the figure eight going everywhere. The center of this figure eight, where the major rail lines cross in an "X," is a small town called Itarsi.

January 11. The days are warm again. I left Khajuraho by bus and headed east to a town called Satna. From there I got my train to Itarsi. I am in what has called the railway retiring room at the Itarsi Junction Railway Station while I wait for my train to Madras tomorrow morning. It is not dirt cheap, but it is not expensive; it is clean, safe, and I can shower and hand wash my clothes a couple of times and hang them in my room to dry. I had a relapse of the boiling gut, but I have still managed to do some chores and I have now recovered a little. Spent some time in the railway cafe, reading the English edition of *The Times of India* and having tea and cigarettes. It is one of my favorite things to do. I read the new Prime Minister is into urine therapy. He drinks it. Surprised by all the personal ads in the back pages for arranged marriages wanted or being offered. Found the bank; it took three and a half hours to cash a $20 traveler's check. I booked a second-class ticket and a sleeping birth for the thirty-six-hour train journey to Madras. It is a cheap long-haul journey and it is costing me under $4, meals and berth included.

About a third of the way into my train journey, I crossed the Tropic of Cancer. I am not sure when another transition happened, but I find myself in a land where most everyone that is carrying something, is carrying it balanced on top of their head.

Itarsi is indeed a small town and the bank is a stone relic from British India. So is the rail station with its wrought iron architecture. It is all very Victorian. The town is under a plague of flies and I have never seen anything like it. Well, only one time before. Flies everywhere covering every surface, everything, and everyone, from the rail station to the town and bazaars. Walking about the town stirs them up like miniature black dust devils. I am lucky my room and most of the station is free from flies. The rail station is large for such a small town, but the adjoining railyard is huge. It is situated a little further down the tracks. The sidings split into numerous tracks and other sidings as far as the eye can see into the haze. This is the crossroads of the Indian railway.

This station is home to a large population of little orphan kids ranging in ages from three or four years old to teenagers. They keep in small groups of a half dozen or so with the occasional solo or duo kids obviously out on their own. They are like an army; an army of orphaned beggars. The large groups do better, and they seem to look out for each other. They are in rags and spend all their time looking for something to eat, begging or trying to avoid the rail station staff and the police. They are often caught, given a beating, and turfed out of the rail station. I have been handing out small parcels of biscuits and fruit to the smaller kids going solo or in small groups. I do not want to be swamped by the larger groups and I told the little kids to keep quiet about it. I used the universal sign and sound for shush. I have given them a few coins as well. Where on earth are all these abandoned and neglected kids coming from? Since arriving in India, I see them everywhere. I am going broke trying to feed some of them.

January 12. I am about ten hours into a thirty-six-hour rail journey. The railcar I am in is taken over and rammed full of Indian schoolgirls from the city of Mysore. They are college kids I think. They are a couple of years younger than I am, and to them, I represent the western hippie they have heard so much about. At least that is what they have told me. Dozens of them all took turns asking me the same basic five questions. What is your name please? What are you doing on this train? Where do you come from? Where are you going? What does your father do? Some of the girls are wary of me and some stared at me like I was a shocking freak show. For the first three hours of this, I played along. Then it was my turn and I did not think I would surprise them with my questions. Are women treated fairly in India? Will you have an arranged marriage? What do you want to do for a profession? Some were reluctant to answer, but most were pleased and embolden with every new question I asked. I showed them my map and they really dug looking at it and asked a million more questions.

The train made a few stops during the day to allow other trains to pass or overtake. Sometimes stopping at a station, sometimes stopping in a field. Stops are made at stations in slow motion and all these stops make for a languid and long journey. Male passengers disembark to piss and smoke until the train starts moving again. Women stay with their children, keeping a watchful eye over their brood. Tea sellers peddle their drinks with loud shouts of chai, chai, chai. Tea is served in disposable clay cups that are passed into the train windows and eventually thrown empty from the train out the very same windows. With every passing mile traveling south, the air grows warmer. The train passed through endless fields and villages, and when the sun reached close to the flat horizon, it turned orange. The green fields turned a deeper green, tinged with a blue hue and the lengthening shadows seemed to chase and keep pace with this slow train.

A young local guy took over the duties of asking the westerner a million questions. However, he was basically asking the same three questions over and over. I do not speak Hindi, and his English was incomprehensible to me. It went on for hours and only stopped when the porter came through to set up the sleeping berths.

I found myself surrounded by the gaggle of young Indian women, each lovelier than the last. I was fully aware that they had no interest in sullying their reputation with a smelly, poor, vagabond traveler like me; I was a mere curiosity. I would have to be traveling first class, wearing perfume, and a suit and tie to garner any real interest from these girls, and any intimacy would have to be first arranged and approved by an army of mothers, aunties, and grandmothers. However, I was acutely conscious that I was enjoying basking in the presence of the innocent full on flush of the youth of India's future. It is quite the buzz. One of the older girls I have been talking with gave me her address in Mysore. Her name is Rene and she invited me to visit if I ever pass through there. She seems intrigued by my journey to Kathmandu and all the places I have been along the way. The schoolgirls had a connecting train to get and departed this train early in the morning. They are on a school trip to somewhere from somewhere and then on to somewhere else before returning to Mysore.

January 15. The hotel I am staying at is in the old quarter near the main rail station. I started out sleeping in the rail station's dorm. I have been in Madras a couple of days now. I went for a night in a hotel, so I could wash and get a good night's sleep. I cannot get over seeing cows everywhere, in the towns and cities just wandering where they please. One wandered into the cafe I was in and the guy at the first table fed it bread sticks.

In general, the Indians I have met are friendly, curious, and usually ready for a *tête-à-tête*.

I have encountered three fellow over-landers. This unlikely trio was made up of a guy from the west coast of the U.S., an elderly man from Australia, and a cat from England. The only name I can recall is the American. His name is Larry. The only thing I can recall about the other two were their stories and one was bald. The English dude said he has been traveling around India, off and on for seven years. More on than off. He said every time he goes back to England, it feels less and less like home. He said that the first time he visited India he was seventeen. The older dude said he was living in England and now he is making his way back to Australia via the long and slow route. He says he is brokenhearted over a relationship that did not work out. He looks as though he meant it.

I have noticed that hanging out with other travelers makes meeting and interacting with locals less likely to happen. They shared many tips on traveling cheap, and where the best type of places to sleep rough are. Stumbled upon a row of tailor shops and went into the shop that looked like it could use some business. I had a hot weather sleeping bag made that covered me from head to toe in hopes of keeping the flies and mosquitoes off me while I slept. It was made from a loose cotton weave that was kind of like mosquito netting. Also got a couple of lightweight cotton trousers and shirts.

I wandered into a downtown area and stumbled upon a large municipal building where a film expo was going on. A middle-aged Indian woman came up to me out of the blue and started telling me her life story. The story ended with her husband passing away six years ago, her kids in their twenties and in college. She said she was from Bombay and I should visit her. I noticed she was wearing lots and lots of expensive jewelry. I asked her if she wanted to buy my camera. She said no, but she knows someone in Bombay who would buy it and she gave me her address. She said she had to go and said she had a ticket she was not going to use for one of the films at the expo. She handed it to me and left.

I went in and found the cinema where this film was playing. Asked around and got pointed in the right direction. I have no idea what the name of it was or what it was about. The place was packed full and the theater was divided into sections. Cheap seats in the back, expensive seats to the front. A "gold circle" section was at the very front. My free ticket put me next to, but just outside the gold circle. Thank god, I would have been too self-conscience to sit there. The film was mad, and I had never seen anything like it. For the first hour, I thought it was a historic drama, lots of Hindu gods and horseback riding and bows and arrows and fourteenth-century-type battles, but it was also some sort of musical, with a few numbers cropping up now and then, sung by the main characters. All in Hindi and no subtitles. The good-looking leading man almost kissed his beautiful leading lady, prompting cat calls and "oohs" and "aahs" from the cinema crowd. Then, in the second hour, a bunch of modern soldiers showed up at one of the battle scenes with jeeps and

A rail bridge to Madras, India. (*R. L. Kreamer, Kodachrome 35-mm print film,* © *1978, 2019*)

tanks and machine guns blazing. Then there was some interlude in a village where the villagers confronted a dude in a gangster suit and tie, and the entire village proceed to beat him to a bloody pulp with sticks and clubs. It ended with a huge cheerful, song, and dance number, where even the gangster shook off his severe beating and took part by dancing like a madman. The crowd went wild for it, and they cheered and booed in what I am assuming were all the appropriate places. It got a massive standing ovation at the end. Of course, I jumped up from my seat along with everyone else and clapped and cheered wildly. I had not had that much fun in a while. My enjoyment and enthusiasm had not gone unnoticed. While shuffling out with the crowd, a group of local young dudes asked if I wanted to go to such and such cafe nearby for a cup of chai. I saw other groups of people looking on, watching for my response to these guys. I readied myself for the onslaught of questions from the curious.

January 16. After yesterday's cinema experience, I went back to my hotel and checked out in the late afternoon. I hiked across the city to the Edmore Rail Station for my train to Pondicherry. The guy at the ticket window was impressed with the fact I had a copy of the timetable for Indian Rail. I had less than a half

an hour to spare and got the overnight train leaving at four. I am riding in the third-class car.

The rhythm of this train journey is like the one I took to get to Madras, albeit a little more crowded. The wooden bench seats have numbers stenciled on them indicating seating for three persons in a row. Reality allows for four or five skinny people to squeeze on in. Floors and gangways are bursting to the brim with people, luggage, and children. Once you find your spot, changing your mind for a different seat is rarely a possibility. A trip to the toilet could result in one losing their seat unless elaborate and extreme deliberations and explanations are made to your fellow passengers that you are not planning to jump from the moving train, never to return, but are only going for a shit and plan on returning soon.

On cue, the setting sun lulls the passengers into a quiet mood and the volume of the conversations around me drops noticeably. We are rolling through fields of rice, villages of straw-built houses, and palm trees. Farmers are driving oxen, pulling ploughs under the setting sun.

January 19. Been in Pondicherry a couple of days now. The French colonial influence is everywhere, from the European architecture to the pressed white shorts

Steam train going south, somewhere in India. (*R. L. Kreamer, Kodachrome 35-mm print film, © 1978, 2019*)

Firewood delivery, Pondicherry, India. (*R. L. Kreamer, Kodachrome 35-mm print film, © 1978, 2019*)

and pith helmets of the traffic cops. This morning, I woke to a strange sound. It was a clattering sound. Like a pile of folding chairs hitting the floor. I looked out the window of my hotel and saw a man standing in the back of a cart in the process of delivering firewood. He was dropping the wood by the handful on the doorstep of the house across the street. The cart was being pulled by two large white bulls. Their horns are painted blue and red. I took a photograph of the scene. I have been staying at the Anivasam Lodge for six rupees a night for a single room, seeing a few of the sights like temples and gates, though mostly taking it easy and resting. The old gut bomb went off and my stomach swelled into a freak beer gut. I was warned by the doctor in Delhi that this could happen, but his warning did little to ease my angst when it did. With any luck, this will not happen too often.

In Germany, I was given the address of an ashram north of Pondicherry in a place called Auroville. I was given pretty good directions and even had a hand-drawn map. I was told to travel up the "old Madras road" along the sea front, so I hitchhiked like the olden days and it felt good. The sun, the sparkling sea and breezes in my hair, I was in heaven. I was told to keep an eye out for a market before the village of Kottakuppam and keep going past the village because then I would know I was on the right track. A mile or so further on down the road, I should be on the lookout for a sign that said, "new school." This, I was told, was a place called "Serenite."

It was an ashram and travelers were welcomed to stay and be fed, albeit for a price. At least that is what I had been told. Fair enough, because everyone knows there is no free lunch. I was thinking it was a cross between a kibbutz, the Golden Temple of Amritsar and a rail station dorm room, with maybe a little enlightenment thrown in with the breakfast tab. I passed some tennis courts that seemed oddly out of place, and I then found myself standing in front of a large modern iron gate painted white. It is like the entrance into a resort or government building or something like that. At this point, I am in front of this gate and still thinking "kibbutz"; it is just like arriving at the kibbutz. I rang the buzzer and happily waited. Up walked some dude and his accent told me he was American. He asked me what I wanted. I think the exact words were "What the fuck do you want." I said I was here to see about the possibility of staying for a short while. After he finished laughing at me, he said this place only was only interested in people with money and whoever could afford it and I obviously

could not afford it, or I would have arrived by car. Oh, and by the way and just for my own information, he was personally sick to death of travelers. At this point, he opened the gate for two middle-aged couples wearing crisp white tennis outfits and carrying rackets looking like a magazine advert. They were obviously on their way out for some lunchtime tennis. As they passed me, they laughed, scoffed, and literally held their noses up. I felt I was some character drawn for their personal cartoon. As the gate clanged shut, I was told to leave. So much for what I had been thinking. I was wandering through the old district when I randomly came across the hotel I am currently staying in.

Saw a weird sight today while walking around; an old local guy with something sticking out of his ears. When I got closer, I had a laugh when I saw what it was. He had decided to embrace the whole hair growing out of the ears of old dudes thing. The ear hair had been braided and the braid was about an inch long and had a blue bead on the end. Now that is a hippie.

Ran out of toilet paper a week ago. I have been cleaning my ass Asian style. Water and the left hand. Soap and water. Left hand for washing, right hand for eating and never the twain shall meet. Left-handed tourists are viewed as disgusting. It took me a while to get used to it, but I must admit it seems cleaner to me now, rather than taking some bits of paper and smearing the shit from my ass.

Ran into one of the guys I met in Madras. We rented bicycles and pedaled around Pondicherry. I do not think he believed my story about the ashram in Auroville and wanted to see it for himself. We pretty much got the same reception from a different gatekeeper, but with less swearing.

He said he had bought far too much ganja in the past couple of weeks, and did I want to take some off his hands for a very cheap price. I said sure. Later, I went with him back to the hotel he was staying at to have a look at his ganja. Holy shit, that dude had a lot of weed. It looked like a couple of pounds and he wanted to sell me half. I laughed and said no way dude. I thought he had a lid to sell or something. In the end, I gave him fifteen rupees for about two lids worth.

January 22. Hot and dry. I arrived in Madurai just before sunrise and immediately set off in search of the bus station and the bus numbered twenty-two. The bus took me into the southern suburbs of Madurai and into a district called Thiagarajar. Ron gave me his parents' address in India and said he wanted me to visit if I ever made it that far south. Last time I saw him, he said he was going to return to India and hang out while waiting for a new job to start in Oman. That seems like a thousand years ago to me now. Traveling this far overland has put me at loose ends. A sort of loss of myself. It is far too easy to misplace one's self on the road. Truly in the wind. He greeted me like a brother and I felt like I was coming home. I am treated like a king. His parents are lovely to the extreme. Their whitewashed house has a thatch roof and its own water well in the back. They even have a couple of milk cows. When Ron described how drinking from this well made him feel, I could not help but feel a little envious at first. He said that it made him feel so good that he had trouble describing it.

January 23. The days are hot. Ron's parents are not rich and I do not want to be a burden much longer. They are Christians and in the minority in this community. Ron has a twin brother named Don and a sister who is married and lives in Ceylon. I enjoy it when the stuff I write about accidently rhymes.

Ron's mother makes a dish called Masala Dosa and it is my current favorite food. It probably will be for a long time. It is like a coconut crispy Indian pancake. I met Ron's girlfriend and went with them both on a walking tour of their town and where they grew up. She took me to a temple and we walked around the old neighborhood. Her name is Ronni and she said she lived in New Jersey for eight years before returning to India. She has had a lot of trouble adjusting to coming back to the old hometown. She has changed, but India has stayed the same. She thinks and acts, looks, and dresses like an American, and she finds it impossible to act in a way that Indian society expects her to act. She says she is hassled no end and she is really tired of all the shit the locals give her, especially the men. So much for the spiritual homecoming. What a contrast to how my buddy Ron sees his own hometown return. For him, it is a comfortable boredom until the next adventure or opportunity arises. For her, it is oppression and pressure to conform. The male-dominated world is at a much louder volume in some places.

The dudes like a chew they call Betel Nut: a concoction of plants that is stuffed between cheek and gum. The dudes spit funky red juice all day, all night, and anywhere they want. Ron hates it. Red splats and streaks everywhere you go, until the next monsoon rain anyway.

January 24. Madurai is a dry state and beer and wine is only sold to tourists. Ron took me to the local state-controlled liquor store. On my passport, I got myself a permit and bought a few bottles, and we had a small party and Ron's dad enjoyed drinking a couple of beers.

Ron played a few of the records he brought back from Germany. We listened to funk and soul late into the night. Ron does not smoke grass and he is paranoid his parents will find out that I do. I had to sneak out for a quick smoke if I wanted to get high, so I gave it a rest. It was weird listening to rock and roll and some disco and guitar stuff. For the past few months, I have been bombarded with whatever local music was around me. Had time to sort out my backpack and its contents. Made sure it was clean and clean. All my magic smoke and clay pipes are in a separate cotton sack inside my Indian shoulder bag.

I find myself carrying a hefty bundle of paper memorabilia and various souvenirs and other stuff I think I need. Wash kit with shampoo, soaps, razors for a shave, a hairbrush and a toothbrush, and boiling gut medicine. Ticket stubs, boarding passes, entry tickets for museums, temples, galleries, and holy places and not-so-holy places. Used rail tickets and bus tickets, brochures and city maps, and maps of ruins and business cards from here to Munich. A rail guide that reminds me of a mini-phonebook. Clothes from Afghanistan and India. Used rolls of film not yet processed and developed, and still containing the ghosts of the people, places, days, months, and moments of my journey. My journal and the camera and second lens. Pen and pencils, airmail writing paper, and envelopes. Boots, clothes, cigarettes, and a sleeping bag and lightweight ground cloth. I am dragging loads of stuff around.

10

An Audience with the Reclining Buddha

January 27. Twenty-four hours after leaving Madurai, I find myself in Ceylon. Well, first thing: it is not Ceylon any more, it is now Sri Lanka.

It started with Ron insisting on coming with me to the train station to see me off. I had left most of my luggage at Ron's house and was traveling light. Just two small shoulder bags. Ditching the backpack, western clothes and camera, gave me some hope of blending in a little more and being less noticeable. Mostly I am hoping to relax and be free of the luggage for a while.

The train from Madurai to Rameswaram was the usual overnight slow train stopping at every stop and I arrived in Rameswaram at 5.30 a.m.; it took me a half an hour to walk to the seaport. Went through a lot of waiting for a three-hour boat ride. Met a guy from Switzerland named Peter and we hung out together during the border crossing into Sri Lanka.

I held my place in line by sprawling on the ground at the entry gate and taking a nap. Peter thought I was a little crazy for doing that, but I did not care. The gates opened at 8 a.m. and we were on the boat by 10 a.m. It was another six hours before the boat sailed and we landed and cleared customs by 7 p.m. The sea was calm and the sun was blazing. Weird scenes on the boat. We arrived just in time to miss the only train to Columbo and ended up spending the night and most of the following day on the beach near the Talaimannar Pier. We had to walk quite a way down the beach to find a stretch of sand that had not been used as an outdoor toilet. Met some other travelers who warned us of tourists having their stuff stolen while asleep on this beach. I think Peter had another sleepless turn at his self-imposed guard duty. I slept like a log.

After finally getting the train to Columbo, I bought a book and a newspaper at the train station. I bid Peter farewell and headed south for Mt. Lavinia and Ron's sister's house.

January 28. Spent a day and a night at George and Ruby's house. Ron's sister and brother-in-law are very nice but religious Christians to the extreme. They enjoyed my stories of traveling through the Holy Lands and all the biblical sites and place names I visited, but very little else about me. I think they saw me as a heathen godless hippie. I was more of an envoy for Ron and his parents, having seen them a few days ago, and I said that they were sending their love and greetings and gave them the news that they were well. I hope I had not sullied Ron's reputation. Lovely people, though. Most everybody seems nice. They seemed relieved when I thanked them for their hospitality and made my way to the station early the next morning.

I am heading south along the coast and all the villages and beaches look inviting. I plan to get off the train in some small village and hang out for a while. I heard about a small village with no westerners called Hikkaduwa.

Anywhere, between here and there, would fine with me. The people here are great. None of the pushing, the shoving, or the hustle and the hassle. Found a dentist to get my teeth cleaned—they were getting funky. He asked about my diet. I told him that since coming down with dysentery, I have been living on tea, ganja, cigarettes, and biscuits and I have lost some weight. He said I looked like I was malnourished and if I kept up with that diet my teeth would turn black and fall out. He recommended for me to try eating some protein, like eggs or fish, and fruit and to lay off the

Rail ticket from India to Sri Lanka. (*R. L. Kreamer* © 1977, 1978, 2019)

cigs and ganja. He then proceeded to clean my teeth with some ancient-looking dental apparatus and sold me a new toothbrush. Still, all in all, it was a fairly inexpensive service. That is enough stories for now. This train journey along the coast and through the jungle is making me sleepy.

February 2. I landed in paradise. I really cannot believe my luck. As I traveled further and further south, the landscape became more beautiful. The jungles seemed greener, the people nicer, the villages smaller, and the beaches more alluring. The air seemed heavy, and moist, warm, and clean. The sea looked cerulean light blue. The train journey seemed spellbinding. To think I was tempted to turn around and go back to India. Columbo seemed a characteristically loud, dirty, crowded shitty city, and I wondered if I had made some colossal mistake as I made my way around the train station looking for the trains going south. Now I wonder what took me so long to get here.

When I saw the station sign for Hikkaduwa, I think I must have just dozed off and the train squealing to a halt woke me up. It seemed like I just woke from a dreamlike state and just got off the train like I was hypnotized, but I was not. I was hyper-aware like I was tripping. I did not even know where I was for a moment. I got down from the train and it must have been noon and it was really hot. I saw a bunch of tourist's brochures in the station and I helped myself to some to read later. It was very quiet. I saw what

looked like a lodge or some small funky hotel near the station, some buildings, cafes, markets, and the detritus of any small south subcontinent town. The market was open, and I bought a straw hat and a couple of bottles of water. This town was kind of a smaller run-down kind of town, but not so bad.

I just kept walking. More like a stroll. I think I was just thinking that I was just going off somewhere to have a nap on some beach or something. I think I walked for a mile, or two or three or four, in and out of the dappled shade alternating between the groves and jungle. There was really not a whole lot in the way of people or dwellings to be seen. Everything was spread out—rural and quiet. The road was mostly dirt, and the ocean was on my right and the railway was on my left. It seemed to get more jungle and have less people around as I walked. I passed the occasional road that seemed to head towards the beach.

I was approached by a middle-aged local man. I could not understand what he was saying, but I knew he wanted me to follow him. I followed him a very short distance past a large hut and into a palm grove. Coconuts. I could see I was a couple of hundred yards or so from the beach and could see the waves through the grove. He gestured around and was speaking, but all I could do was shrug and say something like "I don't understand." I was busy thinking it looked groovy and it was cool in the shade. I thought maybe he wanted to sell me a coconut; he motioned for me to sit and wait, and he hurried off. I walked to the edge of the grove, sat down with my back against a palm tree, and looked down on a large empty beach. I was happy to have a nap here. Empty, save for a few small wooden boats that were beached and had their sails down. I listened to the sound of the waves hitting the beach. The sun was dancing on the water and my brain was dancing in my head. Later I heard voices, so I stood up and looked to see the man returning with someone. I knew this was a translator for the old dude. After the old dude finished talking, the young guy said that the old dude wanted to know if I was looking for a place to stay. I said, "Sure, why not?" Again, the old dude said something and the gist of which was I could stay here cheap. I thought he meant the large hut. Turns out he was offering to construct a lean-to for me to stay in under this palm grove. I asked where I could get water and where could I use the toilet.

An hour later, I had my very own hut in the palm grove for five rupees for a whole week if I wanted to stay that long. There was a well with an old fashion hand pump near the large hut, together with a large fenced in garden. Across the dirt road in a wild patch of jungle was an outhouse and beyond that the rail line.

I watched the old guy string a line of rough rope between two palms and then lash a bunch of palm fronds together, and in ten minutes, I had my own large tent shaped hut. I could almost stand upright inside. My hut is on the far side of the grove in the corner just a couple of trees into the grove from the beach. The sand stretches downhill on a gentle slope for a couple of hundred yards until flattening out the last fifty yards into the ever-rolling surf.

The old guy brought me an old bucket and my translator said I could have water on hand for washing. I was told for a couple of rupees extra a day, they could provide tea and toast in the morning and cook up any fish I buy from the fishermen for me as well. They could add some rice for a rupee. I could get my clothes washed for two rupees. Lots and lots of coconuts to be had, cheaply. The old guy carried over a couple of logs for my table and chair. It is an amazing piece of driftwood that looks like a Salvador Dalí painting come to life.

A small kid showed up out of nowhere with a basket and inside were a couple of pineapples, bananas, and coconuts. For a nickel, he sold me a pineapple, deftly peeled it, and chopped it into bite-sized chunks with a machete that was bigger than he was. I was impressed and had some coconut water as well. I have found myself in heaven.

February 3. Clear and hot days. Last night, I was a little cold sleeping in my hut next to the beach, but the daytime is hot. After my tea and toast, the pineapple kid came by again and I bought one for breakfast. I asked him his name and I told him mine. I watched the fishermen go out in their boats rather early. A couple of boats went out far and I could barely see them after a while. One boat stayed a few hundred yards offshore and a few guys stayed on the beach. The guys on the boat set out a net while a couple of guys swam from the boat and started to string the net out on both sides of the boat. As they swam towards the shore, the dudes on the beach swam out to meet them as they deployed the net in a huge arc, from the boat to the shore. Red plastic floats marked out the huge semicircle of the net. After a while, I noticed the guys on the beach slowly hauling both ends of the net to shore. The two groups were about 100 yards apart on the beach. Four or five swimmers stayed out with the net, pulling back on it apparently trying to keep the wide arc shape as the net was hauled to shore. It was an amazing thing to watch. They were happy to have me join in and hang out and I helped pull the huge heavy net in. The boat slowly followed the net into shore. Some of the guys waded out with large plastic buckets and started grabbing the fish caught in the net. One of the guys who spoke English said the fish were tuna. They must have netted dozens and dozens of them. They were small and about a foot long. They sold me two of them for about 5 cents each. The guy who spoke English said the guy whose grove I was staying in was on one of the other boats and he pointed out to sea where I could barely see the boats from earlier this morning.

I walked back to the hut and gave them to my landlady, and because she did not speak English, I pointed at one of the fishes and then at her and said it was for her. I pointed at the other fish and then at myself and told her that one was for me. She understood right away and seemed happy about it. A half hour later, she brought one of the fish to my hut, gutted and roasted with a little rice on the side, served on a banana leaf with a cup of tea. It tasted amazing and it seemed like rocket fuel, and I really felt like I had more energy than I have had in weeks and weeks. I watched the fisherman down on the beach sell the fish to three guys—well, one guy. The boss man is always easy to spot. Translates into any culture. One guy paid and the other two carried the baskets. They quickly split up the road to Hikkaduwa.

Not sure why I persist in this journal. It gives me something to do while I wait out the blazing afternoon sun in the dappled shade of the coconut grove. The beach was empty save for me and I realized I have not seen a tourist since I got here. Watched an amazing soulful sunset.

Earlier when I came back to my hut and was washing away the sea salt, I decided to make some improvements to my hut before dark. I spent an hour or so gathering up palm leaves and sticks and long grass from the grove and the jungle area across the road. I enclosed the back end of my hut added another layer to the roof and almost completely closed off the front to keep out the cold and damp sea air at night. I made a thick layer of palm leaves and grass for a mattress. Valuables are hidden in a bag under the sand and my bed marks the spot. I am writing by the light of a couple of candles stuck on a lump of driftwood inside my hut, and I already can tell that these small improvements have made all the difference in making this hut warmer. Must be careful with these candles and my smoking; my hut is extremely flammable.

Before bedding down for the night, I ventured out to the edge of the grove to look at the ocean and have a smoke. I have not been in a completely dark environment for a very long time and the multitude and brightness of the stars and the Milky Way took me by surprise. The sea was flat and calm like glass and the reflection of the stars was almost as bright as the sky. It was so dark I could see stars almost to the horizon. To my amazement, the fishing boats I had forgotten all about were still out there, too, on what I was guessing was the horizon. Their little yellow lamps were winking in a broken line and were reflected on the water with a little dance and flicker.

February 4. This shit just keeps getting better and better. This is one of my best days ever on this trip. I got laid today, well, sort of.

The day started early with the boats coming in and the catamarans being dragged up and on to the beach with happy sounding voices. It was early morning and I liked it. I bought a couple of fish offloaded at my threshold fresh from the sea. I think my landlord can see me crossing the road for the outhouse. Not much traffic except for the occasional people walking. The occasional car or bus. I can hear the train; it is twice a day and sometimes it sounds like the surf. Sometimes I hear a distant whistle. When I returned to my hut and had a wash, the tea and toast was not far behind. The pineapple kid was right on time and appeared halfway through my breakfast. He had a couple of bananas in his basket and I bought those as well. Back in my old hometown, he would make a

great paperboy. This is better though. Instead of rolled newsprint full of bad news hitting my doorstep, I have a fresh pineapple hitting my doorstep. Sometimes he comes in the afternoon of the same day and I will have a couple of coconuts. That alone would have made this a great day to be alive.

Later in the day, I was on the beach in nothing but a lungi, reading, sleeping, smoking, and working on a tan. I noticed a couple of people quite far down the beach and I could not tell if they were coming or going. I was stoned and had come to consider this to be my very own private beach—at least in my head. So, I was kind of surprised to notice a half hour later that they had been walking towards me and were now close and probably getting a strong whiff of the spliff I was smoking. They were making tracks right up to me, so it seemed, so I sat up and said hello. They turned out to be two German girls and they appeared astonished to see a tourist way out of town in the middle of nowhere.

They were a pair of sunburnt German girls. I like girls. Later, one of them said to me that because my tan was so brown they did not think I was a westerner at first. Anyway, they asked me if I had any water and I said yes. I was impressed with the sudden realization that they were my age, or a little older, and very good looking, and I had not been laid since the kibbutz and I was very stoned.

I introduced myself and the very nice and very easy-going girl said her name was Iris and the very uptight one said her name was Vera. I immediately forgot Vera's name for about an hour. I told them the water was up there and pointed up the slope of the little hill at the end of the palm grove. We walked over to my little camp and into the grove and I have to admit it looked really cool and groovy and I was thinking anyone would want to stay here. It was cool in the shade and the air smelled tropical. Iris and Vera started speaking low and in German and I did not let on that I could understand German. Not at first. Iris said to Vera it was nice and Vera said to Iris that she did not like it. I said the water well was through the grove near my landlord's house and I pointed in the direction of the big hut, just visible through the palms if you really look for it. I said follow me and led them to the well and antique pump. I started to give it a few pumps and leaned in for a drink, telling them it was cold and clear and nice. Of course, Iris stepped up first and had a long drink with her face in the water. Vera gathered the water in her palms and drank from her hands. I asked Iris to work the pump for a second and I had a long overdue deep drink and finished with soaking my hair, face, and upper torso. I shook the water from my hair and wiped it from my face and I felt like a god. I figured that in reality I looked and sounded like a redneck Robinson Crusoe vagabond from Tucson. I asked them if they wanted another drink while I filled the camp bucket and coconuts I store water in.

I had invented a chore I employed like a ritual and had spent a couple of hours each day sweeping my camp and the path to the water well, smooth and clean with palm fronds used like a broom. I think my landlady noticed me doing it and now, while walking back to my camp, I am glad I did. The place looked like magic.

I was asking them where they were from and what countries and routes they were traveling. On cue, the pineapple kid was walking into my camp as we were walking down the little hill and I turned to the girls and said the paperboy was here. They looked baffled and I said I was only joking, "He is a little kid called Jauni and he's selling fruit." I said I was going buy my usual order of pineapple and bananas, and I invited them to have some of the pineapple. I bought a coconut. I thought offering them some coconut water would be nice. Speaking at the same time, Iris said yes, and Vera said no. I paid and said thank you to the kid. The German girls were looking around like they were in a daze. He proceeded to slice and dice the pineapple and open the coconut deftly with the oversized machete. For him, it was just another day at the office, for the German girls, it was like he was doing a magic trick. They were amazed at the kid swinging his machete. I took a seat near the end of the large driftwood log table. It had the ghost remnants of branches that had been smoothed into table legs by endless tumbling in the endless surf and bleached and baked to a near white with a tinge of gray in the brutal tropical sun, for god knows how long and even I was amazed at how it looked. It took on a life of its own.

Iris sat down, and Vera remained standing. Vera was eyeing the threshold of my hut where I had stacked a couple of paperbacks, *The Times of India*, and my journal and national park brochures from the Sri Lanka tourist board all nice and neat with a pack of Marlboro's on top. Vera was eyeing those American cigs with surprise and I pretended not notice. While watching Iris devour the pineapple, I asked them if they had traveled overland and if they were traveling on their own. Their story as told by Vera, while Iris stayed quiet, was they flew into Delhi from Frankfurt with their boyfriends, saw the sights like the Taj, had hassles with the trains and locals, stayed at hotels and

beaches they did not like, and had fights and arguments and that they were now generally having a lousy time.

I stood up as the diatribe was ending and fetched my cigs and matches and offered one to Vera while placing one in my mouth. While lighting her cigarette, I said, "And now you took a boat and a train here, and this is really nice." She looked embarrassed. I think Vera was maybe changing her mind, but she did seem mad about a lot of things and mad at India and mad at her boyfriend. She liked the cigarette and asked me where I got them. I said they were American and I got them in Bahrain and I save them for nice occasions. They asked where I came from and I gave them a fast run down starting in Munich and the trucks and keeping the story just to capital and major cities all the way to here. I told them that after a week or so of sightseeing on this island, I was going back to India and then by train and bus to Kathmandu. I realized I did not have my map with me. I knew my geography and casually said I was getting ready for the roughly 2,000-mile trip through India to Kathmandu. I ended my tour of the Middle East and India spiel with something about how nice it was to be right here and now in a such a magical place with you nice people. They looked at me slacked jawed. All this took about twenty minutes, from the minute they showed up—the water, the pineapple, the talking, the stories, and the cigarette—to the "It's a magical place" line it was twenty minutes, thirty minutes tops.

Then another Anaïs Nin short story version unfolded—sort of. After all, it is 1978 and I have been on a kibbutz. The lull in the conversation was broken by me when I said, "Can I get you anything more?" Then I said in a casual deadpan voice, "Would you like some more water or some more pineapple or another cigarette or do you want to go for a swim or have sex?" I was only kidding around, and I immediately regretted saying it. I suddenly thought I was being creepy. Iris laughed, and Vera said no, both at the same time. I said, "Sorry, it was such a shitty joke." Vera took the cig I offered and started sternly telling me more relationship woes, the gist of which their boyfriends are upset that Vera and Iris were now a couple, and by the way, she does not want to fuck me. Yikes, however, living in Germany taught me that German girls for the most part do not bullshit and play games, and if they are interested or not in fucking you, they will let you know. After that, you move on as appropriate. I was disappointed, though. Iris said she liked men and was still fucking her boyfriend too. I was really getting off on my new visitors. They started having words in

German in a low fast voice, the gist of it was all from Vera, saying they should not say things like that in front of me and Vera did not want Iris to fuck me. Iris said she did not want to fuck me and stop saying that all the time about everyone they meet. She said she wanted more water and since they had just got there, she liked it and wanted to hang out. In German she said not to worry, she was not going to run away with me.

I lit Vera yet another cigarette and said I was going to get us some tea and I would be right back. I left them having a little squabble and thought of the squabbling I had done with Dave and how unpleasant that must have been for the observers. I was enthralled to see where this little drama was going. I was back in no time with three clay cups of hot chai courtesy of my landlady, and as I passed them around, I noted that I half expected them to have split while I was gone. Vera had been standing the whole time. The light in grove had shifted to bathe the driftwood table in full sun. It lit up like it was made of glass, bright like a white ghost making the shade of the grove somehow darker and cooler. The sound of the surf was the constant soundtrack. I told them I liked listening to the surf. I washed the table and it dried almost immediately, and I got a freshly washed lungi, spread it in the shade, and invited Vera to sit and enjoy her tea. She actually sat down and seemed to relax, sort of, but still annoyed and mad under the surface. Iris said she wanted another drink from the well and asked if I would show her to it. I said sure and we strolled uphill to the pump, and I knew we were pretty much in sight the whole way and Vera was watching. Iris made a big deal out of drinking and cooling off and getting soaking wet. She was really enjoying it and I think she knew I was getting turned on. We were walking back when she said to me in a hushed voice that she liked men. She was walking behind me. She added, "I like to watch men when they come. It thrills me." That was a first for me. I did not know what to say, and by the time I thought of something—anything—to say, we were back in my camp and it was too late, and Vera was eyeing us with suspicion.

I brought back a handful of coconut shells filled with water. I placed them on the table and thought about asking them if they wanted to smoke some weed and get high. I thought, why bother? Whereas most young Germans are liberal about sex and drinking, not many smoke ganja. Odds were these two did not get high, and certainly not the uptight Vera. She could do with getting stoned and so I was tempted. She needs to mellow out.

Iris asked Vera to go for a swim and Vera refused. Returning to speaking German, Iris said something about Vera never wanting to swim, the group never going to nice beaches and that she liked hanging out on the beach and she liked to swim. She said this was the nicest beach she had seen anywhere. Then there was something said about Vera always being a drag. Iris said again in English, "I think I want to go for a swim." She added that Vera did not want to go and then asked if I wanted to go. I said "Sure," and I was hoping I did not sound too enthusiastic. I said it was a nice beach for a swim while handing my pack of Marlboro's and some matches over to Vera. I looked her full in her face and eyes and smiled and said to save me some smokes for when I return. She almost smiled back.

I caught up with Iris halfway to the beach. I said it was calmer over this way and pointed away from the catamarans towards a couple of dunes on our left. I was babbling on. When we reached the spot, I dropped my lungi without even turning around and ran and dove into the water. The surf was not rough, but it was certainly letting you know it was there. I swam out, and stupidly did not think to look if she was swimming out this far with me. When I turned around and looked, I saw Iris was timidly swimming out just a little way, so I did an immediate U-turn and rode a wave in towards her. When I surfaced, she was in front of me naked, wet, and in water up to her knees. She looked incredible. I took her hand and I asked if she wanted to swim out further. She reached over and cool and calm like, started stroking my cock and talking dirty to me.

From the minute they showed up asking for water, up until this point when I was facing the real prospect of sex with a beautiful woman, it has now been almost an hour, an hour tops. I do not think I am smooth and suave, but I know I am lucky and in the right place at the right time. Iris got a little too enthusiastic. Between the salt water and Iris pumping my cock like she was pumping at the water well, it started out a little uncomfortable. In fact, I thought she was trying to yank my cock off. I said ouch, and then I said, "*Langsam bitte*," and gave the game away by speaking German when asking her to go slowly please. I thought she was going to be upset and stop. She looked surprised and had a huge grin on her face. I said I understood almost everything, but I speak German like a ten-year-old. I said, "Whatever you do, don't tell Vera." Iris laughed, and I asked if we could fuck now. I said, "Like from here to eternity." Iris said no, laughed at me, and asked if that was a movie reference. She said, "I want to watch you come." I asked her to suck me, and she said no. I said to spit on my cock and she did and kept stroking my cock. I noticed she was fingering herself and I asked if I could finger her. She said no. I was getting very turned on. She spat on my cock again and she made a cooing sound like a dove and said I had a nice cock. I exploded, and she made "oh" and "ah" sounds, and from her reaction, I was expecting applause. I think she enjoyed herself as much as I did. I was still hard and she was still stroking me slowly and just smiling at me. That had taken all of four minutes, from the time I leapt into the water, until the time she asked if I could do that again. Roughly five minutes after that, I obliged her by doing that again. Very roughly. She was crazy, I was crazy, it was crazy. It was kind of nice.

I had another quick swim and as I came to shore, I saw she was rinsed in the sea and getting her clothes on. I noticed how sunburnt she was in places. I wrapped on my lungi, and as we walked back to the camp, I felt awkward. She said, "Thank you" and I said "No, thank you and can you visit tomorrow?" She laughed and said we will see. Vera was scowling a little when we got back and I am sure she was guessing at what may have happened. She was giving off that vibe. She did not ask Iris, "How was the swim?" Instead she said they had get going and they had been here a long time, and their boyfriends must be wondering where they are. I noticed she moved my stack of reading material. Sri Lanka poetry and Kafka. The important stuff is buried in the sand under my bed and I can tell that was not messed with. I went in to my hut and came out with my straw hat on. In total, they have been here an hour and fifteen minutes and I got two handjobs and maybe almost laid at some future date.

As I watched them disappear up the beach in the direction they came, I dug out my stash and smoked another joint. Vera left me four cigarettes from a pack of ten and I picked up the butts she left in her wake, swept up my camp, and found myself immediately hoping for another visit.

Five minutes later, I got pot paranoid and wondered what if they brought their boyfriends back with them? What if their boyfriends were bigger than me and wanted to beat me up? What if they want to come back and camp? What if this place got overrun with sunburnt Germans and was turned into some sort of resort? I imagined loads of fat sunburnt Germans eating sausages and drinking beer. No, that could never happen. No, it is too remote of a beach, Spartan, without luxuries, and there is nothing much out here and they would never stay here.

February 6. The days are clear and hot. The nights are clear, cool, and amazing. It has been a couple of days since the German girls visit. I have not seen a tourist since then. Must never ever let my mother read my journal.

Went into Hikkaduwa and checked out the market. Was secretly hoping to run into the German girls as it turns out. Too much time to think and write. I was really hoping for a return visit but now realized that was not going to happen. Oh well, they know where to find me, this week.

I have reached a conclusion that the longer I stay here, the least likely I am to leave. It is blissful. So peaceful. The only chatter and noise around here is what is going on in my head and the endless sound of the surf. I have spent the whole day today, wondering now and again, about staying put for a month and forgetting about Kathmandu for a while. I was letting my imagination run away. I had visions of girls from all over the world finding my groovy little beach hut and me having a never-ending cocktail party. On one hand, nothing in this world lasts forever. Then on the other hand, again, it is not every day a girl wants to give me a handjob within an hour of meeting. Bringing people here could wreck the scene and I am not really a never-ending cocktail party kind of guy. A few days maybe. At least not all the time. There is always one jerk, one fight, and that one guy who stays too long and will not leave the party and I do not want to meet or be that guy. I figure it should take a month to get to Kathmandu. I still have a plan. Everyone should always have a plan. I am heading for Raxaul. The northernmost train station on the border with Nepal. Getting to Kathmandu sometime in early March. Yes, I think it could very easily be done.

February 8. The night and day train from Hikkaduwa to Kandy was about twenty-four hours without too many rail changes and it was as easy as it was long. Crawled through Colombo and it did not seem all that bad as I first thought. The rail service is on a smaller gauge of track than in India. I felt sad to be leaving my beachfront castle. I made sure everything was tidy and paid in full. I had a last pineapple and coconut water and gave Jauni a very, very good tip. I made sure I spoiled it for the cheapskates that come later.

To get to Kandy, I passed an endless parade of jungle, rice fields, thatched villages, ponds, rivers, tea plantations, elephants, and people and monks in yellow robes and monks in reddish orange colored robes, carrying sticks or umbrellas or both and a brass begging bowl, hamlets and towns and the capital Colombo and temples all rolling by the train. Even so, it is not the mad overpopulation of India. The locals, as a rule, are not pushy and that is a nice flow to go with. I would say there is a more mellow and spread out feel to Sri Lanka than India or anywhere else I have been since leaving Munich.

Elephants—some being ridden, some put to work moving logs and stuff or just wandering around in a small herd or alone in the distance. It is something about having elephants around that makes me feel I am in a natural clean environment. As long as they are not mistreated or killed for the ivory or killed by some asshole hunter who gets off on killing. Have not seen any being mistreated. I was regretting leaving my beach hut and the prospect of getting laid. I am trying to find a good reason for leaving, but that is the whole point to this trip really in a way. Keep moving forward.

At the Kandy rail station, I was able to wash the black train ash, coal, smoke, steam train grime from my body and change clothes. These trains chase their own pollution around and it settles on everything. I walked around town and saw the clock tower, lots and lots of monks, all kinds of people and even some tourists that seemed to have hired a car, cafes, hotels, lodges, and guesthouses, shops and markets, and the bus station and all the people needed to make it all run and have purpose. I even had time to take in Kandy lake, all in a couple of hours. Kandy was lovely and colonial cute but not my cup of tea at present. I was sitting alongside the Kandy lake and I heard a splash in the water that caused me to look up and see that a pigeon fell into the lake. The pigeon did not flap around after hitting the water. It was like it just fell dead from the sky and floated on the calm lake. It was more like a large pond than a lake. The ripples the falling bird made were traveling outward from the floating carcass. I turned around and saw a guy off to my right, some monk dude wearing sunglasses, just standing there about 30 feet behind me and just seeming to stare forward across the pond and not saying a word. Surely, he must have noticed. No reaction. I wonder if he threw it in the pond.

I went to a nice hotel just for a cup of tea, and to see if they had an English language newspaper I could read. It is a beautiful day and all outdoor tables are full save for one. A little old man with a hearing aid was sitting by himself at a large table for six. He looked like an antique. He looked like an American, so I politely asked if he spoke English and I asked if this end seat was taken and would he mind, and may I please join his table so I could drink my tea outdoors

on such a nice morning. Isn't it just? I thought I was being super polite about something I really did not have to be super polite about, and I could have sat down without a word. Maybe I was too polite. He looked up at me and in a loud whine shouted, "Why pick on me?" Then he got louder and put a higher pitch into his whine when he repeated himself. "Why pick on me!?" I said something like, "Thanks a lot numb nuts, I'm just waiting on a train. I'll have my tea inside." He looked shocked. When I finished and was leaving for the rail station, I noticed the old guy was gone. Times like these I always miss my beach paradise.

February 9. The trains are great. They are cheap, easy, and frequent. They are slow and rock back and forth like they are about to derail, but they get there. It is narrow-gauge lower-class rail fare wooden bench cheap and the light is always on. It is a pain trying to write, but journal entries can kill a lot of time in transit. It could be the early hours of the tenth, but it is late and I am on the train heading for the ferry crossing. Met the engine driver and he let me ride in the cab. He saw me getting off the train at stops and then leaping back on board once the train starts. At one of those stops, he waved me over. He gave me his address in Anuradhapura and said if ever I found myself there, to stop in for a visit. The Kandy to Polonnaruwa train took me west around the central highlands.

Arrived in Polonnaruwa early and basically followed the brochure I had picked up in Hikkaduwa. It had a crude map, and in essence, it said that near the station I could rent a bike and peddle to the stone-carved Buddhas and monuments in a nearby park, which is near a large lake and a nature reserve. It sounded groovy. The morning found me pedaling to Polonnaruwa and there was not a lot of people or traffic. The village or town was only a mile or two from the station and the park entrance was next to the town. It has been a pilgrim site for centuries.

The park was fairly deserted save for groups of monks and Buddhists in yellow and orange robes, some local tourists, and me. I was not the only person on a bike. The Reclining Buddha was twelfth-century amazing. Spent a while looking at it and came back to it as I cycled around the park. Easy flat cycling. It made me think about the Buddha of Bamiyan and all the amazing things I have seen. Felt good about being on the move again and all the possible things out ahead of me on the road to Kathmandu.

The park and all the carvings and monuments were deeply moving. It really did feel like a place of pilgrimage. I was really digging it. Surprised the

British had not carted it off for the British Museum. I was approached by a young dude in brown robes with a stick and brass bowl tied to his wrist. He had a small shoulder bag and a well-rehearsed spiel. He did not speak much English, but his recited lines were understandable. He said, "My name is Devadas and I am on a pilgrimage. My guru has sent me to India and I have secured a letter."

I thought he said David at first. He went on about his guru and going to see people. He wanted to secure help for his journey and he was searching for a sponsor. I told him I had very little money, but I could give him something. Then he had a heart to heart talk, with me, with himself—I am not sure, but I could tell by his voice. I could only understand half of what he was saying. I thought he said I was a parade. He offered me a drink of a honey and lemon and pepper concoction he carried in a bottle. I tried it and it was nice. I gave him the coins from my pocket. He said he knew magic tricks and offered to show me some. He asked if he could show me a trick on my bicycle. He handed me his stick and bundle. I watched him climb aboard the bike and peddle furiously down the straight dirt road of the park. I could see quite some ways down the road and I watched this guy literally disappear with my bike. I was thinking I could not believe he stole it. Then I saw what was in my hands. I knew I had to stop jumping to too

many conclusions—the fat lady had not sung. I think that may have been his magic trick. At that instant, it seemed he was coming back, but he was still far away, and it was hard to tell. A few moments later, he came flying past me, no hands and standing on the bike seat and grinning like a nut. I hung out with him for a while and he wanted to talk a lot and ask a lot of questions. I could not understand half of it, though I did not mind, and he was mellow and quietly curious, and then he asked for a ride to Polonnaruwa. I thought I may have a train travel companion. Instead, he wanted to get dropped off at a friend's house or the house of a potential sponsor. I agreed, and he rode sidesaddle on the crossbar. It took me a while to get the hang of it and when I finally did, he said "Stop," and we were there. It was sort of on the outskirts of town, at a semi-busy afternoon intersection. He hopped off the bike and I followed suit and was wrestling the bike up the curb. When I looked up, he was gone. I could not see him anywhere. That whole encounter played out quickly and I pedaled back to the Reclining Buddha.

When the tide at last is slain and the fishermen dry their nets in the sun, the moth returns to burn in the flame, and the mistress of the moon is won. The night casts its long black stain along the running sand where she slides, and for everything she gives a name, slain in the deep by the tides.

11

Bangalore to Mangalore

February 10. On the boat to Rameswaram. Thank god, I kept hold of the old canceled traveler's checks. I would not get in without them. Goodbye to Sri Lanka and hello India.

February 14. Hung out with Ron for a few days and put the still valid tourist liquor license to good use, enjoying bottles of beer with Ron and his dad. I told them stories of Sri Lanka, leaving out certain parts. Ron got his job in Oman and was leaving in a couple of weeks. It was easy to see Ron's dad was sad about it.

February 15. Took the time to quietly take stock of my finances. I have enough money to live in Hikkaduwa for six months, and then I start begging. I have enough money to get to Kathmandu and hang out for a couple of weeks, and then I start begging. Maybe I should start begging now. I wrote to my parents asking to borrow 200 bucks and asked if they could send it to Kathmandu as a backup plan. I have to sell my camera. That is a realistic plan. I have been calling it the albatross since Kabul.

This village suburb of Madurai has one phone for a couple of hundred houses. It is located in the post office. On occasions, I can hear it ringing in the still, breezeless hot afternoon. Ron misses Germany and talks about it a lot.

February 16. I tried to help with a bunch of tasks as much as they would let me. Fetching water and getting stuff from the market. The idea of me keeping a journal amuses Ron no end. He laughs at me when he sees me writing. Ron is amazed I brought my camera all this way. It is not top of the line but it is pretty good. Nikon body with Minolta lenses. He has lived in Germany for a while and knows the variance of economies. East meet west and west meets east. He

worked for the Agfa color film labs, and he knows something about cameras. He asked what I paid for it. He said that was what his dad earned in a year and no one really has things like these. He said it is not like Europe where everybody has a camera. He laughed and said if I could have seen him when he was fifteen, he would have begged to hold it. He said, "Of course everyone would want to check it out if they saw it."

February 17. Ron said a friend of Dave's had been hanging around and could I leave with this guy so he is not hanging around when Ron goes off to Oman in a couple of weeks. I am thinking Dave is giving out addresses that are not his. Dave blew through town while I was in Sri Lanka. The gist of it is, Ron said, Dave jettisoned a kilo or two of girlie magazines along with this Canadian dude named Rick who kept showing up every couple of days. I wondered, but it was not the same Rick. Ron was thinking trains. He said he is trying to convince this dude to go to Kerala. There are no straight easy trains back to Madurai. I get where he wants me to go with this. And take Rick along. Maybe this cat is a proficient cool traveler. I do not relish the push and shove of traveling in India on the cheap again. I may not get to the cape.

February 19. The days are hot and the nights are cool. Ron is such a great guy. I wonder if we will ever meet up again. Ron was very happy to see Rick and myself off at the station on the night train to Quilon. I am running third-class rail and living as cheap as I can. I cannot get over that the locals love something called beetle. The dudes chew it like tobacco and it is spicy and turns red. There is red spit everywhere. Dudes grin at you with red teeth like a polite vampire. Rick is ok; he just seems a bit slow and unaware of what is around him—at least for now.

We waited at the pier for our boat to Alleppey. The tourist board brochures sealed the deal for Rick. I heard good things about this part of India and it is wonderful. It would take months, and money I do not have, to explore and travel the state of Kerala. The boat was like a waterbus, and it spent the next ten hours picking people up and dropping people off, while navigating a maze of canals, lakes, ponds, and rivers. It was the best public transport ride of my entire trip. I was mesmerized, and I mentioned to Rick that this was pretty cool being on this waterbus. He kind of looked at me and grunted. I could not tell from the minute we got aboard, until we climbed off the boat, whether or not he hated it or liked it. He sat with his backpack on his lap almost the entire boat trip. What a weirdo. A one point I said he could set his bag down if he wanted.

In Alleppey, I told Rick that I had heard there were some really groovy and nice beaches north of here towards Cochin. Rick said, "No, I don't like beaches." I said, "Rick, you don't know what you're missing dude." Turns out that Rick does not like boats either.

I am going to try to hang out with Rick and maybe to help him adjust his attitude. He is a lump of a downer. I tell him I am going to Bombay and then Raxaul. He does not ask why or anything.

We were in Alleppey and I was trying to impress upon the lad that there was an endless buffet to choose from. The adventure does not start until you choose, but choose you must or there is no adventure. I said the beaches were a good option. He had a stack of India tourist board brochures and he showed me one for a place in the hills called Ootacamund. Did not like beaches, did not like boats, well what about hills then.

February 20. Rick seems oblivious to the need to figure out how to get somewhere. I explained that to get to Ootacamund we needed to catch a bus then a train and then another bus. He seemed perplexed that the Indian rail did not run from where he was standing, all the way to where he wanted to go. Sometimes they do. I said I checked it out and it seemed straightforward. A bus to Kottayam and then the train to Coimbatore. I gave him my Indian rail times book. He could not make heads nor tails out of it. At one point, I thought he was going to turn it upside down. How did he get way the fuck out here? People helping him, I guess. Could be this is how Dave thinks of me? Holy shit. No fucking way. I have a map and a plan. I have been places.

The train journey would have been a challenge for anyone experienced with overland travel. For Rick, it was a bad trip drag. I have heard about and seen worse, but this was weird and heartbreaking. The heartbreaking part happened about an hour into the journey. At one of the many stops, a woman crawled on the train just before it departed. She is in rags and is wailing. She obviously just had one of her legs amputated. It was a fresh and still bleeding wound. It was truly shocking to everyone. She was crying, begging, and crawling through the cars. Some of the local dudes said in English that she did it to herself to get more money when begging. The train had left the station and was rumbling into this woman's tragic future. The sight of her on the floor made me almost cry. I gave her a handful of coins; there was no more I could do, and that made me sad too. Rick was glued to his seat in the crowded car and he looked like he had seen a ghost. The woman crawled off the train a few stations later.

An hour after that, a crazy-type guy boarded the train and sat next to Rick. He was tall, big, and beefy for an Indian. I mean most local dudes are thin and reedy like me. I was sitting across from Rick, so I found myself under his wild-eyed gaze. He said he was from Calcutta. He spoke rapidly, calmly, and furiously all at the same time. If I did not know any better, I would say he was tripping on LSD. His rapid-fire monologue got a little loud and angry at times. I really had not said anything other than "Hello." Rick looked like he was about to shit a brick. Rick was in his usual pose with his backpack in his lap. The gist of this monologue was something about world education. I could not tell if he was for it or against it. He said we were on parade. I immediately remembered the crazy nice bicycle monk in Sri Lanka said the same thing. I also tried to immediately remember his name. Shit, it is not David. He was asking us questions as if we were taking a test in school, but he never waited for an answer. He seemed to be annoying everyone else on the train. He was attracting a lot of attention to himself at this point. He called us fools, fools, fools. The only time I spoke to him was in reply to the fool's comment. I threw my hands in the air and shouted in his face, "Yes, we are fools, we are all fools." I laughed, and he did not. He looked shocked and did not say anything. The train guard came by and told him to shut up. At least that would be my guess at the meaning of the volume and body language. I told the guard he was ten minutes too late. The man from Calcutta got off the train an hour later. What a grumpy morning commuter is to me is a demon crazy man from hell for Rick.

I sat next to Rick and talked to him for a while after the weird shit had calmed down. I think I was really talking to myself. I said something about not trying to take the chaos personally. I turned to him and spoke in a slow and low voice. I told him if we had caught a later train or were 300 miles east of where we are now, who knows what kind of scene is going on, or what other people and travelers are out there to meet. We would have missed this weird scary dude and possibly met up with someone worse. Who knows what is out there? What kinds of cities and temples must fill the plains, the hills, and the beaches? I glanced over and noticed Rick was looking even more frightened. Big help I was. We caught the bus and wound our way the last few miles to Ootacamund. It was a lovely ride, snaking upwards into the forests and into the cool air. Rick does not like Ootacamund.

February 21. The days are hot. Despite this bummer barnacle stuck to my ship, I managed to meet a pretty groovy Australian girl, Lea. I was digging the scenery and what a beautiful place Ooty is, and I met her in the market. We discovered we were heading in the same direction and we decided to go as far as Mysore together. Ootacamund to Mysore by bus. I did not even say anything to Rick and he just sort of tagged along, which was alright by me.

I noticed the bags of rice and luggage and young kids getting packed on the roof as we shuffled up to the bus. It was not going to be a high-speed voyage. I passed my backpack up to guys stacking the roof rack and found the driver. I collected a small crowd as I told the driver I wanted my seat, but I was going to ride on the roof for a few hours and when I got down, I wanted to have my seat again. He understood. He could double sell the seat for a few hours. The locals were chattering about it and translating it. Lea wanted the same ticket deal I was having. Rick found a seat inside the bus and I imagined him sitting with his bag in his lap. I climbed the back ladder.

Lea was a seasoned savvy traveler who even adopted local dress and headscarves. She was going to meet up with some old traveling buddies in Mysore. She had come over from Thailand and did not know how much further towards the Middle East she was going. I noticed her sort of looking me over and after looking at my feet, I realized how grubby I looked. My feet were really dirty and sooty. The dirty threadbare cotton pajama trousers did not help. I realized I had not had a wash in a while. She asked where I was from and where I was going and so I gave her the truncated version of the overland from Munich story. It had a new part

about Sri Lanka. She was impressed. I said something about not having a bath since Jerusalem. I said I was on my way to Kathmandu. She has been there. I told her I was very envious, and she laughed at my use of the word envious and she spoke for hours about Thailand, and a place called Bhutan. She talked a lot about Nepal and gave me the name of a hotel she said I should stay in Kathmandu and even recommended a trek into the mountains. I wrote it down. I told her that a few weeks ago I wanted to travel from Bangalore to Mangalore just because of the way it rhymed. She laughed and said yes, it seemed that way sometimes.

I said, "I bet you keep a journal." She looked at me and said, "Of course I do." I said, "You can be in my journal if I can be in yours." She laughed at that. We hung out chatting on the roof of the bus for four hours. I do not think she has done this mode of transport before. She was digging it. You can lean back on a sack of rice and watch the world roll by. Back in the bus before sundown and we rolled into Mysore. Lea said "see ya," and was gone like smoke.

Rick was still moping around with his brochures. He said something about wanting to see a local sandalwood plantation; the first time I have seen Rick close to being animated. Turns out sandalwood is tightly regulated and controlled. I wanted to buy a lump of wood for a souvenir. Rick wanted one to carve. I think Rick woke up. We got there too late and they were closed for a few days. *No entrada.* Rick was bummed.

I thought about looking up the college girls I met on the train heading south. I had Rene's address. No way could I explain Rick. I said I was getting the train to Bangalore and then another train north in the direction of Bombay and he could tag along if he wanted to. He said, "Ok I guess." We found ourselves in the waiting rooms of the Bangalore train station. We met a couple of gregarious dudes from Rome. One of the dudes was rattling on about Ginsberg, Kerouac, Dylan, and American music. Traveling will do that to you. These guys would have been my never-ending party dudes at my beach hut. They were great. One of the dudes said I must be Bob from Tucson. Turns out, he met Dave on the boat from Sri Lanka to India. He said it is a small world. I said I must have been described well enough for a line up.

Rick said he wanted to see sandalwood trees. Rick announced he was going back to Mysore. He wanted to know if he could pick up a piece for me while he was there. He said he was going to go to Kathmandu later and would bring it to me and keep in touch via *Poste Restante*. I told old Rick to be careful and get a decent hotel, like the Retiring Rooms at a large rail station in a big city, like Mysore. It was the only advice I could give him. Rick seemed inspired. We exchanged addresses. He wanted to get there ASAP and wait until the plantation opened. I had never seen him hustle his ass that fast before. As a man on a mission, he was on the platform waiting for his train to Mysore two hours early. I told him to take care and have a safe trip and I wished Rick well. At least he did not wait until he got to Bombay to decide. Three hours later, I was on the train north to Hubli. Five hours later, I knew I would never see my $5 or Rick again. Six hours later, I was thinking I should have been the one who returned to Mysore.

The train rolls through the huge landscape of southern India, from farms and fields and towns and stations, and the endless villages with the dirt road crossing the tracks with people waiting as the train hurtles by.

I am aware as the train departs Hubli, I am a stone's throw from the shores of Goa. The hippie Mecca—or one of the hippie Meccas. I did think it would be a good jumping-off point for a coastal journey to Kerala. Head south to the beaches and avoid the crowds. I am tempted. The tall tales call like a siren, and I have heard them since living in Europe. Alice's Restaurant. You can get anything you want. Free love and cheap weed. The stronger than rum addicts keep the smack and coke business afloat. Boom times ahead with the never-ending summertime cocktail party parade and I may get laid.

The reality is creepy, super seedy, grimy, and risky. On cue at the first stop, three tourists climb into the railcar and compartment I am riding in. The one girl and two dudes that make up this trio were agitated and brittle. After a while of chatting to them, it transpires that the three of them have been in Goa for a few months and doing a lot of opium and only just realized they have not had a shit in five weeks and they are rushing home to France to see a doctor. Flight from Bombay I think. I think I will remember the opium the next time I get the shits like I did in New Delhi.

Met a really cool tourist on the train. Helaine is from Sao Paulo; she was meeting friends in Bombay and knew what she was doing and where she was going. We talked for hours and she volunteered her phone number and said if ever I was in Brazil.

February 23. I was hit with a stick. While sleeping on the rail platform at the Victoria Terminus in Bombay. At any given time, there are a few dozen or even a hundred or so people waiting on trains in various poses of repose.

The nights are scary and the worst with the cops walking around with their bamboo staffs, picking on the beggars and poor travelers and dishing out bamboo whacks. They walk around stabbing at the concrete floor with their staffs and making a sound akin to jackboots marching. Whacks on backs, the back of the legs, and wrapped knuckles and whacks on hands that are upstretched and beg for mercy. I have watched the cops grab beggar kids by the ears and throw them around. I have watched them at their routine for a couple of days and nights now. Again, the poor travelers huddle in the dark corners of the station.

It was around 3 a.m. when a couple of cops were rousting people. With my backpack in left luggage, I was wrapped in my cotton sleeping bag and looked like a local. When I got whacked, I popped up and said, "Hey man," and added, "Why are you hitting me?" They were immediately shocked and contrite.

I went to the address of the woman I met at the film expo in Madras. She said to stop in for a visit when I was in Bombay, she said she knew a buyer for my camera. However, her housekeeper butler dude had other ideas and told me in no uncertain terms to take a hike. Mrs. Tayson is not receiving visitors.

This plan to sell my camera in Bombay is not looking likely. I have taken to perusing the camera shops and the odd electronic shop, but there are not that many around. I dashed up here as cheap and as fast as I could, sort of. I am down to $200. Did a little sightseeing. Saw the house Gandhi lived in. Lincoln slept here. The Gateway to India. The tourists flock to it like pigeons. A couple of museums. The money I am saving sleeping rough pays for normal tourist stuff, and I even mailed some postcards. Stopped at Poona on the way to Bombay. Another stop on the parade route. Heard it was a supposed hippie nirvana. Lots of Sadhus so it must be on a pilgrimage site or route. Five rupees to take a photo. Orange and crimson color for robes, scarfs, and turbans and head wear. Little possessions save for a weed pipe, trident, designer sun glasses and a human skull. Some sort of gray powder rubbed on the arms and faces. Cheap lodgings and weed. Did not see many hippies though saw some tourists. Stayed a day.

While riding on the train I saw a fruit seller with the proverbial thousand-yard stare. I asked him if I could take a photo of him. He said I could as long as I bought some of his fruit. He made change from the coins he kept in his ear.

Sadhu posing for money, Poona, India. (*R. L. Kreamer, Kodachrome 35-mm print film, © 1978, 2019*)

Fruit seller on a train, somewhere in India. (*R. L. Kreamer, Kodachrome 35-mm print film,* © *1978, 2019*)

Saw an elderly woman pass away in line waiting for train tickets. She was in the Ladies Only line and she reached out and said, "Oh baba, help me." She clutched my shirt with a vice-like grip as I lowered her to the ground and I shouted for a doctor. I knew there was little to no likelihood of a doctor being near. Her friends were with her. People ran from the scene and people ran to the scene. She held my hand and I held her hand until the end because I did not know what else to do. I cried.

February 24. There are cows everywhere and I watched a large black bull blocking traffic at a major intersection. Everyone was afraid to go near it. I am still sleeping in the Bombay Victoria Terminus. It is kind of grubby. I discreetly left very early in the morning and tried to sell my camera. No directory or yellow pages, so I asked and wandered. At night, I checked my stuff in with my backpack at left luggage. I returned to the station around 9 p.m. The station has inexpensive wash facilities and retiring rooms. Late trains and early trains have a chasm of quiet and uncertainty between them. The night sees the beggar children long scattered and now hiding at their place of rest.

February 26. On the train to Daulatabad. That is my *entrada*. The rock carvings and caves of Ajanta and Ellora—that is my route. This is about eight hours by train.

Turned a corner on an arbitrary street in Bombay and chanced to notice a shop with posters for film and cameras. The posters were sun bleached and void of the color red, and what was left was fading pale blue images and faded writing. I am surprised I recognized it as a camera shop. He was a middle-aged guy. The shop had no lights on and it was dark with pale blue light filtering in. He was describing to someone on the phone the camera body, lens, and filters that were laid out on his counter in front of him. I walked out with $360 U.S. cash. He said he was saving his client money because of the luxury tax in India. I did not even haggle. I even had the instruction books to hand over. It was like a miracle. I had Ron's dad's year's wages in my Indian cotton pajama pocket. My total holdings were increased significantly. Sometimes you have to sell the family silver. I could get back to Hikkaduwa and live on the beach in comfort for a year or two.

After converting most of the money into traveler's checks, some in rupees, and keeping some dollars, I mailed the rolls of exposed film, some gifts, clothes, souvenirs, and ticket stub-type maps and stuff back home to Germany for $15. They stitched the box up tight in cotton cloth like a shroud, tied it with coarse string, and sealed it with a big lump of wax on both sides. It had its custom forms and postage stamps glued on it and I made sure it was franked. Goodbye to carrying too much shit. I washed and put on clean clothes.

February 27. Ajanta and Ellora were more than worth the visit. Magic. Magic and very hard work carving intricate and huge temples and figures from solid rock for a thousand years. Ancient and holy sites for sure. They are about 40 miles apart. It is like an ancient anchor.

Met a French-Swiss guy at the Daulatabad station cafe and he was going to Ellora. He called himself Michael. We hit it off and traveled to Ellora and Ajanta by bus, and spent the day sightseeing together. First time in a while doing some sort of sightseeing routine with someone who enjoys it and is cool and easy going about everything. It was all cool. I think he really does speak some English. I think we understand each other for some reason. We spent some time wandering some ways, away from the tourists, and having a discrete joint or two—his stuff and then my stuff.

We exchanged a rundown of capital cities where we have been to, as a kind of Rosetta Stone. It was a friendly contest he started, and it seemed he was eager to play. Him in French and me in English. We had a lot of European capital visits in common, but he did have more than a few on me. He was used to winning his little game. Running away with it. When we got to capitals like Beirut, Tehran, Kabul, Colombo, and a few more, I garnered a little surprised disbelief and maybe a little admiration from him. He was not used to a spirited return volley. I thought I broke even. It was a surreal day; the tourists we met and greeted as if we were some sort of ambassadors were amused, perhaps a little surprised, and maybe a little envious. He is one of the few cats I have met that I would look forward to meeting again somewhere in this crazy world. He does not like my name. He was puzzled about Bob being from the name Robert. He asked me to write Robert down, and when he saw it, he said row bear. He said, "Yes, I forgot, the English say Robert and the French say row bear." He called me row bear the entire time.

He asked me a lot of questions about Sri Lanka. He kept asking me about it, so, I told him. I left out some details but left in the important ones. He could find the beaches south of Hikkaduwa effortlessly. The Reclining Buddha and hills around Kandy. Narrow gauge rail. I found myself saying it like I wanted to go back. I showed him my rail timetable book and rail map. This was another Rosetta stone. He thumbed through it like a kid who grew up using trains. He even made some notes for his own journey. I was impressed. He said he was going to get this timetable. I said that he could do it in a few days, maybe on a beach, feet in the water somewhere well south of Colombo in a week. He liked the idea of using the train and retiring rooms like a hotel. He asked me about the trains in Sri Lanka; he did not like the idea of riding third class to save money and traveling with the great horde.

Rough road and long bus ride to Jalgaon. Michael found his train to Bombay. With the obligatory exchange of addresses, he was gone. With the obligatory regret of not taking Michael up on his proposal to travel together to Sri Lanka, I found my train to Itarsi. I had a few hours to mull things over.

12

Crossing the Ganges and the Road to Kathmandu

March 1. Traveling is severe. Traveled while sitting on my bag near the train door. Near the toilet. The gut and butt volcano came back. Long ride with lots of stops.

Good seat for watching all the coming and goings. Watched a woman leave a child on the train platform of a large town. Her child, whose child, I do not know. She gave the child a little push away on to the platform as the train started to pick up speed as it departed the station and the kid fell off the train. The woman calmly walked back through the car and kept going. I said "Hey, what the fuck." Everyone around was quiet, pretending not to notice. The last view I had of the platform was with the child picking himself up with a bewildered and frightened look on his face. Now I know where all the train station children came from.

March 2. Trying times. Still freaked out about yesterday. This train journey is a pain in the ass. Had a short while to walk around Itarsi again. The second place in India I have been twice. The plague of flies had departed. Feeling a little battered by the push, shove, hassle, and hustle.

I was having tea in a cafe and watching the road outside. I noticed a group of cows in the street, and one starts to pee an enormous stream. Some dude runs out of a neighboring shop and takes a long drink from the pee spout. Another dude runs up too late for a drink. Commiserations offered to the dude who was too late by the guy who bogarted all the wee. Wow. I remembered reading in *The Times of India* that the new Prime Minister of India is into drinking urine. Wow again. Boarded my train at 9 p.m. It was packed shoulder to shoulder everywhere until 4 a.m., even the floors. Three of us found our way to the mail car while searching for relief from the crush of people.

Katsumasa, a dude from Japan, a local kid, and me all found seats on the mail sacks. We had been there for a couple of hours and had been talking.

A fat middle-aged fat sweaty fat guy in a suit showed up in our car and started kicking and shouting at the local kid. The gist was color coded. The fat cat wanted the local kid to give up his seat because the fat cat was of a higher caste. Katsumasa spoke up in protest. I was right behind. The locals sided with the fat man. It got a little ugly and the Mexican standoff lasted an hour. Some people got off and there was room for the fat man and his cronies to sit down. The fat man spent a long time glaring at us and wiping the sweat from his face. The local kid spent a long time looking scared.

Time and distance jettisons and receives the riders from the train, at stations large and small, like the fragile throwaway clay teacups the chai sellers pass around like communion. They ride for a few hours, take a bow, and are replaced with a new ensemble. All except for me, for now. Not so sure about anything. Late in the afternoon, I saw a kid on a camel walking faster than the train. I had a déjà vu moment and I could not remember if I saw that kid on a camel a couple of months ago, or just now. On the way into Varanasi, I passed a town and station called Robertsganj. I liked it and decided I was now more a Robert than a Bob or a row bear.

March 3. The train discharges you in the middle of it all. Downtown Varanasi. Got a bicycle rickshaw. The Sadhus, people toing and froing, the cows and people everywhere crazy crowded. It is a place of pilgrimage. The Sadhus usher the ash of the dead into the river. They will tend the pyre to the end. They will break your skull.

Staying at the Government Tourist Bungalow. Went out for an early walk. Old man gave me a walking stick; I asked him why, and he said it was for the dogs. He said there are corpses in the river. Sometimes bachelors or the children who die do not have a pyre; their bodies are put in the river and sometimes come to shore and are eaten by stray dogs—docile during the day and aggressive at night. All are wary of a person with a stick. The river seemed wide, muddy, flat as a pancake, and hardly flowing, and I encountered some dogs along the way. In the distance were some men by a small fire. As I walked past, I said hello and they said hello. The Sadhus were naked save for ash and face paint. The small fire they tended had a perfect unblemished foot sticking out that they were gradually feeding into the flames. The sun still had a couple of hours before it rose. I hustle for your money, I will hustle for your head, and when I am lowered in the ground, I will hustle for the dead.

March 5. Train to Sagauli was slow and not very crowded. No train to Raxaul, they said it was late. A man with a bucket and a few clean-looking towels was walking through the train carriages, offering to provide a shave for one rupee. He had one eye. I waved him over and after explaining I wanted to keep the moustache and mutton chops, he unwrapped his trusty cutthroat and razor strap. He did a very good job with no nicks or cuts. A large group of people gathered to watch. You would think they had never seen a one-eyed man shave a gringo on a moving train before. Rode on the roof of a bus with fifteen other people into Raxaul Train station and found it had a place to wash and change into clean clothes. Noticed my hiking boots were missing. Somewhere between here and Mysore, they have gone missing. I know I packed them at Ron's place, and I cannot remember a change in the weight of my bag.

Crossed the border into Nepal. Found the bus to Kathmandu.

March 7. Long bus ride. Night driving through the hills. Arrived at 5 a.m. and wandered from the almost-empty bus station through the almost-empty streets to the main post office in the grey of early morning. There were a few people going about their business and everything is closed. I found a park and propped myself against a tree and dozed. I woke some time later to the sight and sound of the latest recruits to the Nepalese army learning left and right. Left and right. Everything is open now, and while still waking up, I made my way to the post office. I walked from the light into the dark post office building. My eyes were adjusting

when I heard a voice say "Bob." It was Dave. Dave said, "Bob, your brother is here." Nothing registered. I said something like, "How's it going Dave?" It was genuinely good to see him. Dave just repeated himself and led me to a side counter window. There taped to the other side of the glass among the various notices in Nepalese and English was my brother's Arizona driver's license.

I was served by a clerk with an extra finger on each hand working stamps at the Poste Restante window. I had four letters sent to me in care of Kathmandu. When we left the post office, Dave said he was staying at the Mustang Lodge and it was this way. He pointed. I asked how much he was paying for a room. He said it was a dorm style. I said I had heard from someone about this other hotel, and she said it is on Freak Street, just off Durbar Square. I said I think it is this way. I told Dave that I was going to wash and read my letters and maybe sleep. I told him I just got in and said that we should meet up later. I gave him a hug and said, "Good to see ya brother"—and I meant it. I still find hard to believe. I made it to Kathmandu.

March 8. Staying at the Hotel Manang. It is laid back, cheap, and I have my own room and key—it is groovy. Kathmandu is everything and more than my little brain could imagine. The heart of the city is old and made from wood. Lots of ornate carvings. Must be one of the few medieval cities not to have burned down because of a careless baker. I am staying right off Durbar Square. Ornately carved wooden building and temples are otherworldly.

Spent part of the day yesterday tracking down my brother. It was great to see him. He had flown out from Europe without any of the rigors of overland travel and had just completed a trek from the Kathmandu valley to the first Everest camp. He looked fresh and well fed. He said he flew back in a light plane. He said it flew over the miles and miles of his constant uphill or downhill walk over endless valleys and hills that he had just spent a couple of weeks hiking.

He has had his share of mishaps with the locals since I have been hanging out with him. He is wearing a crisp white polo shirt like he is playing tennis. We are walking through crowded streets; there is a man with a long pole that he is maneuvering sideways through the crowd, laden with heavy baskets of fruit and vegetables that are hanging from the pole. I have to go with the pole guy on this. Everybody saw him coming through but one. My brother was being inattentive, and the pole lightly poked him in the chest, but hard enough to leave a black greasy stain. His exclamation of "Hey!"

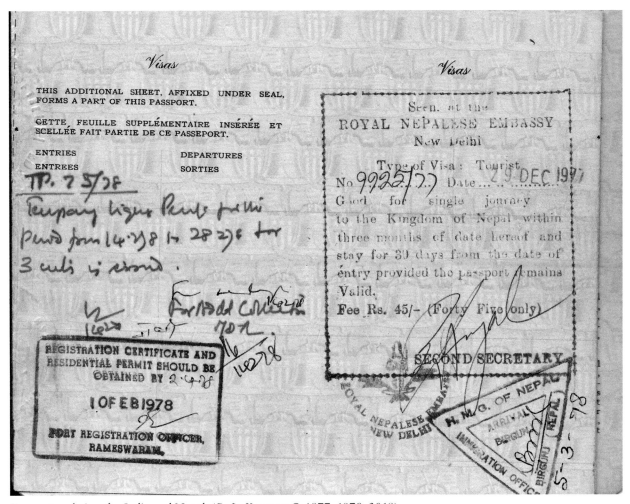

Passport and visas for India and Nepal. (*R. L. Kreamer © 1977, 1978, 2019*)

caused the man to stop and set down his burden. My brother is talking about a dry-cleaning bill. The man thinks he has made a sale and holds up a melon. I asked my brother what he wanted to pay for the melon. We continued along the streets and a woman leaned out from an upper window and blew her nose into the air. Unfortunately, it landed on my brother, Dave. He said "Hey," and let it be known that he just had this shirt cleaned. I said, "Dave, that's not what I would call a lucky shirt."

He has made a point of calling me Bob. I had called myself that for a couple of years now, but the family per se never cottoned to it. It is a different name I use out in the world I suppose. It was something separate—sort of. Bob coming from him, does sound weird though. We have made an *ad hoc* plan for trekking. Right now, it is Dave, Dave, and me. We are going to the Langtang. I mention it was one I had heard about from somebody who went to Bhutan. My brother, Dave, said he would look into it. The weather is supposed to be good for it.

I bought maps and it is a bus ride and couple of days hiking to get to the start of the hike.

The letters I received were wonderful and were really welcomed. It was like I had been at sea for ten years. Those months of sending postcards had a return. I got a letter from my old flame. I am dumped for sure. Still, her letter made me want her even more. I am sure my letters to her have been too needy and I should have stuck with the overland travel stories. My mother sent me a letter; she included $180—I am so grateful. I got a postcard from my buddy, Dave, about my brother, Dave, being here in Kathmandu. He was not sure if we would run into each other. It was a postcard of the Treasury in Petra. I even got a letter from my buddy in Tucson I have known since I was fourteen. Damon wrote, "Dear Robert, this is senseless because you will never receive this letter."

March 9. We need our trekking permits and it is something my brother and I got on to right away, just like a competition. We got ours before lunch. The other

Dave is now in the big after-lunch trekking permit queue. My brother and I went for a walk. It started weird, but it ended pretty cool. It took a little while for my brother to relax a little. He had his map out and was finding north like a scoutmaster. I pointed out we could see across the valley and there was Swayambhu on the only hill for miles. He was OK with me suggesting he may want to stop flapping the map around, relax, and try not to look so touristy. So we went to the monkey temple.

I had been forewarned about the monkey's fondness for snatching glasses, hats, books, bags, food, lit cigarettes, and anything else they can get their hands on from unsuspecting tourists. I mentioned this to my brother. At the bottom of the long flight of stairs up to the temple, we stashed anything that could get snatched into our bags. As we climbed the stairs, we talked about the litter of twisted and broken sunglasses, a torn book, a tourist map, and bits of paper on the left side of the stairs in the dirt. We could hear and see the monkeys in the trees above. There was a pair of glasses hanging from a tree.

I surprised my brother when I offered a banana to a solo standing monkey. I surprised the monkey too I think. I said, "It is a monkey temple, one of us had to bring an offering."

It took us about two and a half hours of walking to get to these steps. He talked about getting a degree and now he is getting another one. He likes science and he is having girlfriend troubles. News of my siblings and parents. I am shocked how old he looks; he must be twenty-seven. He spoke about his trek up to Namche Bazaar and how different everything was. He wants to do another trek and then he has a plane to catch. It forces me to think of my return. My version of the rat race. I told him about my travels. It was an amazing temple. As we descended the stairs, we heard

the cries of tourists being deprived of their goods by the monkeys. My brother spent some time explaining how to keep things from getting snatched after the fact to the tourists. I could have sworn the monkey I gave the banana to saluted me.

We were supposed to meet the other Dave in the large park in the evening. The other Dave brought along two girls. The other Dave was showing a map to the girls. My brother was lounging on a bench with another more-detailed map of Langtang route. I noticed the dude right away. A harmless little old man was carrying a brass tray and had stumbled into our circle. He was a Sadhu and seemed a hundred years old. For a few pennies laid on his antique tray, he would put a smudge of color on your forehead. The exquisitely engraved tray held a small butter lamp, flowers, coins, and a small pot of smudge. I gave the old man a few coins, said an amen for our little trek, and thanked him. I must have over tipped. He decided to give everyone a dot on the forehead and started for my brother who was blissfully unaware behind a map, deep in study. I thought I was being helpful when I warned Dave with a "Heads up brother." He peered over the map and lord knows what he thought of the little old man with an outstretched finger of red rouge and a huge grin under a long wispy beard. Dave was startled and yelled "Hey," and held his map up like a shield. Instead of Dave's forehead, he put a dot right on the Langtang valley. I took it as a good omen.

The other Dave, the girls, and myself all got dots, and later my brother did, too. I got to talk with the girls a little. The other Dave was way aggressive about the blonde girl. She is like an R. Crumb drawing. After asking, I told the other Dave the girls needed to get their trekking permits and how about tomorrow morning. There is only one afternoon bus.

13

The Roof of the World

March 12. Bus to Dhunche took all day. Rode on top. The girls Dave is traveling with are nice. Canadian and French Canadian, I think. Walked a couple of days to Rimche, though it felt like three weeks. We met other tourists trekking and we walked at our own pace through the day. There are any number of guest type teahouses to stop at along the way. We are walking towards the Himalayas and it is an awesome sight. The vista slowly changes and comes slightly nearer as we cover the distance. The view is right in front of us, and we are walking into it.

After a couple of days, I slowed. I am pacing myself. The ski knee from Kashmir and the Delhi gut is bothersome. This trail is a busy foot highway with people and yak traffic. It would be hard to get lost. My crew is out ahead by half a day as I plod along. It is starting to rain. I try to clear my mind.

March 14. Cloudy, cold, and raining. I caught up to everyone. I thought they were being nice, and they had waited for me; turns out, they were out of breath with the climb in altitude and they had not paced themselves. My brother is going on and on about the dangers and symptoms of altitude sickness. The vistas and views are awe-inspiring, with every corner turning into a grander backdrop than the one before. I said my ski knee and my gut are much better thank you and I felt great. The other Dave looked at me mystified. We were stopped at a tearoom, hotel-type place. It looked like a large wicker basket turned upside down and someone cut out a door opening on the side. At our outdoor seats with a view, I fired up a joint and asked Dave if he wanted to get high. My brother said he did not smoke, and the other Dave said maybe later. The girls got high with me. We marched out of the forests of monkeys and rhododendrons and headed up into the steep sided valley. Crossed a huge scree slope from a massive old landslide then climbed into a treeless landscape. Staying at a rather large lodge with a large open space dorm for sleeping. It is crowded with locals and tourist trekkers, and it is cold and wet. My cheap Indian sneakers have bled the cheap blue dye into my feet. While drying my socks and shoes by the stove, I find myself constantly reassuring someone that I do not have frostbite. I bought some candles from the guest lodge and melted the wax on to my shoes in hopes of making them waterproof.

We passed some local traffic on the trail. People heading up and down from the Langtang carrying all manner of stuff and herding yaks as well. It seems every time we pass a yak, it wants to head butt and nudge Dave's blonde girl friend off the trail. She is beginning to take it personally.

Some tourist trekker at the lodge tells a tale like a ghost story. I had heard this in Kathmandu. A couple was out on a trek back in the late '60s and the woman gets kidnapped and spirited away into the wilds somewhere, without a trace of her anywhere—God knows where in these mountains—so the man she was with returns every year to search for her.

My brother is a real comedian. One afternoon, my brother was hiking behind me. He spent hours picking up tiny pebbles from the path. He would then creep up behind me and place the rock carefully and gently in the fold, or under a strap, or on top of my backpack, taking the utmost care that I would not notice. That I would not notice both the gradual increase in weight and my brother leaping about behind, mimicking my movements to time the placement of the rock just so. I

Buying knives while trekking to the Langtang Valley, Nepal. The Ganesh Himalayan mountain range is in the background. (*Photo kindly lent by David Kreamer, Fuji Color 100 disposable camera film, scan from old print,* © *1978, 2019*)

took my pack from my back and watched the cascade of pebbles hit the ground. It was over 10 pounds of extra weight that I was carrying. He said he did me a favor because trekking will seem easer now.

From a group of local dudes and kids, I bought a couple of really old Gurkha knives. They huddled together as a group to decide the price. I did not even haggle. They have carved wooden sheaths. Dave's friend Mimi was there and my brother took a photo of us with one these kids. The views of the Ganesh Himalaya are astonishing. The water in the streams and rivers flow from glaciers and is freezing for washing. Prayer flags fly everywhere.

It snowed. We had reached the Langtang valley. My brother and I did a little side trek to the foot of a glacier. The other Dave came along. We are 6 miles as the crow flies to Tibet. My brother has a little disposable camera and he took some photos after we put the zinc cream

on our noses. The Langtang Valley; it is the greatest thing I have ever seen. We heard a boom like thunder, followed by a distant rumble. Looking around we saw the tail end of an avalanche across the valley miles away. We saw a second avalanche start and waited for the sound to reach us.

The other Dave suddenly noticed I did not have my camera. He said, "Hey Bob, why don't you take a picture?" I told him I sold my camera a long, long time ago back in Bombay. This raised loads of questions. I told the other Dave his questions spoiled the view. We were warned about more snow. The afternoon we arrived at Langtang, there was talk about it, though that was hours before we decided to go on a hike for a few miles. By evening, everyone in the upper valley was on the move down to lower ground and it was snowing. We followed like the proverbial last ones out. The other Dave and the girls took off right away. Locals

My brother, Dave, and I at the top of the Langtang valley at 16,000 feet above sea level. (*Photo kindly lent by Dave Kreamer, Fuji Color 100 disposable camera film, scan from old print © 1977, 2018*)

emptied their teashops and hotels of goods and such and started down with a few yaks. Then it suddenly snowed more. A big red-haired dude, a tourist, carried a little local kid down on his back. A group of six or seven people found themselves thrown together hiking through a snowstorm. The snow was about a foot deep not quite whiteout medium falling. I showed my brother a solitary flip-flop frozen into the trail that someone had walked out of and not noticed. It took a few hours, but our little group made it out to the Langtang village and found shelter and lodging at the first stone building that was housing wayfarers we could find—it snowed all night.

My brother spent the many, many hours we were snowed in, gently and with a good-natured persistence, instructing our local roommates how to cover your mouth when you cough and why it is so important. He took on two unwilling students to tutor. The captive duo of my brother's unappreciated benevolence rolled their eyes and looked like they were searching their past lives for whatever misdeeds brought them to this

calamity. The look of "why me" translates into every language. It seemed obvious to all but the oblivious. The wind was beginning to pick up a bit and it blew snow over the door. It eventually drove my brother to frustration that all his hours of tutoring were rewarded with the hand coming to the mouth after the cough. When my brother braved the snowstorm to have a pee, everyone went back to coughing, hacking, and spitting as normal. Sure, we all noticed it when he left the room. The other Dave pointed this out and laughed. Sure, it was amusing. Sure, it has been going on for hours. I found myself about to revert to old roles and old reactions. I can make fun of my brother but fuck if you can.

I told Dave I was going to call him the other Dave from now on. His spot was perfect for three, but with twelve of us rammed in here, he has been pushed, nudged, and elbowed to the official worst spot in the room. Someone had to have it. The problem was that, in this case, he overcommitted too soon to some vague middle region of the room near the smoky wood stove.

I think he thought he was going to have the place for himself and his harem. I kind of feel sorry for him now squeezed by the crappy door, the victim of everyone's midnight run to the outhouse, getting thudded by the door and the blast of icy wind and snow. All night, the wind was howling wild.

March 15. Stopped snowing this morning and the sun is out. Little local kids are running around barefoot in the snow. They occasionally pee on their own feet to keep them warm. I was outside drinking tea and shaving, and a local dude, who later turned out to be a village boss man elder, noticed I had scissors and asked if I would cut his hair. Of course, I said "Sure." Two hours later, I had given him, a few of his buddies, and a few others haircuts. It was just the dudes and they made it easy by all wanting the same Beatle haircut. They wanted bangs. Looking up, it appears the peaks of the Langtang are right above us.

March 17. Had a talk with the other Dave and everything is cool. I think he is respecting me a little—probably not. He headed down trail with the girls before me and my brother did too. The vista of the Langtang peaks is stupefying and beautiful. The rays of the sun hit the peaks with soft rose gold light an hour before the sunrise. We were only a few hours behind them and caught up to them easily. The prayer flags mimic their surroundings: yellow, green, red, white, and blue—earth, plants, mountains, peaks and clouds, and sky. They are around everywhere. Everywhere is around me.

My brother and I encountered a troop of monkeys that were driven down valley by the snow. They eyed us from the large rocks and trees near the trail. They made me nervous. There were a lot of them and they quietly eyeballed us and trailed us for what seemed like hours but was only a minute. We then encountered an

Cutting hair in the Langtang village, Nepal. (*Photo kindly lent by David Kreamer, Fuji Color 100 disposable camera film, scan from old print*, © 1978, 2019)

angry local middle-aged man standing off trail. Looked like he was collecting wood. He started shouting and pointing back the way we had come. He was waving a rather large Gurkha knife around in a threatening manner. I shouted back some gibberish that ended with me saying his taxi was on its way. He did not like my jokes and I had no idea why he was annoyed at us in the first place. The monkeys spooked me. The angry old dude spooked my brother.

The trip downhill took a third of the time it took to cover the distance going uphill. On the way down, my ski knee gave me trouble. I was on a mountainside soaking my knee in an icy stream and the view was the stuff of dreams. Dave and the girls overtook me. I was embarrassed I had forgotten her name, as she was the first to stomp by. I said "Hello," and the blonde girl looked sweaty and annoyed. She stopped and said hello and threw her pack down, with Dave and the French girl close behind. They must think I am like a total pothead. Every time they see me, I am smoking a joint. Dave wanted to know if I was waiting for them and insisted that I was waiting so I could follow him. I said I was soaking my ski knee. He seems to have forgotten my misadventure on the ski slopes. It was great taking in the views and I smoked with Dave and the girls. I still called him the other Dave and said we should take off now. I told him we were meeting up in Rimche before dark. Dave marched off followed by the blonde girl and then the French girl. I quickly lost sight of them.

Down in a deep ravine, I was overtaken on the trail by a local kid playing a harmonica. I was sitting down, and he offered to carry my bag up to Rimche, like a Sherpa or a porter. He blurted out a price: two and a half rupees. That was way over the going rate. At that price, I could get a real Sherpa for a half day, and they carry crazy heavy stuff like sacks of rice or iron stoves for guest lodges a long way over mountain passes and other herculean tasks. I once saw a Sherpa carry a chair on his back with some guy sitting on it. I said OK and the kid put my pack on and took off playing the harmonica. It was so much easier without the pack, but I still had trouble keeping up. I had to tell him slow down a couple of times. It took a little over two hours and my knee liked the uphill; it does not like the downhill anymore. I caught up to the other Dave as I got to Rimche. The kid played the harmonica the entire time, even when I was paying him.

March 18. It is a long walk back to Dhunche. I thought the trek was incredible. One of our party seemed rather blasé about it, was unhappy, and did not seem to like our trek. I was blown away by the sheer enormity of the visual feast and was hooked on the polite laid-back Buddhist culture vibe, and I chattered about it endlessly. I had more energy at this lower elevation. I am glad my brother liked it. More science lessons from my brother. He has been talking again about how we are walking into more oxygen as we descend and we are getting a runner-type high. I kept going on and on about everything we saw and all the creature comforts someone had to carry uphill. I said, "We had tea at eleven thousand feet, who carried those glass cups and the tea pot, and the tea leaves up there?" They thought I was mad. Someone other than me carried a hell of a lot of firewood uphill above the tree line.

March 20. The couple of days it took to reach the bus was a cool part of the trek because we were just hanging out and getting back to Kathmandu and in a really good place. The good views were behind us now, but we only had to turn around.

March 25. Spring is coming to the Kathmandu valley. Cool nights. Caught up on my random volley of postcards. My brother got his flight. It was great to see him and sad to see him go. Got my room back. In the cafe downstairs, I occasionally drink my tea and meet and watch the tourists. It is now easy for me to tell who has been trekking and who has not. Everyone is friendly. There are so many different types. They fly in, like my brother. Flies. Money and a plan. I never did ask him where he got the dough to fly to Kathmandu and stay in the swank hotel area. The shell-shocked overlander, the trekkers, students, travelers, the climbers—from Europe, America, China, and Japan—everyone has a budget. I heard the climbers leave their garbage behind and just walk out. Been hanging out with the other Dave and it has been nice. I tried to talk to him, and I have no issues with the dude and he does not really remember either one of us being a dickhead, especially him. He is oblivious. Nothing matters, except for one thing: he wants me to stop calling him the other Dave.

March 30. I have walked everywhere in Kathmandu twice. I like hanging out in Durbar Square. There is a pyramid of steps in the corner of the square with a small temple on top. The locals sit there a spell, so I do as well. Found a shop in a back street making and selling woodblock prints on rice paper. I bought a few. Dave and I have walked all over the Kathmandu valley together. Spent a couple of days doing it. You can get chocolate bars from Europe, and hash, weed, and decent imported cigarettes. Dave is shocked I still have packs of the American Marlboro's. I save them for selling or trade or pass them around on special occasions like cigars. He now thinks I am frugal. He now thinks I am holding out on him. I have been smoking local cigarettes since Jordan, now I smoke bidis. Talked about doing another trek, but of course, it comes down to money. Dave cannot afford the trekking permit and cannot afford this, that, and the other. He started to ask for a loan. I reminded him I had a promissory note in a letter from him back in Germany giving me possession of his $2,000 stereo system if he fails to pay me back the loan I gave him for this trip by a certain date. I said, "Sorry dude, I was hoping you could start to repay me early. You don't have to, but a couple of hundred bucks would help me out."

Dave has been staying at his same old lodge. Thank God, he has not discovered the girls that hang out in the cafe below my hotel. Seems to be an early lunch scene. I am still staying down the end of Freak Street.

We went across town and ate at a cafe with some friends of Dave's. It was late, and we were going to a pie shop we heard was open. I think Dave felt sorry for me. I would on occasion hang out at my hotel on my own and he wanted to be my social ambassador and master of ceremonies. Get me out of what he thought were my doldrums. I was only melancholy about knowing I was soon to leave Kathmandu.

A pie shop has different meanings in different cities, but this was a pie shop. Dave regaled everyone with tales of our overland journeys. Where we had been chased by five kids throwing rocks, his version had fifty villagers chasing us into yet some other adventure. The car crash in the Sinai sounded like forty years of Moses wandering the wilderness searching for a way out. It all sounded wonderful and long ago. From the pie shop, we split up. Dave's friends hurried back to their nearby hotel, and Dave and I were heading south through the quiet nighttime city. We had a large chunk of Kathmandu to cross.

We heard dogs barking behind us in the distance and we both shut up at the same time, and we started walking faster. Very few streetlights and few lights from windows. We heard barking again and it was still behind us, only closer and joined by more barking

off to the right. Dave said, "I think we're being chased by fucking dogs." I knew he was right, and a shot of adrenalin had us running. That must have caught them by surprise because it was a while before we heard them again. We were down to a walk and I was smoking a cigarette. We were getting near to the Mustang Lodge, and Durbar Square and Freak Street were just a little way beyond. Then we heard the barking a bit too close. At the time, I swore to Dave these were the same dogs chasing us cross-town all night. The barking was familiar like a voice. The strays are so passive during the day and aggressive at night. The same story from here to Istanbul. Stray dogs.

We ran again, and the dogs were right behind us. I thought of the old man and the stick in Varanasi. I had no stick. This would not be happening to those old Sadhu dudes thrice my age. In the darkness, I saw a vacant lot with little mounds on it like small piles of dirt. I called to Dave as the dogs sounded like they were 50 yards away and bearing down on us. I was frantically searching for a stick, but I was grateful for the rocks. They were getting close enough now to hit with a rock, but I was sure that would not deter them for long. I climbed on one of the little hills and yelled, "Fucken hell find more rocks, Dave," and then the little hill moved. By the time the twenty or so of the cows were awake, up on their feet, and milling and shuffling around making noise, the dogs were quickly losing interest. They seemed to know that stirring up the cows would stir up the locals.

Sure enough, by the time two dudes showed up with sticks, they had time to see me throw a rock at the retreating pack as the dogs melted away in the darkness. The dudes were yelling at us like it was our fault. I showed them the rocks and pointed at the street where the dogs disappeared. I said we were saving the cows. I knew they did not give a shit the dogs were after us. Do not involve the cows he seemed to shout. My weird translator in my brain made all his words understandable. When he got sarcastic sounding, and was waving his stick, he was clearly saying to me, "You think you know everything tourist, so where is your stick dumbass?"

April 1. Got the bus from Kathmandu to Pokhara, which was about 120 miles west. Having a good time hanging out with Dave. We stopped at Trisuli Bazar along the way. I started calling it Truly Bazar. The vista of Annapurna range is astounding of course. Of the ten highest mountains in the world, three are right in front of me. Huge trekking scene is freeze-dried, oxygen under the big top expensive tent scene. Sometimes it looks like a competition. Thankfully, it employs Sherpas. The sun was on the peaks early and I woke up extra early for it, but I am without a trekking permit for this area of Nepal. Dave actually suggested that he could talk his way past a police checkpoint, and he maybe did not need a permit. I let Dave know everything was cool and I was getting the bus back to Kathmandu. I said that instead of getting a trekking permit for the Annapurna, I was going to look into plane tickets—standby or something cheap. I think he looked shocked. I think he thought I was going to buy him a trekking permit. I let him know that it is the best trip ever and I am running out of money. It is time to think about heading home soon. I said we will hook up in Kathmandu. I said I thought we were going back to West Germany together.

April 8. This place gets more and more wonderful. It has always been wonderful. I have just discovered Kathmandu is indeed my favorite city. I could stay for months or years. Travel between here and Sri Lanka forever. I got laid. The mountains are like an aphrodisiac and all week the cafe under my hotel has buzzed with the couples and people and groups back from trekking. It was something I sort of noticed the first time I stayed here. They look different from people yet to venture into the Himalayas.

I met her in the cafe. It was the first time I have used Robert in a long time. She said she was Anna from Austria. We had a tea, a great chat about trekking. She trekked around Annapurna. I said how lovely, Anna from Annapurna. She blushed. She went on and on and I was getting the buzz she was on. She flew in from Austria with a group. Her group had weird complications and or something about a boyfriend. I swear that every traveler goes through this same old shit. We were pretty much affected the same way by walking up close to big mountains. We talked for hours.

She was surprised to see me in the cafe the next day. I said I was staying in the hotel above and pointed up. I said, "What brings you back to my neighborhood?" She sat down, and she was still buzzing from her trek like before. She seemed to ring like a bell. I said I was relaxing after a long trip. She said, "Yeah the Langtang, you mentioned it." I said no, it was getting here, going through Sri Lanka, India, and Kashmir. I found myself giving a rundown of countries and cities with a detached boredom. I told a good story or two when she asked. She got a buzz from the travel stories and trekking. Asked about the mountains in Kashmir and Afghanistan.

She talked about the mountains in Austria for an hour. She talked about the group she is traveling with and all its sticky gossip. It was cool, I guess. Made me think of all the shitty travel times I have had. Then she surprised me. She said I smelled like weed and cigarettes and I stank. She said in a thick German accent, people would like me better if I did not stink. I was flabbergasted, and I excused myself. I said, "Watch my tea please." I went upstairs to my room at a run and smelled my shirt and, yes, my shirt did stink of cigs. I felt like I was back at school and I was six and I shit myself. I washed myself with the sandalwood soap I got in India, while brushing my teeth at the same time and all the while wishing she is just being nice to me in a mean weird way, and not just fucking with me mean. Two minutes later, I climbed into clean clothes believing she has left by now and rushed out the door and back to the cafe. There she was.

I sat down next to her and not across. I leaned in, our noses almost touching, and asked if I smelled better. I stayed close and she blushed and said something about wanting to trek to Langtang. Then she asked why I did not ask.

In another ten minutes, we were up in my room. She said she knew when I came down clean that I wanted to have her. I said I was thinking that yesterday. She said after the trek, it seems she has been hyper-aware. Hypersensitive to things. She brought a condom out. She said she made her boyfriend wear them and he hated it. Hated her. All I could think was how fucking beautiful she is, and I told her that and "Oh yeah, sure, I'll try the condom as well." I had a little trouble with the condom at first. We made out, caressed, kissed forever, and got into heavy foreplay. Then she wanted me sit on the bed and she wanted to sit in my lap facing me. I her told about the temples of Khajuraho.

It was kind of weird and hard to get into, and the condom was feeling weird and my mind was feeling weird and I thought I could not do it. Somehow, it all suddenly clicked, and it was one of the most amazing fucks I ever had. She really enjoyed it and got kind of loud too, and that kind of freaked me out because I first thought something was wrong. She said, "Stupid boy, that's the sound of something right." She said with any lover, the first time is the best. She said after that it is not new anymore. She must have enjoyed it. I asked right away if we could do it again. She said yes. I almost blew it by saying too much stupid needy stuff. I even asked if she wanted a boyfriend. If looks could kill. For a second, I thought she might leave.

Quickly recovered thanks to my brother, Dave, and his endless science talk in the Langtang. For some reason, I suddenly thought of the long science lessons about high altitude and frankly I did not know what else to do. I moved close to her and in a low voice started to recite a science lesson. I told her she felt great because she had been hiking at 10,000 feet above sea level for a week or two. I gently caressed her left breast and said I could feel her heartbeat. She was looking at me surprised. I said, "Back in Kathmandu at 4,000 feet your heart is still pumping a little harder

than normal, and that your brain is flooded with more oxygen now and you feel great." I started to kiss her. I stopped. "You have a climber's high," I told her. "It's science." I said, "Be aware of the symptoms of altitude sickness and always descend when they occur." I recited most of them. "You acclimate to your current altitude over time, but everyone does it at different speeds," I said. I started kissing her again. I just parroted the information I learned, and I felt pretty stupid after doing it. She thought I was a genius. "It's science," I said again. I told her that when she has acclimated, she would feel normal or even low. What was genius, however, was how I got the conversation back on to the erotic temples of Khajuraho.

April 10. Saw Anna yesterday at the cafe again. I was surprised and sort of was not. She was very talkative. I was having tea. I was even double washed and in clean clothes. Told me a funny story about the group she is with. In a nutshell, she gave them the high-altitude spiel and told them that Klaus was not given hashish in his food on the trek and why this other woman had bad headaches and now she feels better. She said she made them realize how stupid they were being. I think she is in charge now. Information is power. Yikes. Today her trekking buzz seems gone and she needs another fix. She is off with her group to go trekking. I told her to tell the Klaus dude that no one would throw money away by placing hashish in his food. She was telling me all this in a low voice. She was even drinking her tea in a determined way. She wanted to go up to my room.

She commented on the fact I smelled good. I was feeling stupid that it has taken me twenty-one years and a brutally honest girl to realize smelling funky is not something most girls like. Now she was the one talking too much. I asked if she still wanted to come up my room. She came up to my room again and it was great, but she is right about it being special the first time around.

I said I was getting a standby ticket and was going back to Germany soon, and maybe we could look each other up. She said she hoped I would be here when she got back, or I could come along. She said, "The Langtang maybe?" I momentarily saw myself as their stoner tour guide, sashaying through the rhododendrons, putting hash in Klaus's dumplings, and fucking Anna and her girlfriends. I could move the party to Sri Lanka.

I have all my shit together. I have a week left on my visa. I am now double packed, and my bag is clean. No weed or hash. All my contraband is out on my hotel room table.

Sold my sleeping bag and sleeping pad to a trekking company. Dave did the same. We got paid the same money. I was surprised at how much I got. He was surprised how little he got. Later, I went back and sold my folding buck knife and sheath. I was surprised how much they gave me for it. We may leave as early as in two days. Dave is low on money and is freaking out. I know how he feels.

April 11. I have my ticket with a Russian airline. I fly Kathmandu, Calcutta, Bombay, and Tehran to Moscow overnight, and then fly Moscow to Frankfurt. We could leave tomorrow. I am paid up and ready to wait. I am going to miss this cafe. I went for a long walk. Sent a few postcards and felt great about everything and actually felt good about leaving, sort of.

Gave away my hash and ganja. This hippie dude I had met in the cafe weeks ago wanted to give me money for it. I said that would defeat the purpose of giving it away. I thanked him for getting rid of it for me and doing me a favor. He just looked at me like I was crazy. I said I did not want to get busted taking it to Europe.

April 12. What a crazy flight I am on. It is like a weird version of the Magic Bus. I am flying with Aeroflot. We had to disembark the plane in Calcutta. That annoyed Dave more than it should have. We were herded on board and the plane was half-full at the start of the journey. Then two guys with gasmasks came on the plane and started spraying everyone and everything with something from aerosol cans. We flew on to Bombay and picked up passengers and we stayed on the plane. We flew on to Tehran, refueled, took on more passengers, and stayed on the plane. It was now dark. Then two guys with gasmasks came on the plane and started spraying everyone and everything with something from aerosol cans, again.

I told Dave what I was thinking. It was mind blowing to me as I thought about all those miles we traveled for all those months, and there they were, rolling beneath this jet plane below us. He said he was broke and needed to think about getting a job when he gets back.

The plane is a crazy mix of people: weekend hippies, business guys, dudes from India and the Middle East, travelers, overlanders, diehard hippies, and students— all coming and going. Some look like spies but are probably normal business dudes. We are supposed to get to Moscow sometime in the morning. I write, I sleep, I walk back to the smoking section and stand in the back and have a cigarette. I wash off the stink of the cigarette and think about those miles. I think about all the people I met and all the people I cast my eyes over.

I am about the only one not drinking booze. Chatted to a couple of girls sitting near us. They are nice. Later Dave butted in as subtle as a wasp. I do not care, I am in a different mode to him, I think. I feel like I need to be doing something different now or doing the now differently. I am twenty-one and I rent a room from my parents. That has got to change. I need a girlfriend. Smart girls are cool. I have to shit or get off the pot and think and decide on universities, job prospects, and where I want to undertake my endeavors. What are my endeavors? First is to survive the coming rat race. Five-year plan and back to traveling? Ten-year plan? Holy shit, I will be thirty-one. An old man. Holy shit. I am suddenly beat. I suddenly feel like I ran all the way to Kathmandu just to catch a flight back to where I started. I am suddenly bone weary. I am done writing on this long night flight.

April 13. Wow, in the U.S.S.R. Of course, Dave and I sang "Back in the U.S.S.R." as we descended with all the passengers down the stairs they had rolled up to the doors of the plane and we walked across the tarmac singing. We landed at around 9.30 a.m. It was fucking cold.

Weird scene from the start. Some weirdo was shouting nearby in the terminal. I did not think he was from our flight. We were clearing customs and getting our luggage and he was shouting, "The German man is better than the American man." Dave thought he was shouting at us. I did not feel he was being personal about it. He did not know where I was from. I was not being loud. Like in a movie, three dudes approached him and gave him a shot in the neck with a needle full of something. Dave and I could not believe what we saw. Later some dudes in white coats took him out on a stretcher. Again, just like in the movies.

Everything is freaky big and sometimes new or old and rich and poor and Europe a go-go. I am having some culture shock. Huge buildings looking like tombs. We are staying at the Aeroflot Hotel. They assign two people per room. We get breakfast first and Dave is eager because it comes with the room. It is free with the plane ticket. Two breakfasts, a dinner, and an overnight in their hotel. It was a really cheap ticket.

We shuffle into a type of canteen or cafeteria. It is like they expect us to sit in rows and march in and march out when we are finished. Like the opening scene from the musical *Oliver*. Some sort of toast, butter, not half bad cheese, coffee, some sort of sour juice, and eggs. Saddle up to the greasy spoon Russian style. The eggs are cooked and served single, sunny side up, in a small aluminum pan. Most were burnt to the bottom of the pan. Cooked with no butter or oil. The eggs were cold. Like metal poison. Dave was hungry. He kept asking, "Are you going to finish that?" "Are you going to eat your egg?" There were plenty of untouched eggs for Dave to choose from.

Dave was still angling with the girl from the plane. He told me he did not want to share the double room with me. I said I was OK with anything and rolling with it and I was planning to sleep anyway. We shuffled up to the desks for the hotel. In no time, rooms were assigned and we were ushered to the six-floor squatting monstrous box that was the Aeroflot Hotel. By bus. Its name affixed to the front. I climbed two stories to my floor. Now room number. There was a large matron sitting at her desk who pointed with a stern finger down the hall. I looked down a large cavernous dark hallway, badly lit and lined on both sides by the rows and rows of closed hotel room doors running the length of the hall. I found the room I was assigned and instead of the girl I saw in the line, it was a dude who would have passed easily as a rock drummer. The dude had a cool afro and the girl I think everyone saw.

He said he was from Holland. He asked if I needed to use the W.C. I said I was from Arizona, and "no, go ahead man." He ran in, barely closed the door, and sounded like he came down with Delhi belly. I was a little concerned and he ran the water for a long time washing. He finally came out and said, "Hey man, how's it going?" Like nothing happened and I could not hear him. He sat down on the bed I was not sitting on and said, "You want to get high?" Apparently, he is carrying a quantity of hash only restricted to what he can fill into a condom and can tolerate shoved up his ass while sitting on a long flight and patiently waiting through a tediously crappy breakfast and room assignments. He seems keen to take the size down somewhat before he must reinsert his special souvenir tomorrow for transport.

He rolled up some towels and stuffed them under the door. He smoked a lot of hash in about an hour. Did not seem to take the size down at all. If anything, his pile of stash seemed bigger after I got stoned and I would not, could not, do what this cat has done. No way. We talked a bit and I got way stoned. I should not have got stoned. Too stoned for having just got back from Nepal and India. I said I was taking a nap and zonked out right away for a couple of hours. I woke up and he was still going at it. Smoking. I put the T.V. on, and it had one station in black and white. The T.V. was showing a war film and the Russians were winning. The guy from Holland was into it. I had

some of my Marlboro's left and I made him a joint, Lebanese style. He really dug it. I had a couple of small tokes and said I was going for a walk. I got my down jacket on and left.

Smoked a cigarette for a cover smell and walked down the hall to the matron who was sitting at the desk at the end of the long hall. I asked if she spoke English and she said no. I tried anyway and asked if there were any parks or nice walks. She looked at me and said no. I said I was going out for some air. I was walking around the hotel and around the back there was this factory gate. Boots, hardhats, grubby overalls, and coats, gray and black. The dudes walking out were definitely not happy to see the likes of me. It all seemed pretty hostile, and I scurried back around to the hotel entry. I caught my reflection in the glass of the hotel. I looked at myself and thought I looked really noticeable. The parody of a hippie. Kind of silly. I saw there were no cows or holy men, or horse-drawn carts on the streets. It was noticeably cold to me. From my down jacket and Afghani hat, to the shirt, Indian cotton trousers and wax-covered crappy blue Indian sneakers, I had not adhered to my habit of dressing like the locals, and I had a noticeable Indian scarf on to boot.

Got to my floor and the matron was gone. I went back to the room and the cat was still smoking. I changed into the most somber clothes I could find and took off my hat. I mentioned the walk I just took. He did not answer just stared at the T.V. The Russians were still winning. The cat from Holland was laying low.

Dave was not downstairs at dinner. What was on offer reminded me of the tinned stew we bought in Jordan, only thinner. I keep thinking it was not like him to pass on a free meal. It was not like him not to be in the bar crowing like a rooster when it meets a new hen. My roommate hotfooted it back to the room after dinner. I wonder if he sleeps with that thing in place. I hung out at the bar and waited around for Dave. I think he must have been down earlier. He must be busy. I quietly toasted to myself and Dave, and to the best adventure and to many more. I had another beer and waited. I thought about all the cities I have been to. I toasted those cities and everyone I met along the way. With a little help from my friends.

I tried to find out what room Dave was in but no luck. I went back to my room, and the roommate was back at it. Smoking and watching another war film. I made another Lebanese joint. This one I did fast, and we were both impressed. I went back outside for a wander. Went back to the bar again. This time I turned right when I went out the hotel doors and down a street. It was not at all like my last encounter with the locals. I bought some weird Russian cigarettes and went back to the hotel room. My roommate asked if I wanted some hash. I said, "No, thanks. I'm cool. But thanks." I said I was broke. In the morning, he was flying to Amsterdam and I was flying to Frankfurt—early. I just smoked a load of hash and I am stoned and cannot sleep; I am writing like a madman.

April 14. What a strange trip it has been. Light breakfast. Still not touching the egg. I put my cigarette out in the yoke. The waitress glared at me and my improvised ashtray. Coffee and this time a cold rubbery croissant and some cheese. I go outside, smoke, wait, and eventually I got on one of the buses that leaves the hotel for the airport every fifteen minutes. No Dave. I am thinking that in about twenty minutes, he will be cutting it close. I got assigned a seat and I was beginning to think I was about to leave without any sign of Dave. The plane was not boarding for a while and I had time to think of the phone calls, the people I will have to speak to, the embassy, all when I start asking the airline if they have seen him. Then all of a sudden, Dave showed up with this girl and told a convoluted tale.

Seems after devouring eggs like Cool Hand Luke yesterday morning, he gets to his room, doubles up in pain, and is sure he is dying. I said welcome the world of Delhi belly. He said this was the first time he was ill since leaving Munich. His roommate does not speak English and the operator does not speak French, and they cannot speak Russian and they spent fourteen hours trying to find someone who speaks all these languages at once to get a doctor. Dave barely took a breath as he told his story.

I told him I was in the bar downstairs last night. Anyone could have found me by asking the bartender. I said I tried to find his room, but I could not get information from anyone. I said I could have knocked on every door. I asked, "So what happened." He said he spent fourteen hours curled in a ball, in pain, and when the doctor was eventually checking on him and while pressing down on his gut, he farted a loud and terrible smelling fart and suddenly felt much better.

His lady friend was looking for a way out from all this hard work and seeing me talking to Dave, takes her leave with a roll of the eyes and takes her place in the queue to board. I tell Dave about the dinner he missed. I said it was like all those cans of stew we ate in Petra. He said he would have liked that. I tell a brief tale about my roommate from Holland. I think he is envious of all the hash I have been smoking while in Moscow. I think Dave last had a shower in Kathmandu. He stinks really bad. Dave got a seat assignment somewhere else.

It is about a four-hour flight. I am caught by surprise at how quickly some things end. It seemed like in no time we were on the curb in Frankfurt and contemplating our options at high noon. The Friday hitchhiking was fast, and Dave and I were chattering with the old gusto of nine months ago. It is a straight through ride, one hour then dropped off drive.

Dave had a long haul to get to his rented room in the groovy mansion twelve people shared on the far end of town. Down river. We made plans to meet up for a beer on the Untere Strasse. The public transport is easy and after living here for a couple years, I could do these journeys with my eyes closed, and sometimes I think I have.

Just off Romerstrasse by 2 p.m. and I am back at my parent's apartment. No reply to the bell. I retrieve the key my mother hides in the hall, as I try to recall where I last remember seeing my keys. I walk in and note the comfort of seeing familiar things: the living room; the consistent ceiling; electricity; art on the walls; my LP collection near my dad's stereo. Everybody is out. I check what is in the fridge, and I am staggered by all the food I see. Then I am staggered by the notion that I have never noticed all that food before. I see my package from India arrived and it is slightly opened. I grab the spare keys to my room on the fourth-floor row of ancient maid's quarters. I grab my package, my backpack, lock up, re-stash the key, and run up three flights of stairs. My room looks small. Looks the same. A quick rummage tells me nothing is missing from the parcel. I find some clean street clothes I left behind. The old communal shower on the fourth floor I used to sniff at for being too old and worn is delivering gloriously hot water. In half an hour, I am dressed like its Monday morning, ready for a shift at my old job in the registry—or its Friday night and I am ready to hit the bars.

The noise from the stairwell tells me my family are home. After the usual familial welcome, we had a talk and I said it was a great trip and told of a few highlights. I asked how they were all doing, and I said I saw Dave in Kathmandu. My mom said she liked the cards from the Holy Land. My little brother seemed a little disappointed he was not getting my room after all. I gave my mom the $180 she sent me, and the old man was surprised. I said "Thanks, it was really needed if I didn't sell my camera, but I got lucky." My dad said, "You sold your camera?" Like a judge, his stare could not be ignored. I said, "Yeah, it helped me out of a tight financial jam." "What jam?" His growing interest was just getting started.

I described the bumbling into the Persian Gulf, needing a flight out, the airline cost, and describing the camera as an investment that came in handy later. I think he was impressed. I added that after hitchhiking through Iran, we started taking buses and then trains and the transportation costs mounted up. I said, "A few months after I'm back to work I can get another one." I left out the part where I lost my wallet. I knew that look from my dad. He knew I handled myself well in my travels. He knew I knew. He knew I was bullshitting a little. He wanted to know my plans and I gave them a rundown of prospects from university to even getting my old job back. I left out mention of my plans to see Dylan play in Nuremberg in July. I saw the posters on the way in from the airport.

I gave my mom her gift. A souvenir from a time and place that will take me a while to figure some of it out—India? I could not imagine the little wooden and intricately carved bookshelf could hold all the things I wanted to say and all the things I will never want to say. I gave my little brother a T-shirt with the eyes of Buddha on it. It was copied from the Boudhanath Stupa in Kathmandu and was a semi-motif of the city. I realized much too late it was a little too weird for him and he gave it a look that said he would not be caught dead wearing it. I gave my dad some woodblock prints from Kathmandu. He used to do woodblock prints in art school. He liked the skill it represented, but the religious theme was not to his taste. He said not to forget the rent is coming up on my attic atelier. I told him I had a little travel money left over, so I could cover it. He looked impressed, and in my head, I was thinking this was going to be a great summer. He said he was happy I made it back safe and had an amazing journey. He said I seemed smarter and more grown up now than when I left. I did not know what to say. I should have seen it coming. I said, "Thanks, maybe you're right, maybe I am."

He said, "I hope so, because the knucklehead who went to Kathmandu left his window open and the light on in his room."